Population Economics

Titels in the Series

Jacques J. Siegers Jenny de Jong-Gierveld
Evert van Imhoff (Eds.)
Female Labour Market Behaviour and Fertility

Hendrik P. van Dalen

Economic Policy in a Demographically Divided World

Springer-Verlag
Berlin Heidelberg New York London Paris Tokyo
Hong Kong Barcelona Budapest

Dr. Hendrik P. van Dalen
Erasmus University Rotterdam
Department of Mathematical Economics
P.O. Box 1738
Burg. Oudlaan 50
NL-3000 DR Rotterdam, The Netherlands

ISBN 3-540-54727-4 Springer-Verlag Berlin Heidelberg New York Tokyo
ISBN 0-387-54727-4 Springer-Verlag New York Berlin Heidelberg Tokyo

© Springer-Verlag Berlin · Heidelberg 1992
Printing in Germany

2142/7130-543210 - Printed on acid-free paper

To Dirk and Dook van Dalen-Mekenkamp

PREFACE

This book was inspired by one plain observation: the population in the developing world grows at a faster rate than the population of the developed world. However, simple facts may have complex causes and implications and this stylised fact was no exception. When I started writing this book I felt there was a need to analyse such demographic division and my hunch is that in decades to come the issues treated here are bound to rank high on a policymaker's priorities list. At the time of finishing the book I was far from convinced that I would have said the final word on such issues as international debt, migration, development aid, and fiscal policy. The models and subsequent analyses presented in this book are personal choices of how economies work and how economic policy should be conducted and as such they should function as debating topics focussing attention on real world problems that are in dire need of an answer. Optimal growth models figure prominently in this book since they are, in my opinion, quite suitable in framing the policy questions of a demographically divided world. Its prime selling point is the intuition one gains in understanding the mechanisms of economic development and the principles of economic policy. While working on questions of optimal economic growth, one encounters many limitations of the models used. In that respect one can arrive at the rather paradoxical thesis that excessive concentration on interior solutions makes one especially aware of the boundaries of economic models. Bearing this *caveat emptor* clause in mind I hope the reader will find enough food for thought.

The research for the present book, as well as the actual

writing, was done at the Tinbergen Institute and the department of Public Sector Economics at the Erasmus University Rotterdam. I am greatly indebted to Jo Ritzen and Evert van Imhoff, who both had a marked influence on the project and who were most generous in sharing their insights and experience. The book also owes much to discussions with colleagues and friends. Lans Bovenberg, Sukhamoy Chakravarty (who unfortunately passed away much too early in August 1990), Gerbert Hebbink, Carla Naastepad, Otto Swank, Herman Vollebergh, Frans van Winden and Maarten de Zeeuw provided me with constructive comments and suggestions. Needless to say, they cannot be blamed for any remaining errors in the text and neither can Edith de Vries, who checked the English of the dissertation.

Finally, I would like to thank the production factor that no growth accountant until now has been able to detect or measure: my parents, Corinne, my sisters and the rest of my 'extended' family: my friends and colleagues at the Erasmus University.

Rotterdam, August 1991

TABLE OF CONTENTS

LIST OF TABLES

CHAPTER 1: INTRODUCTION

Economic theory addresses extensively the question how to allocate scarce resources to attain given ends. For the sake of convenience, functions describing tastes and production technologies are assumed to behave elegantly and resources are assumed to flow preferably at a constant rate into the economic system. Unfortunately real world problems seldom come in such convenient forms. The occurrence of shocks in tastes, technology, endowments and the rules of the game are all the more common.

This thesis applies the question of resource allocation to one particular kind of shock, viz. demographic shocks. Shocks or fluctuations in the demography of a country come in various forms and influence the economy in various ways. The reason why population growth is a particularly difficult aspect of growth models is that populations play an ambiguous role. On the one hand, a population is treated as an endowment of an economy. People represent the human wealth of a country. On the other hand, people are decision making units and their mere number makes it necessary to take account of present and future market participants. A further complication concerning the role of population growth is caused by the choices involved in the determination of the population growth rate itself, viz. choices that influence the rates of fertility, mortality and migration.

It is outside the scope of this thesis to entertain thoughts of endogenous population growth. To keep the analysis at a general level I will restrict the attention to the effects of the population growth rate on economic policy decisions in a world with and without an explicit public sector. The title *Economic Policy in a Demographically Divided World* has a ring to it that reminds one of the times of grand designs and king-for-a-day questions. It has not been my intention to give this impression. The central question this thesis examines can be summed up quite generally as:

> *How should economic agents allocate scarce resources efficiently in an interdependent world economy, when each agent differs with respect to his or her technology, tastes or endowments?*

The attractiveness of this problem is that it is a very practical question as well as a theoretical one. The finance of public outlays of an ageing society could place a heavy burden on future generations, if current governments do not take measures to countervail the detrimental financial effects of ageing. At the same time, the present international debt problem will surely continue to play a dominant role in the development of the international capital market. If there is one thing, that models of interdependent world economies make clear, it is the fact that welfare of today and in the future depends just as much upon one's own actions and endowments as on the actions and endowments of a trading partner, now and in the future. Nonetheless, the reader who catches in this introduction a glimpse of the words such as 'international debt problem', 'ageing economies' and 'economic policy' might get the impression that this thesis will give some exact answers as to questions about the size of the twin deficits (i.e. government and trade deficit) of the U.S.A. in the year 2026. My intentions, however, are modest. The various chapters of this thesis should be looked upon as exercises in optimal growth theory and are aimed at gaining intuition and insights in intertemporal aspects of economic policy. Perhaps a book that tries to cover such a broad topic as a demographically divided world economy should be accompanied by the warning one may encounter in novels with fictional intentions:

> *The characters and situations in this work are wholly fictional and imaginary, and do not portray and are not intended to portray any actual persons or parties.*

Economics is an artificial[1] science. At conferences and workshops one may encounter from time to time the puzzled faces of colleague social scientists who try to imagine everyday life, preferably their own, in the models of economic growth. Of course, economic theory tries to come to grips with the problems of *actual economies*, but the analysis is always performed with average or representative persons and not actual persons. Models of economic growth are no exception. They are constructed to answer only a limited set of questions, viz. to establish a better understanding of propagation *mechanisms* of economic development and *principles* of economic policy. The models should, however, be in touch with the 'facts' of economic life. Nicolas Kaldor [1961] established the tradition to start theorising from a set of stylised facts. The mere act of calling something 'stylised' implies that economic theory intends to construct theories about economies *in general*. This introductory chapter is set in such a Kaldorian fashion and is mainly directed at gaining insight in the relevance of examining the world economy as a demographically divided entity. I will first present some stylised facts concerning demographic and economic developments which are relevant for later chapters. I will briefly expand on the methodology of analysis in section 1.2. And after that I will present an outline of this thesis and of

---

1. The term *artificial* has in this context the meaning 'man-made' as opposed to 'natural' (see H.A. Simon [1982]).

the research questions it tries to answer (section 1.3).

1.1 STYLISED FACTS

The history of the world population has been fundamentally discontinuous in nature. The theory of demographic transition, as pioneered by Notestein [1945], Davis [1945] and Thompson [1929], stresses the importance of innovations such as industrialisation, medical progress and wars in the explanation of discontinuous population growth. At present, the world as a whole is in another period of high population growth rates. After millennia of low growth rates, with deaths largely offsetting births, innovations in medical care and a rise in living standards induced rapidly declining death rates, and with birth rates remaining high in developing countries, this development gave rise to a steep increase in population growth around 1950. After taking more than 100 years to double from 1.25 to 2.5 billion in 1950, it took the world population only 37 years to double again from 2.5 to 5.0 billion people in 1987. The demographic developments did not occur simultaneously in the different parts of the world. The industrialised countries preceded the less developed countries in the demographic transition. Table 1.1 presents a quite clear-cut picture of the current extent of demographic division of the world economy. The dividing line in demography should also be seen as an economic division. Generally, less developed countries (LDCs) are rapid growth regions, whereas more developed countries are characterised by slower population growth rates. The difference in population growth rates is reflected in the age structure of the two regions. Developing countries have a relatively young age structure, whereas developed countries are ageing: the

TABLE 1.1: A DEMOGRAPHICALLY DIVIDED WORLD

	Population size 1989[a]	Average annual change (percent) 1985-90[a]	Age structure 1990[a]		
			0-14	15-64	65+
Africa	626.0	3.02	45.3	51.7	3.0
North and Central America	423.5	1.38	27.9	62.8	9.2
U.S.A.	246.3	0.86	22.1	65.7	12.2
Canada	26.5	1.01	21.3	67.4	11.3
Mexico	87.0	2.39	39.1	57.2	3.7
South America	291.2	2.08	38.6	56.4	5.0
Asia	3,009.1	1.63	31.8	63.2	5.0
China	1,110.8	1.18	25.4	68.7	5.9
Japan	123.3	0.51	19.2	69.4	11.4
India	813.4	1.72	34.5	60.9	4.6
Europe	497.2	0.27	20.1	66.8	13.1
France	55.3	0.31	20.3	66.7	13.0
Germany	60.4	−0.18	15.2	69.7	15.1
Netherlands	14.7	0.34	17.9	69.5	12.6
U.K.	56.2	0.02	19.0	65.4	15.6
U.S.S.R.	298.3	0.93	25.1	65.5	9.4
Oceania	26.1	1.43	26.7	64.3	9.0
World	5,162.4	1.63	31.9	61.9	6.2

a) The years 1989-90 are forecasts. Age groups are expressed as a percentage of the total population.

Source: World Resources Institute [1988]

number of youngsters decreases and the number of elderly increases. Growth rates and age structures are of course interrelated. A high fertility rate results in a relatively

young age structure. For example, the proportion of the LDC
population under 15 is currently about 40 percent of the LDC
population, almost twice that of the more developed world. The
questions demographers and ecologists ask is whether population
developments will sometime converge and whether this development
is viable. Table 1.1 is not suitable for understanding the
interaction between population growth and economic growth since
it is only a freeze-frame. If one wants to understand
demographic developments one should look at the demographic
history of countries and recognise patterns and conditions
inducing those patterns. On the surface, the study of demography
is merely an accounting science and as such it appears to be
quite simple. This apparent simplicity, however, is at the same
time its prime difficulty. Single demographic figures cover up
the history of a population and in summing up demographic
stylised facts one may well be tempted to engage in wishful
theorising, whereas the figures could be meaningless. Unraveling
figures till they have meaning seems to be the task of a demo-
grapher and it cannot certainly be seen as an easy job. The
aggregate population growth rates of Table 1.1 *suggest* a demographically divided world. However, one needs to disaggregate
this growth rate into aspects of fertility, mortality, and
migration, preferably by generation. Despite the fact that
demographic and economic development are closely intertwined, a
separate discussion may serve a purpose in keeping a clear mind.
I will therefore start with some demographic stylised facts.
After that, I will discuss the stylised facts that concern the
interaction between economic development and demography.

1.1.1 AGEING AND DEMOGRAPHIC TRANSITION

The term *ageing* expresses a motion in time. The ageing of a
population is in fact an increase in the share of older persons
in a population and is associated with an increase in the median
age of the population. As this definition already indicates,
ageing is a subjective term, since the characterisation of an
older person is left undefined. The usual distinction between
young and old age is set at the mandatory retirement age. In
industrialised countries this age ranges between 59 and 66 years
of age (see Hagemann and Nicoletti [1989]). The ageing of a
population can be caused by reduced fertility, increased life
expectancy or simply the net emigration of youngsters (or net
immigration of elderly). The process of ageing is a part of a
broader class of demographic phenomena, known as *demographic
transition*. It primarily describes the development of mortality
and fertility over time. Countries are assumed to develop
gradually from a high population growth rate to a low population
growth rate. The change in reproductive behaviour is said to
occur during the transformation of a society from a traditional
to a highly modernised state. The postulated change is from near
equality of birth and death rates at high levels to near
equality of birth and death rates at low levels. In the absence
of migration flows, this would imply that the aggregate
population growth rate in the two steady states does not differ
significantly, whereas the growth rate would show considerable
fluctuations during the demographic transition. Another feature
of the transition which leads to an acceleration in the
aggregate population growth rate is that a decline in mortality
normally precedes a decline in fertility. In the past, this
sequence created a gap between the death rate and the birth
rate, a gap that was closed only after a delayed reduction in

fertility. The large reductions in death rates in LDCs have
contributed overwhelmingly to the increase in aggregate population growth in those countries. The reduction was greatly
enhanced by the available technology, as developed in industrialised countries. As a consequence, the rate of reduction in
developing countries has been four to five times as fast as that
experienced in Europe in the nineteenth century. Table 1.2 gives
an impression of the development of life expectancy in the
Netherlands.

TABLE 1.2: CHANGE IN LIFE EXPECTANCY AT BIRTH IN THE NETHERLANDS

	Male	Female
1840	36.2	38.5
1905	51.0	53.4
1951	70.6	72.9
1968	71.0	76.4
1985	72.8	79.4

Source: Mackenbach [1988]

A number of innovations in preventive and curative medicine in
the 18th and 19th century contributed to lower mortality, such
as vaccination for smallpox, the invention of aneasthesia and
the spread of a more empirical approach to medical care. As
illustrated in Table 1.2 the change in life-expectancy has been
formidable: in a timespan of 150 years, life-expectancy has

doubled in the Netherlands. An aspect which is often neglected when discussing changes in life expectancy is the expectancy of the number of years living in good health. Table 1.3 modifies the picture considerably by showing that although women, on the average, may live longer than men, men live slightly longer in good health. Averages may, however, be misleading: there are differences in mortality among the various social and economic classes (see, e.g., Ehrlich and Chuma [1990]). One of the most difficult questions one has to face, now and certainly in the future, is "How should one value life?" People live longer, but more frequently come upon the choice of ending their life because it seems to have no social or physical value any longer. The valuation of life is, of course, more an ethical question than an economic one, and I will let this question rest. It stresses, however, the fact that technical progress, just as population growth, can have an ethical dimension.

TABLE 1.3: LIFE EXPECTANCY AT BIRTH, WITH AND WITHOUT DISABLEMENTS IN THE NETHERLANDS (IN YEARS), 1980-85

	Male	Female
Short term disruptions	3.4	3.8
Long lasting disablements	8.9	15.0
In institutions (hospitals, etc)	1.0	2.5
Number of years without disruptions in state of health	59.5	58.2
Total life expectancy	72.8	79.5

Source: Van Ginneken et al. [1989]

The rapid population growth in LDCs and its dismal ecological consequences forces one to give thought to one of the open questions of demography: will the demographic transition in LDCs be completed in decennia to come? To get an impression of the state of demographic transition Table 1.4 is presented.

This table indicates two of the most important components of population growth, viz. fertility and mortality. To start with the latter component, mortality focuses on numbers and rates of

TABLE 1.4: POPULATION GROWTH COMPONENTS IN THE WORLD ECONOMY

	Crude Birth Rate (per 1000)		Crude Death Rate		Life Expectancy at Birth (Male)		Child Death Rate[a] (1-4 years)	
	1960	1985	1960	1985	1960	1985	1960	1985
Low Income countries	44	29	24	10	42	60	27	9
China/India	43	24	24	9	42	63	26	6
Other Low Income c.	47	43	24	15	42	51	31	19
Middle Income c.	43	32	17	10	49	60	23	8
Lower Middle	46	36	20	11	44	56	29	11
Upper Middle	40	28	13	8	55	64	15	4
High Income Oil Exporters	49	41	22	8	43	61	44	5
Industrial Market Economies	20	13	10	9	68	73	2	0
East European Econ.	23	19	8	10	65	65	3	4

a) Per 1000 live births in a given year.

Source: Worldbank [1984,1987]

death. The crude death rate (CDR) represents the number of deaths per 1,000 inhabitants in a year. The crude birth rate (CBR) represents the number of births per 1,000 inhabitants in a given year. The number gives an impression of fertility across all age-groups at one point in time. The age structure is therefore of influence on these crude rates. The ageing of a population can affect the crude rates as follows: with constant reproductive behaviour and a decreasing number of deaths the CBR will falleven though fertility is constant. The same goes for a constant life expectancy but a falling rate of fertility; under those conditions, the CDR falls even though life expectancy has remained constant. To get a complete impression of fertility one should supplement this figure with the total fertility rate (see Table 1.5). The total fertility rate (TFR) is defined as the average number of children that would be born (per woman) among women progressing from age 15 to 50 who are subject to the age-specific birth rates *as currently* observed in the population in question. A permanent TFR of 2.1 (i.e. replacement level) will eventually lead to a stationary population. The present situation in the world is that of a general fall in TFRs. However, to a large extent, the global fall in the TFR is the result of family planning efforts in China. TFRs in Africa, South America and India remain high. The frustrating aspect of population policies is perhaps that even a slight change in fertility behaviour, e.g., in China and India (where 37% of the world population lives), could dwarf the effects of population planning efforts elsewhere. Theories concerned with fertility choice are therefore of vital importance in the understanding of diverging population developments in the world of today. The TFR still has the drawback that it is time-dependent and figures should be obtained on desired and completed family size.

TABLE 1.5: TOTAL FERTILITY RATE IN THE WORLD

	1965-1970	1985-1990
Africa	6.60	6.22
North and Central America	3.53	2.62
U.S.A.	2.55	1.91
Canada	2.51	1.75
Mexico	6.70	3.98
South America	5.17	3.60
Asia	5.69	3.14
China	5.97	2.11
Japan	2.02	1.83
India	5.69	3.69
Europe	2.47	1.83
France	2.61	1.83
Germany	2.34	1.40
Netherlands	2.75	1.43
U.K.	2.53	1.78
U.S.S.R.	2.42	2.37
Oceania	3.49	2.56
World	4.86	3.28

Source: World Resources Institute [1988]

The third component of population growth, migration, has always
played a prominent role in economics, although the motive for
migration may not always have been an economic but rather a
political one. Although the net migration flow may be a small
percentage of the population, migration cannot be called a
negligible phenomenon. Countries like the U.S.A., Canada,
Australia and Israel have thrived on the inflow of migrants.
Considerations of political stability and economic opportunities

are the main motives for leaving a country. Aspects that make migration such a complex phenonomenon are the social welfare consequences of such a flow. International migration may have an economic impact far greater than the impact caused by its mere number, because of its effects on the transfer of skills and technology, savings behaviour, international monetary remittances and social adjustments. The big question about the economic consequences of migration is therefore: "Who gains and who loses from migration?" Governments reflecting on migration flows have to consider the character of migration, temporary or permanent, and its contribution to national or domestic welfare. Compared to the historical rates of emigration, present-day permanent emigration rates are small: between 1970 and 1980 emigration absorbed roughly 3 percent of the population growth in Europe and Latin America and less than 1 per cent in Asia and Africa (see Table 1.6).

Permanent emigration has only a limited effect on the reduction of the labour force in developing countries. To illustrate this, if 700,000 immigrants a year were admitted to the major host countries (i.e. Australia, United States, Canada and New Zealand) up to the year 2000, and all came from the LDCs, less than 2 percent of the projected population growth in the LDCs between 1982 and 2000 would have emigrated. By contrast, these same 700,000 immigrants would account for 22 percent of the projected population growth of the industrial market economies and for 36 percent of the projected increase in the major host countries. One may be tempted to call the effects on the reduction of the labour force in developing countries of a limited nature. If the country of origin is large, such as India, the relative effect on the total labour force is bound to be small. However, one should make a distinction between the growth rates of various human capital stocks of the country of

TABLE 1.6: PERMANENT EMIGRATION IN ECONOMIC HISTORY
(as a percentage of increase in populations of emigrants'
countries)

Period	Europe	Asia[a]	Africa[a]	Latin America[a]
1851-1880	11.7	0.4	0.01	0.3
1881-1910	19.5	0.3	0.04	0.9
1911-1940	14.4	0.1	0.03	1.8
1940-1960	2.7[b]	0.1	0.01	1.0
1960-1970	5.2	0.2	0.10	1.9
1970-1980	4.0	0.5	0.30	2.5

a) The periods from 1850 to 1960 pertain to emigration only to
the U.S.A.
b) Emigration only to the U.S.A.

Source: Worldbank [1984, p. 29]

origin. About 11,000 university graduates leave India every year
for advanced work or study abroad, about 2,500 will remain
abroad permanently. The largest number of emigrants move to the
United States and Canada. In addition, between 1977 and 1979 the
total number of professionals who migrated to the U.S. was 8,035
(see Ommen [1989, p. 414]). These numbers are not that high
compared to the total labour force, but they are high when one
compares them to the total stock of a particular category. Each
year, the permanent loss is about 2.6% of university graduates,
7% of doctors, 7% of engineers and 2.5% of scientists. The
governments of many sending countries feel that emigration is a
loss to their country, because they subsidise the emigrants'
education but lose their contribution to the national income and
productivity and the opportunity to tax their incomes.

1.1.2 ECONOMIC DEVELOPMENT

The theory of economic growth, or development economics, is concerned with the long-run time path of key economic variables such as consumption, investment and production. The puzzle that development economics has to solve boils down to the plethora of questions Table 1.7 raises, for instance: "What has spurred Japan in becoming one of the wealthiest countries in the world, while up and till the second world war it still belonged to the category of developing countries?", "Why have the Netherlands and the U.K. not kept up with leaders in growth such as Germany and the U.S.A.?", and "What was the contribution of immigrants in establishing economic growth in the U.S.A.?" These are questions that deal with the 'wealth of nations' puzzle. There is considerable consensus amongst economists about the underlying determinants; however, the exact contribution within

TABLE 1.7: GROSS DOMESTIC PRODUCT PER HEAD OF POPULATION (in U.S. $)

	1870	1913	1950	1960	1973	1984
France	1,542	2,878	4,147	5,933	10,514	12,643
Germany	1,366	2,737	3,600	6,985	10,899	13,267
Netherlands	2,290	3,298	4,884	6,703	10,581	11,710
Japan	560	1,060	1,486	3,136	8,987	12,235
U.K.	2,671	4,101	5,000	7,093	9,902	11,068
U.S.A.	1,962	4,657	8,261	9,608	13,741	15,829

Source: Maddison [1987, p. 683]

the variety of factors is debatable. Four factors are often named as factors of economic growth, viz.: (1) the labour force, or in more general terms, human capital; (2) physical capital; (3) technical progress; and (4) natural resources. All of these factors have a demographic element and I will briefly discuss each factor.

Although the present thesis cannot cover all of these consequences, I want to discuss in short the major points of interaction between demographic changes and economic development. In addition to the four factors mentioned, I want to add the public sector as a fifth factor, since its role and influence has become so dominant in industrialised countries that no growth theory can play down the real effects of government.

LABOUR FORCE DEVELOPMENTS

The economic consequences of a change in the rate of population growth for the labour market are not as straightforward as one might think. The 'direct' effect of a decline in fertility rates is a *delayed* decline in the size and structure of the *potential* labour force. The reason for this delay can be found in the education of the labour force. The 'time to build' human capital takes about 16 to 30 years in industrialised countries, hence it can take a considerable time before the newly born can become a member of the effective labour force (see Ritzen [1987]). A shock in fertility can therefore propagate a business cycle merely from the simple fact that it takes 'time to build' human capital. This is analogous to the business cycle theory rooted in the construction time of physical capital (like in Kydland and Prescott [1982]).

The consequences of a population decline for the labour
market depend predominantly on the labour force participation
rates of men and women. Table 1.8 clearly shows four stylised
facts with respect to the participation rate of various age
groups: (1) the labour force participation among men of all age

TABLE 1.8: LABOUR FORCE PARTICIPATION RATES IN OECD COUNTRIES

	Males				Females			
Age:	15-24	25-54	55-64	65+	15-24	25-54	55-64	65+
Canada								
1950	79.2	98.3	86.6	40.9	45.0	23.4	12.0	4.5
1985	71.7	94.8	75.0	13.8	61.5	61.6	34.3	5.1
France								
1950	86.2	96.4	83.4	37.2	53.5	35.3	39.3	14.3
1985	61.3	95.0	54.2	5.6	50.0	62.3	29.8	2.2
Germany								
1950	88.7	96.1	81.4	27.5	75.5	39.5	26.0	9.6
1985	71.3	95.5	63.2	4.7	60.9	55.5	24.8	3.1
Netherlands								
1950	82.4	98.1	89.0	31.5	53.8	21.0	14.9	5.5
1985	50.0	94.3	67.2	4.3	46.6	38.2	15.4	0.9
Japan								
1950	74.0	96.2	85.7	54.5	58.0	50.9	41.0	21.6
1985	45.7	98.2	88.4	42.7	44.2	56.8	43.9	14.0
United Kingdom								
1950	91.5	98.9	95.6	34.4	72.5	30.3	20.1	6.1
1985	74.6	97.0	83.1	10.6	59.2	61.7	39.4	3.6
U.S.A.								
1950	70.7	96.8	87.0	45.0	38.6	36.4	27.3	9.9
1985	69.3	94.5	71.1	18.3	57.4	64.4	40.4	7.0

Source: ILO [1986]

groups has steadily decreased over the years; (2) the participation rate among women of the pre-retirement age group has steadily increased in most cases; (3) the labour market activity of the older age group (65+) has rapidly dropped over the years; and (4) the participation among men and women differs substantially. Men have always participated more actively in the labour market than women. The only exceptions to this rule are Sweden and Finland, where the participation rate of women in the 25-54 year age-group approaches the rate of men of the same age[2]. A fifth, and perhaps trivial, fact is the divergent labour market developments across various countries. For instance, the participation rate of men in the age-group of 65 years and over

TABLE 1.9: LABOUR FORCE PARTICIPATION IN THE WORLD ECONOMY

	Males				Females			
Age:	15-24	25-54	55-64	65+	15-24	25-54	55-64	65+
More Developed Region[a]								
1950	81.9	96.4	87.0	44.1	58.9	45.0	32.3	16.8
1985	64.2	95.4	68.0	15.6	55.0	68.2	28.8	5.2
Less Developed Region								
1950	87.6	97.8	90.5	67.7	50.8	52.9	33.5	16.9
1985	74.8	96.7	80.4	44.8	48.7	52.3	25.8	10.2

a) The more developed region consists of Japan, Northern America, Europe, Australia, New Zealand and the U.S.S.R.. The less developed region amounts to the rest of the world.

Source: ILO [1986]

---

2. The figures are for these age groups in 1985 for Sweden: male 95.2% and female 88.9%; for Finland: male 93.5% and female 86.7%.

was less than 5% in the Netherlands and Germany, in 1985, while it was well above 40% in Japan. Given the extraordinary position of the Japanese labour market, one might even wonder whether or not leisure is a normal good in Japan. The divergence in labour market developments across the world is even more clearly illustrated in Table 1.9. The participation rates in LDCs lag behind the developments in the more developed countries (MDCs). The only rate that does not differ across the two regions is the participation rate of males in the age-group of 25-54 years.

A last remark on developments on the labour market concerns the increasing complexity of household decisions. The traditional household, with its clear-cut habits, role division and life cycle, seems to belong to the past permanently. The modern household comes in various forms, and economic decisions cover children's education, recurrent education, the timing of births, the choice of job locations, labour time/household time scheduling[3], etc. All these activities have their price in 'real time', and the pressure of an ageing population may not only have its consequences in material welfare but in terms of leisure as well. Lee and Lapkoff [1988] present some illuminating figures on the cumulative time costs of a child. As one can deduce from Table 1.10, an additional child will reduce, on average, the mother's lifetime leisure by 1,130 hoursand the father's by 2,050 hours and hence a combined leisure reduction of 3,360 hours is the result. There are, however, learning effects present in raising a child. Turchi [1975, p. 92] finds that a second or third child increases the mother's worktime at home by 4,500 hours over its first 18 years, while a first child

_____

3. This aspect also covers the issue of the allocation of sleep and work time, as analysed by Biddle and Hamermesh [1990].

TABLE 1.10: AVERAGE TIME COSTS OF AN ADDITIONAL CHILD (expressed in cumulative hours over the first 18 years of a child's life)

	Change in housework	Change in market work
Mother	+ 5,860	− 4,550
Father	+ 640	+ 1,410

Source: Lee and Lapkoff [1988, p. 650]

increases housework time by about 9,000 hours. To obtain the time cost of a third child in Table 1.10, we can assume that the second and third child have half the effect of the first. In addition, families reported in Table 1.10 have three children on average, so if we multiply the average cost of 3,360 by 0.75 we obtain the time cost of a third child, viz. 2,520 hours.

CAPITAL MARKETS

The relation between demography and capital markets is pivotal to determining the financial and economic consequences of ageing. Individuals differ in their savings behaviour and their life-cycle productivity profile. Whether ageing leads to sharp increases in real factor prices depends to a certain extent on the availability of capital. Standard neoclassical growth models associate capital-deepening with a decline in population growth (see Pitchford [1974] and Van Imhoff [1989a]), and, other things being equal, an older population should therefore have a higher per capita income than a younger population. An ageing population needs less investment than it used to: although the

capital/labour ratio rises as a substitution effect, due to a
slower rate of labour force growth, less investment is needed to
keep the capital stock in line with the labour force. Simulations by Van Imhoff [1989a, p. 187], for an overlapping
generations model with human capital, indicate that in the
beginning of the 21st century there is a sharp drop in the
optimal savings rate. In the new steady state, consumption per
capita is significantly higher than in its old state. The
welfare effect of ageing is, however, not so easily determined.
What is consumed and saved depends to a large extent on the
intergenerational links between family members. The change in
age-distribution of a population could affect a country's
private saving if the consumers of different ages consume and
save in accordance with the life-cycle hypothesis (LCH), a
theory initiated by Modigliani and Brumberg [1954]. In its most
simple form, one can imagine an individual that lives for only
two periods. In the first period he works and earns an income,
in the second period he is retired and consequently receives no
income from work effort. In order to smooth this unregular
income pattern, the life-cycle theory of consumption asserts
that saving occurs in pre-retirement years, so as to finance
consumption during retirement. The household's consumption is
therefore determined by current and expected income, the date of
retirement, the expected length of life and net wealth. The
attraction of the life-cycle hypothesis is that it seems to
reflect adequately conventional wisdom as to how saving
decisions are made within the household. The LCH enables one to
make straightforward predictions. A growing number of old-aged
in an economy will lead to a reduction of aggregate private
saving. The LCH has, however, been challenged by models of
infinitely-lived representative agents or dynasties. In the LCH,
bequests are believed to play a role of minor importance in the

accumulation of wealth. Kotlikoff and Summers [1981] broke the consensus about the ideas of life-cycle consumption behaviour. They argued that the bulk of U.S. wealth accumulation is due to intergenerational transfers. Life-cycle savings account for only one-fifth of existing wealth, whereas intergenerational transfers account for the remaining 80 percent. There are, however, conceptional problems as well as measurement problems[4]. Are bequests intended, as argued by Kotlikoff and Summers, or does a large part of bequests correspond with the precautionary motive, where wealth in retirement years serves to hedge against the uncertainty of lifetime? The main difference between the two theories hinges on the degree of altruism within the family. Modigliani and his followers assert that, by and large, intergenerational gifts and bequests are not sufficient to transform the finitely-lived family into an infinitely-lived extended family. To state their position bluntly, they argue that 80 percent of wealth accumulation is the result of life-cycle savings and the remaining 20 percent represents gifts and bequests within the family. In short, they take the opposite view of the dynastic consumer model. The prediction of the economic consequences of ageing with the dynastic consumer model, are not as straightforward as the predictions made with the life-cycle model. The representative agent never retires and wealth changes do not necessarily lead to an immediate reaction, but the consequences are spread out in time. The predictions made with the dynastic model come very close to the predictions made with Friedman's [1957] permanent income theory of consumption. A permanent increase in income will lead to an

---

4. A discussion of the problems encountered in life-cycle consumption analysis by leading players in the field can be found in Kessler and Masson [1988].

immediate and permanent shift in consumption. A temporary and unexpected rise in income is, however, not completely consumed at once. The surplus is spread out in time. Consumers prefer a smooth consumption path to an irregular path of hardship and splurges. As pointed out earlier, ageing is a temporary phenomenon which does not necessarily affect the steady state rate of population growth. If one favours the dynastic consumer model, the central question one has to ask about the economic consequences of *ageing* is then "Does ageing imply a *temporary* rise or fall in income?" At the same time one should be concerned with the consequences of the *steady state* of an older population: "Does an older population lead to a *permanent* increase or decline in income?" These questions touch upon the surface of how population and technical progress are interrelated, a question which is postponed to the next (sub)section.

Neither view of consumption is quite true. On the one hand, there is growing evidence (summarised by Kotlikoff [1988]) that the elderly do not dissave to the extent the pure LCH predicts[5]. On the other hand, the degree of altruism actually found within families does not seem to support the dynastic model of consumption (Altonji *et al.* [1989]). There are many puzzles to be solved in consumer theory before one can predict satisfactorily the economic consequences of demographic change. Nevertheless, both types of models will co-exist in modern macroeconomics, since they provide two polar archetypes of a consumer; an artificial consumer of which we know that the 'real' consumer is a

---

5. In addition to this observation, Börsch-Supan and Stahl [1991] show that West German elderly of 70 years and older do not dissave but *increase* their wealth holdings; a fact they explain in terms of health and age-related consumption constraints rather than desired bequests.

mixture.

TECHNICAL PROGRESS

The history of economic thought seems to be characterised by persistent *déja vus*. The interest in long-run dynamics by economists at present is an interest shared by fellow economists in the sixties. It was Robert Solow [1960] who tried to explain the stylised facts of economic growth with his now well-known one-sector growth model. One of his estimates of the determinants of economic growth was that 87½ % of improved productivity was due to technical progress. Technical progress was then a phenomenon that came like mannah from heaven. Twenty years later the interest is again concentrated on the long-run development of economies. Despite the tremendous research efforts of the past 25 years, technical progress is still the "measurement of our ignorance". As the accountants of economic growth (see, e.g., Maddison [1987]) point out, there is more to productivity growth than the mere usage of capital goods and labour. Various forms of natural resources and public capital goods (see Aschauer [1989]) could just as well be included in the production 'function' of a nation. But even then a large share of productivity increase cannot be explained and further refuge should be sought in theories of technical progress. Capital theories of recent date include technical progress as a factor that is embodied in the vintages of physical or human capital (Romer [1986,1989] and Lucas [1988]), while some look for the externalities of a particular organisation of capital (e.g. the experience structure of the labour force). Learning-by-doing or training-on-the-job (as in Arrow [1962] and Stokey [1988]) seems to be another plausible explanation of productivity increases. And finally, some argue that a theory of technical progress has to describe the core of the process, viz. the modelling of the product/process innovation technology (see Schmitz [1989]). The majority of these theories is of such recent date that it has not yet been empirically tested, and at this stage some economists seem to be skating on thin ice when they derive policy recommendations from these first generation theories.

The interaction between the age structure of a population and the rate of technical progress is still one of the most puzzling causalities. Some believe, notably Julian Simon [1986], that the rate of population growth has a positive effect on the rate of technical progress. The reasoning behind these theories is quite simple: the larger the population, the bigger the chance that inventions and innovations will occur. To say the least, this theory is quite unbalanced. On the one hand, a plausible theory of endogenous technical progress should be related to other production factors. On the other hand, one must admit there is an element of common sense in the Simon theory, because a growing population has a larger number of young people than a stationary population. Younger people are assumed to be more innovative than their older colleagues. If we were to take the aggregate stock of knowledge as a separate production factor, a growing population might be advantageous since 'two know more than one'. This issue of technical progress and population hinges on a number effect. One can model this as follows: let the size of the population be denoted by $N(t)$ and let $h_j(t)$ be the amount of knowledge of individual j, where individuals are not necessarily identical. The aggregate stock of knowledge would then amount to:

$$(1.1) \qquad H(t) = \sum_{j=1}^{N} h_j(t)$$

In the production of human capital one has to recognise the public-good character of knowledge as represented by H. The production of goods by the individual j, y_j, is therefore affected by this externality as follows:

$$(1.2) \qquad y_j = f(h_j, H)$$

The stock of knowledge is given to the individual, and it would be in the interest of a benevolent government to see to it that the optimal amount of knowledge is produced. Prescott and Boyd [1987] hold the view that the productivity of human capital depends not only on the productivity of the worker himself but also on the productivity of his co-workers. The externality of an experience structure in the work force seems of particular relevance in predicting the consequences of ageing. Given the existence of an optimal age structure, the question with respect to ageing then becomes: "Is an older age structure of the work force below or above the optimal age structure?"

NATURAL RESOURCES

The interaction between natural resources and populations is perhaps one of the most classical relationships economists have dealt with. Political economists like Adam Smith, David Ricardo and Thomas Malthus made lasting impressions on this point. In their time, economies were primarily based on the contribution of agriculture to the national income, hence it was quite natural that economists of that time focused on the scarcity of land and the abundance of population and labour. The dominating theory of that time was the Population Thesis of Thomas Malthus. Malthus' population thesis was founded on two "postulata", viz.: (1) "That food is necessary to the existence of man".

(2) "That the passion between the sexes is necessary and will remain nearly in its present state" (Malthus [1798, p. 70]). The second assumption amounts to the view that fertility is exogenous. Taking the assumptions (which Malthus calls "fixed laws of nature") as granted, Malthus goes on to conclude that,

> "the power of population is indefinitely greater than the power in the earth to produce subsistence for man. Population, when unchecked, increases in a geometrical ratio. Subsistence increases only in a arithmetical ratio. [..] This implies a strong and constantly operating check on population from the difficulty of subsistence. This difficulty must fall somewhere and must necessarily be severely felt by a large portion of mankind" (Malthus [1798, p. 71]).

Malthus' population thesis found an application in classical economic theory through the *wages fund doctrine* developed by Smith and extended by Ricardo. This doctrine implied that if the real wage of labour rose above the minimum subsistence wage, this would result in an increase in population, and this increase would, in turn, eventually bring the wage rate back to its former subsistence level. A cross-section analysis by Boyer [1989] for early nineteenth century England proved that birth rates were indeed related to child allowances, income and the availability of housing. Malthus could, of course, not foresee the technical changes to come, but his theory might still be of some relevance for studying problems of resource allocation in developing countries.

The modern theory of the allocation of natural resources goes beyond the simple Malthusian model on some points, though on other points - such as endogenous population growth - it still shows some caveats. An exception to this observation is a study by Eckstein *et al.* [1988,1989]. They show how long-run per capita consumption depends on assumptions of technical progress and fertility choice in a model with a fixed amount of land. When parents only care about the number of children and not about their children's welfare, the equilibrium would be such that the family would choose one child for each adult, hence a zero population growth rate. The remarkable result is that when fertility is subject to choice, there exists a competitive equilibrium which avoids the gloomy Malthusian outcome, and the economy converges to a steady state with a constant population. The Malthusian result hinges quite strongly on exogenous fertility. With exogenous high fertility, a decentralised economy eventually vanishes, possibly in finite time, although the path is likely to be Pareto optimal.

Eckstein *et al.* used the fixity of land as an approximation of a natural resource, but this modelling strategy sidesteps the issue that dominates the entire discussion about natural resource allocation, viz.: are natural resources exhaustible or renewable? Renewable resources offer no problem as long as the rate of population growth does not exceed the growth rate of this resource. This was essentially Malthus's concern, but today it appears in a new form. The choices that society faces depend to a large extent on the degree of reversibility of changes in the environment (see Arrow and Fischer [1974]). When development of a natural resource is irreversible and one is uncertain about the pay-offs of such an investment in developing the resource, one should underinvest rather than overinvest, since underinvestment can be remedied later, whereas overinvestment cannot. The difficulty society faces is that natural resources which *appear* to be renewable are gradually transformed into exhaustible resources. Contemporaneous examples of such a transition can be found in desertification, overfishing and declining rain forests. Ecologists call this theshold level the 'carrying capacity' of an ecosystem. The carrying capacity focuses on the interaction between a population, its activities and the surrounding environment, and it highlights natural thresholds that might otherwise remain obscure. Biologists can calculate rather precisely the carrying capacity of a particular system. Some developing countries have gone well beyond their carrying capacity and current generations have to deal with the problem of the allocation of exhaustible resource such as forests, fisheries or, in general, the entire ecosystem. Normative theories of exhaustible natural resource allocation are essentially 'cake-eating' problems: for how much of the world's endowment of exhaustible resources is it fair for the current generation to use up and how much should be left for the generations to come who are not actively participating in contemporaneous decisions? Hartwick's [1977,1978] rule provides a useful rule of thumb: a society that invests the competitive rents on its current extraction of exhaustible resources in reproducable capital, will enjoy a consumption stream constant in time. However, this rule works only under conditions of *no technical progress* and *no population growth*. Besides these two factors, the discussion of exhaustible resource allocation centers also on the *substitutability* of natural resources and other factors of production and the *size* of the reserves. Empirical estimates on the extent of substitutability are hardly reliable, and at present we must admit that we simply do not know. Uncertainty about the extent of depletion is of particular relevance to the present day world economy, depending on oil and related resources like gas. How should one use up a natural resource which is subject to shocks such as a war or the discovery of new oil fields? The social planner who tries to answer this question continuously faces the question whether he should live like a monk or whether he should adopt the lifestyle of a king. With hindsight, taking either position may be regrettable. The intertemporal use of Dutch natural gas is a case in point. Using the proceeds of gas to finance *permanent* government expenditures is, of course, wrong, but from the point of view of the initial decision maker, it was undoubtedly right, perhaps because changes in public spending were seen as temporary. However, one cannot blame the entire dismal state of Dutch public finance on the discovery of gas. Kremers [1986a] argues that Dutch fiscal policy rules (viz. the endogeneity of public spending) as initiated in the late 1960s turned out to be unsustainable.

PUBLIC EXPENDITURES AND TAXATION

Public debates suggest that the financial consequences of ageing are mainly a concern of the public sector. A substantial number of goods and services that are related to needs of the old aged are provided by the public sector. Public expenditures are therefore very sensitive to the age distribution of the population. Relatively young populations make intensive use of education and child care facilities, while older populations absorb large quantities of medical care and the tax burden of public pensions becomes quite distinct. Tables 1.11 and 1.12 give an impression of the asymmetry in public expenditures per age group (in per capita terms). The health care expenditures of old aged are quite high compared to the younger part of the popula-tion. Of course, the coverage of public health care differs per country, with low ratios for France and Germany and quite high ratios for Sweden and the U.S.A.. A population that ages will reduce the per capita consumption of education and family assistance programmes and steadily increase the amount

spent on health care per capita. The implicit assumption of this
prediction is that user propensities per age-group are constant,
as well as the cost per public expenditure category. The latter
assumption may lead to false conclusions, because a category
like health care depends largely on human capital. With
dependency ratios increasing from 'one pensioner supported by
four workers' to 'one pensioner supported by three (or even two)
workers' real wages could rise substantially, thereby raising
the relative price of medical care. Costs in public health care
could then consume a substantially larger part of the national
income than one might think at first.

TABLE 1.11: RATIO OF PER CAPITA PUBLIC HEALTH EXPENDITURE ON
ELDERLY TO NON-ELDERLY IN SELECTED OECD COUNTRIES

	Year	Expenditure ratio: Persons aged 65+/ Persons aged 0-64	Persons aged 75+/ persons aged 0-64
Australia	1980/81	4.9	8.0
Canada	1974	4.5	6.7
Denmark	1983	4.1	4.8
France	1980/81	2.4	2.8
Germany	1975	2.6	3.1
Ireland	1979	4.5	6.0
Japan	1980	4.8	5.3
Netherlands	1981	4.5	6.2
Sweden	1983	5.5	9.2
U.K.	1979/80	4.3	6.6
U.S.A.	1978	7.4	-
Average		4.3	5.9[a]

a) Average of 10 countries

Source: OECD [1988, p. 33]

TABLE 1.12: PER CAPITA PUBLIC EXPENDITURES BY AGE GROUP IN SELECTED OECD COUNTRIES IN 1980 (in units of national currency)

	0-14	15-64	65+	65+/0-14	65+/15-64
Belgium	117453	74503	242017	2.1	3.2
Canada	2462	1772	6535	2.7	3.7
Denmark	20589	14483	42259	2.1	2.9
France	15529	7975	40902	2.6	5.1
Germany	5823	3464	18409	3.2	5.3
Japan	435874	191868	1022829	2.3	5.3
Sweden	20860	8974	48871	2.3	5.4
U.K.	918	490	1956	2.1	4.0
U.S.A.	1874	1254	7135	3.8	5.7

Source: OECD [1988, p. 34]

On the expenditure side, questions that are in dire need of an answer amount to "Which resource allocation mechanism is best suited to cope with shocks in demography?". The public budget mechanism is sometimes automatically seen as the only mechanism through which age-related expenditures, such as health care, can be financed. The household or the family is, however, equally capable of coping with demographic shocks. The ultimate answer to the question of who provides age-related goods and services depends then on the manner in which individuals take account of future and/or uncertain developments, and the excludability and rivalry of 'public' goods.

The largest category of demographically related public expenditures is public pensions. Public pensions can be financed by two schemes: a pay-as-you-go (PAYG) system or a fully funded system. In the PAYG system, retirement benefits are financed by contemporaneous taxes, so that in each period the budget is balanced. In general, the taxes are levied on the workers' earnings, part of which may be collected from the employer and the rest from the worker, so that production factor labour has to bear the burden of the finance of public pensions. This is a clear disadvantage of a PAYG scheme. The sole reliance on a contemporaneous tax base is alleviated by the fully funded scheme. The pension premiums are set so that the present value of all contributions paid by a generation equals the present value of the future liability engendered by that same generation. The fully funded pension system is therefore a neutral system, i.e. there is no wealth redistribution between generations. For a *social* security system this might seem undesirable, since generations differ in endowments and the (inevitable) shocks they encounter[6]. A public pension system that can spread out the wealth of a nation over generations is likely to be a more just system. This implies for models of intertemporal economic policy that a government's objective function should show (limited) complementarity of consumption levels between present and future time. An aspect one must not neglect with social security analysis is the effect its introduction or its method of finance has on population growth. Poeth [1975] and Van Praag and Poeth [1977] have shown for primitive economies that the fertility rate decreases as more weight is given to a PAYG system, compared to a primitive pension system, where retired parents are supported by their children.

Table 1.13 shows how over the years, the demographic state of countries has contributed to the growth of public expenditures

---

6. E.g., Pozdena [1987] has shown that between 1977 and 1983 a significant shift has taken place in the U.S. age distribution of financial wealth towards older households. The unexpected high rates of inflation had given rise to increases in home values, social security income and other sources of wealth from which older households benefited disproportionately.

TABLE 1.13: IMPACT OF DEMOGRAPHIC CHANGE ON THE GROWTH OF PUBLIC EXPENDITURES IN OECD COUNTRIES, 1960-1981

		Annual Percentage growth in real expenditures[a]		Per cent attributable to demogr. change[b]	
		1960-75	1975-81	1960-75	1975-81
Canada	Education	8.4	1.0	16	-
	Pensions	8.3	6.8	29	49
France	Education	-	1.0	-	-60
	Pensions	7.7	8.7	25	9
Germany	Education	7.2	1.6	8	-56
	Pensions	6.3	2.1	49	43
Nether-lands	Education	4.3	1.1	16	-45
	Pensions	10.3	5.2	26	38
Japan	Education	5.7	4.1	-4	-
	Pensions	12.7	13.7	27	27
U. K.	Education	5.0	-2.0	12	20
	Pensions	5.9	4.5	27	22
U.S.A.	Education	6.1	0.4	18	-
	Pensions	7.2	4.4	25	57

a) Average compound growth rate in expenditure at constant prices.
b) Rate of growth in client population divided by growth rate of real expenditure; client population are: persons aged 0-24, and population aged 65 and over.

Source: OECD [1985], Tables 6 and A.

in two large categories of public spending: education and public pensions. Both categories entail intergenerational transfers. Changes in demographic structure have made a substantial contribution to the growth in public pensions: 30 percent of the growth is attributable to the growth in the age group of 65 and over. In addition to the age-related use of public outlays, there is some reason to expect a larger increase in public expenditures than presented here. It should be noted, for instance, that most of the increase in pension expenditure is attributable to better pensions and pension coverage rather than more pensioners. Ageing societies will encounter a larger group of people (say people over 45) who might influence the alloca- tion through their political pressure. People over 45 will not only gain a voting majority due to an increase in life expec- tancy, but there is also the asymmetry in voting age: people are generally qualified to vote at the age of 18. Another interest group which is likely to dominate ageing populations is the female population. Life expectancy of women is far higher than that of males. Provided they use their voting majority, ageing societies may well encounter increasing feminist pressure. Changing sizes of political pressure groups makes the public choice analysis of an ageing society especially noteworthy. Renaud and Van Winden [1987] show for a simple public choice model for the Netherlands that the numerical strength of social groups has significant empirical meaning for the determination of the overall tax rate and the relative government expenditure[7].

On the revenue side, governments are quite anxious to obtain knowledge about how the various tax bases develop. This is necessary in order to design principles of fiscal policy. Questions of tax reform in an ageing society should therefore be addressed in dynamic general equilibrium models in order to evaluate and design tax structures. Auerbach and Kotlikoff

_____

7. A more general public choice model of government finance is presented in Van Velthoven and Van Winden [1990].

[1987, ch. 5] evaluate various tax bases in terms of their allocative and distributional effects in the form of simulations. The difficulty with a tax reform question is that certain taxes perform a dual role. The present build-up of the effective tax rate on labour income in Table 1.14 shows more than clearly how various taxes can affect the price of labour.

TABLE 1.14: TOTAL MARGINAL TAX RATES ON LABOUR INCOME, 1983[a]
(per cent of total compensation)

	Effective tax rate	Pay- roll tax	Employers' contri- bution	Employees' contri- bution	Personal income tax	Indir. tax
Canada	42.72	0.00	0.00	0.00	29.40	13.32
France	59.70	4.64	30.24	9.68	5.61	9.53
Germany	57.02	0.00	15.61	14.60	18.57	8.25
Japan	39.93	0.00	10.15	9.07	16.15	4.55
Netherlands	73.47	0.00	19.68	31.17	16.99	5.63
U.K.	54.53	1.25	9.34	8.05	26.82	9.07
U.S.A.	42.64	0.00	7.83	6.18	24.29	4.34

a) Per cent of total compensation including payroll taxes for a single-earner married couple with two children, with income equal to that of the average production worker.

Source: McKee *et al.* [1986]

Straightforward calculations[8] of the finance of social security and age-related public expenditures show quite dramatic increases in payroll taxes. Developing rules for taxation remains a difficult task. Questions, such as, "Should a

---

8. See, e.g., Halter and Hemming [1988], Hagemann and Nicoletti [1989], Ritzen [1989], Masson and Tryon [1990] and Wildasin [1991].

government balance its budget each and every period or should it smooth the tax rates and balance the public budget only in a present value sense?" and "Is a tax reform necessary to absorb the demographic transition, if so, what is the optimal tax structure?" are subject to a great deal of uncertainty, since they demand a great deal of knowledge on how tastes, technology and population[9] develop and interact.

1.2 METHODOLOGY

The methodology used throughout this thesis is that of the *dynamic general equilibrium* approach: this approach assumes that markets are continuously cleared and agents have rational expectations (which boils down to perfect foresight under conditions of certainty) concerning the entire time path of prices and endowments. Perhaps I should also add the tacit methodology used in this thesis. Some people argue (notably McCloskey [1985]) that the rhetoric of mainstream economic theory is dominated by the language of mathematical economics. The reason for this domination is thought to be the feeling amongst economists that one can only persuade a colleague economist by means of a technical analysis. This, of course, is not true. Verbal arguments can be just as strong as technical arguments. But mathematics has the unequivocal advantage that one has to be precise in defining an economy. A general

---

9. E.g., the U.S. federal income tax has a feature that implicitly affects the decision to have a child, viz. the personal exemption for dependents. Whittington *et al*. [1990] have estimated the effect of personal exemptions on the birth rate per thousand women between ages 15 and 44. It turns out to be small but significant.

equilibrium model is usually constructed, since statements made on the sign of effects to certain shocks simply surpass the calculating capabilities of the human mind. As an example of such a mathematical exercise one may consider the analysis of comparative statics. This type of analysis may give an impression of how the system works and how large some effects are. When tractability of the model is at stake, simulation may offer an insight into the mechanics of economic development. Verbal theories, on the contrary, engage in the use of vague and undefined words which meanings change constantly throughout the analysis, and the use of more or less metaphysical expressions that can mean anything one wants. Verbal analysis simply lacks precision of argument, although economic prose may be more enjoyable than endless sequences of assumptions, first order conditions and three-dimensional phase diagrams. Mathematical economics can on that same account be very elegant and rigorous, but completely lacking in content. This might be seen as Friedman's [1949] grudge against Walrasian economic theory. He sums up the state of the art of Walrasian economic theory as he sees it:

> "*Abstractness, generality and mathematical elegance have in some measure become ends in themselves, criteria by which to judge economic theory. [..] Theory is to be tested by the accuracy of its 'assumptions' as photographic descriptions of reality, not by the correctness of the predictions that can be derived from it*" [1949, p. 490].

The Walrasian or general equilibrium approach stresses the interdependencies of markets. According to Friedman, Marshallian economics, or the partial equilibrium analysis of a single market is better suited "as an engine for the discovery of concrete truth". Marshall's methodology of 'partial' equilibrium analysis helps to focus on a manageable bit of reality, ignoring or summarizing those parts of which the influence on the problem at hand is small. The 'ceteris paribus' condition is central to the partial equilibrium approach. Partial equilibrium analysis is to be regarded as a special case of general equilibrium analysis because, as Arrow and Hahn [1971] argue,

> "[t]he existence of one market presupposes that there must be at least one commodity beyond that traded on that market, for a price must be stated as the rate at which an individual gives up something for the commodity in question. If there was really only one commodity there would be no exchange and no market" [1971, pp. 6-7]

Modern day Walrasians, like Lucas, Prescott and Sargent, are of the opinion that one can only understand *macro*economic phenomena if behaviour is microeconomically founded. Their preference for fully interdependent systems is therefore understandable. The dividing line between Walrasians and Marshallians is however not that clear. On the one hand, if one wants to practice meaningful macroeconomic theory one has to invoke a general equilibrium model of analysis to stress the interdependency between consumers, producers and government. On the other hand, economic theory is not practised by flat characters only. For instance, the general equilibrium analysis of a *closed* economy with *one* representative consumer/producer, who enjoys a *composite* commodity is just as partial an analysis as the Marshallian cross of demand and supply reflecting the market for cereals in Zimbabwe. Or to give an example of the real world of academia, the *Marshallian* Robert Lucas [1990a], who analyses the question why capital flows between rich and poor countries do *not* come about, differs quite distinctly from the *Walrasian* Robert Lucas, who examines formation of interest rates in a two-country world economy [1982]. The everyday economist is merely pragmatic: different problems require different models. If pragmatism is tantamount to adequate abstraction, we can all be considered Marshallians.

Debates on questions of economic principles are generally centered around the degree of realism of the assumptions employed. Realism incorporates the belief that there is an objective world which exists independently of consciousness but which is knowable by consciousness (cf. Lawson [1987]). Given the arbitrariness of 'an objective world' and what is 'knowable by consciousness' an argument about the realism of assumptions is bound to end up in a discussion led by the rules of argument of a christmas pantomime. The practice of economic theory should surpass the exchange of "Oh, yes it is!" and "Oh, no it isn't!". It is the economist's task to clarify the conditions under which certain phenomena will appear and change and design principles that are practical, robust and welfare enhancing. The axiomatic approach to economics has enabled one to screen economic and ethical reasoning by performing experiments without any real societal costs. This approach has, however, led on several occasions to objections. Critics assert that mathematical economists, such as Arrow and Debreu, are chasing the will-o'-the-wisp. Indeed the preface of Debreu's *Theory of Value* seems to suggest this:

> "*Allegiance to rigor dictates the axiomatic form of the analysis where the theory, in the strict sense, is logically entirely disconnected from its interpretations [1959, p.x]*"

The axiomatic method gives rise to a formal structure and it is legitimate to analyse it merely as a formal structure. However, to call axiomatising the product of creative acts of human imagination, where *economic* axioms are chosen independently of interpretation, does not appear to be a truthful description of the practice of economic theorists. Two doctrines dominate attempts within traditional epistemology to provide foundations for knowledge: *empiricism* which stresses the primary role of sensory experience in knowledge and *rationalism* which claims a primary role for *a priori* reasoning in knowledge. Of course, the two are interrelated: rationalism presupposes knowledge while empiricism cannot function without a priori knowledge. It is basically the debate about 'measurement without theory' versus 'theory without measurement'. The axiomatic structure can become particularly *a priori* if assumptions for convenience are made merely to achieve mathematical tractability. It must however be stressed that this is the art of theorising. One has to make a simplification, otherwise one will end up with the enlightened opinion that 'anything goes'. True, general equilibrium theory is not the pinnacle of description of modern-day economies. It is, however, reasonably realistic in the enhancement of understanding principles and mechanisms.

One can, of course, argue that it is no good quarrelling over the meaning of the realism of assumptions and follow the F-twisted methodology of Milton Friedman: realism does not matter as long as a theory predicts well. The strong version of this methodology is absurd or twisted, because one wants to understand predictions and, in the absence of perfect foresight, why they do not materialise. The F-twist amounts to the claim that "it is a positive merit of a theory that (some of) its content and assumptions be unrealistic" (Samuelson [1963, p. 232]).

The weaker version is standard practice in economics and not very controversial. Perhaps there is only one objective yardstick by which one can measure the degree of realism, viz.

the acid test of economic research: research directed at creating ideas that are detached from reality is bound to fall into oblivion.

1.3 RESEARCH QUESTIONS AND OUTLINE

As the stylised facts suggest, the strategy to model the world as two *demographically divided* and *interdependent* entities seems worthwhile. The term 'demographically divided' can, however, also refer to a closed economy, in which regions or groups in society differ in their rate of population growth, preferences, state of technology or initial endowments.

The questions this thesis examines can roughly be divided into, on the one hand, central decision making problems of a social planner who has a complete mandate of its constituents, and, on the other hand, questions of policy design in an indirect manner (i.e. the government can only influence the behaviour of consumers/producers by affecting relative prices and redistributing resources across agents and across time), on the other hand. The first part is better known as the theory of *optimal economic growth*. The normative theory of optimal economic growth was pioneered by the Cambridge mathematician Frank Plumpton Ramsey[10], who published his seminal article "A Mathematical Theory of Saving" in December 1928, just about a year before his untimely death at the age of 26. His analysis was considered at the time "one of the most remarkable contributions to mathematical economics ever made" (Keynes [1933, p. 295]) and indeed today it remains one of the most fundamental papers in economic theory. The research question

---

10. See Newman [1987] for a short overview of Ramsey's fundamental contribution to economics and mathematics.

that he posed can be summarised as:

> *How much should a nation save and invest in order to enjoy the maximum amount of utility of consumption over its entire lifetime?*

The importance of this question is perhaps best illustrated by questions one comes across in everyday policy debates: "Why is Japan's savings rate so high?", and "Is saving too low in the U.S.A.?" The degree in which a country saves is seen as one of the central policy problems of today. By calculating the optimal capital stock, one can compare it to its actual counterpart and

TABLE 1.15: DIFFERENT MEASURES OF GROSS FIXED CAPITAL FORMATION (as a percentage of GDP, average of individual year ratios, 1970-1984)

	Conventional measure[a]	(1) + Education	(2) + Research & Development	(3) + Consumer Durables
	(1)	(2)	(3)	(4)
U.S.A.	18.1	24.2	26.2	30.1
Canada	22.0	30.9	31.9	37.2
Japan	31.9	36.1	38.0[b]	39.9[b]
France	22.2	25.9	27.5	32.4
Germany	22.1	26.0[b]	27.9[b]	n.a.
Italy	19.8	24.9[c]	25.7[c]	29.0[c]
U.K.	18.5	23.0	24.9[b]	28.4[b]

a) The conventional measure amounts to gross savings as compiled by the Bureau of Economic Analysis of the U.S. Department of Commerce.
b) 1970-1983
c) 1970-1982

Source: Lipsey and Kravis [1987, pp. 47-50].

determine whether capital is over or underaccumulated (a related approach can be found in Christiano [1989] and Abel *et al.* [1989]). The simplicity of these questions is perfidious. First of all, saving and investment need not be equal to each other in an open economy; by borrowing or lending on the international capital market a country may smooth the time path of its policy objective (in mainstream theory this is generally the time path of consumption). Secondly, there is a measurement problem. Once one has determined the optimal investment rate and tries to compare it to actual rates, there is a difficulty in obtainingthe right figure. Table 1.15 shows some different measures of fixed capital formation. The prime difficulty with measuring investment rates is their mixed character. Investment in education is a case in point. Not all expenditures on education are inspired by investment motives. Education is one of those goods that exhibit production as well as consumption characteristics.

Last but not least, there exists considerable disagreement on what the objective of a nation should be. Some argue (such as Meade [1955]) that a government should strive for the Benthamite goal of the greatest happiness for the greatest number. The argument of the objective function - consumption - is therefore expressed in total terms. Others (such as Pitchford [1974]) are more concerned with average happiness. The argument of the objective function is therefore expressed in (unweighted for the size of generations) per capita terms. The normative statements concerned with the population size and growth resulting from these two types of formulations are exact mirror images. For instance, the proponents of the total utility criterion would like population to grow at the fastest rate, while proponents of the per capita utility criterion would like the population to grow at the smallest, preferably negative, rate. Both criteria are at fault with ethical considerations of optimal population sizes. Optimality implies that there is a trade-off. To prescribe a corner solution might be called optimal, under certain conditions, but with populations this is an entirely different matter. If one proposes a negative growth rate, who would enjoy welfare in the end? A positive growth rate is, however, equally indefensible since the world has only finite space and resources and in the end one has to solve cake-eating problems of a rather morbid nature (see, e.g., Koopmans [1974]).

In chapter 3, I will take a closer look at the question of development planning of transferring resources from the developed world to the developing world. This chapter serves as a background for the problem of optimal economic growth of chapter 4. In chapter 4 I will look at the question of optimal capital flows between two countries with decentralised planning. In the first part I will look at the standard model of optimal growth to examine the exact conditions under which patterns of international lending and borrowing come about. A more general model with endogenous time preference formation is introduced in the second part of chapter 4. Time preference is assumed to be dependent on current utility of consumption.

In chapter 5 the welfare consequences of selective immigration policies are examined. The question that induced the research is:

> *Under what conditions can two social planners execute a selective immigration policy to make at least one party better off, without affecting the welfare of the other in a negative way, compared to the autarkic welfare level?*

The economic analysis of the *brain drain*, as the phenomenon of the outflow of trained individuals is called, is of some interest to the world of tomorrow. On the one hand, pressure will be build up in ageing countries to alleviate domestic labour market tension by 'importing' foreign trained labour. On the other hand, developing countries are still in dire need for skilled labour. In the past, questions of migration have often been examined in a partial equilibrium setting[11]. One need not have an accountant's eye to see that this is a false research strategy. Gains embodied in labour for one country could imply losses for the source country and the appropriate modelling strategy should be a two-country model.

Chapter 6 serves as an introduction to models of indirect government control. In this chapter I will discuss the relevance of the Ricardian theory of public finance to economies charac-terised by demographic changes. Ever since Robert Barro [1974] published his paper on the question "Are government bonds net wealth?", the public finance community has debated about the relevance of this fiscal theory on several occasions. The research question posed by Barro can be translated into a variety of alltime public finance questions, such as "Is public debt a burden for future generations?", or "Does fiscal policy matter?". Refuting the first question certainly gives us a comfortable feeling, but replying 'no' to the second question must indeed be a shock to a benevolent government and a relief to the civil servant enjoying the quiet life. In this chapter I want to take a closer look at some of the assumptions of the Ricardian theory of public finance and see whether a Ricardian world is a possible world.

To do justice to actual economies I have tried to answer a basic question of economic policy design in a second best world. It marks perhaps the genius of Ramsey that he was again the one to pioneer the second strand of economic policy questions,

---

11. See, e.g., Simon and Heins [1985].

better known as the *theory of optimal taxation*. In his article in the *Economic Journal* of 1927 he examined the following policy problem:

> *A government has to finance its expenditures at one point in time by using proportionate tax rates on a variety of consumption goods. How should these tax rates be set when the objective of the government is to minimise the welfare loss the individual consumer incurs as a consequence of changed relative prices?*

The welfare of the consumer will of course be higher in case the government has access to lump-sum taxes. The deviation between consumption bundles under the regime of lump-sum taxation and distortionary taxation is called *deadweight loss* or *excess burden*. The main deviation from the theory of optimal economic growth is the presence of individual competitive behaviour. In the case of distortionary taxation a government will generally affect the welfare of the consumer in a negative way. Questions that are addressed are, amongst others: "Should tax rates be constant across time?" and "Which tax rate is best suited for absorbing shocks in public spending and demographic change?". These are the low brow spin-offs of high brow economic theory and they are addressed in chapter 7 for a small open economy. In addition, the discussion is extended to the use of public debt and distortionary taxation in an interdependent world economy. Questions of time consistency of fiscal policy and the pros and cons of cooperation are discussed.

Chapter 8 is the final chapter in which the main conclusions of the thesis are summed up and in which some qualifications are made to the results obtained, and possible extensions to the presented models are suggested for future research.

CHAPTER 2: ELEMENTS OF A THEORY

> *"All theory depends on assumptions which are not quite true. That is what makes it theory."*
>
> Robert M. Solow [1956]

The demographic state of an economy has such a pervasive influence on the performance of an economy that it may be worthwhile to disentangle the various elements through which demographic changes work and the way in which we evaluate certain allocations that result from such changes. The way in which an economist analyses economic problems shows some resemblance with the everyday practice of a detective. Just as any good detective goes about his work, the economist tries to establish his case by reconstructing the 'crime' called economic activity. The motives can often be summarised by pointing to utility and/or profit maximisation. But these motives are merely used as hard-core assumptions, which yield falsifiable predictions. In general, the economic motives in conjunction with preferences, endowments, technology and, last but not least, the rules of the game describe an economic system. But again, the task of an economist does not end here. Histories of economic activity can only be traced in conjunction with fluctuations in relative prices. The difficulty economists encounter in establishing the applicability of a theory *beyond a reasonable doubt*, is the observational equivalence of theories: different theories can be equivalent in terms of explaining a dataset. At all times, it is therefore of prime importance to choose credible and useful simplifications. The art of choosing good simplifications is often overlooked in the creation of ideas. Successful social scientists are not valued for their mastery of some or other technique but for their contribution in choosing plausible simplifications and building simple models; models that reflect an idea. 'Simple' models refer to an accurate and tractable formalisation in this context. As John Maynard Keynes once wrote in a letter to Roy Harrod:

> "Good economists are scarce because the gift for using 'vigilant observation' to choose good models, although it does not require a highly specialised intellectual technique, appears to be a very rare one."[1]

My 'vigilant observation' has led me to choose general equilibrium models of economic growth as the basis for discussing the economic consequences of a demographically divided world. One should, however, keep in mind that every model of the real world is a personal choice.

In these introductory remarks I will give some reasons why I have chosen these models to analyse demographic changes. Two aspects of formulating the theory stand out as being characteristic for the optimal growth analysis. One aspect is the dynamic formulation. The second aspect refers to the general equilibrium nature of the solution. Dynamic economic theory makes the time structure explicit and stresses the fact that decisions today influence the outcome of tomorrow. General equilibrium analysis derives behaviour under the restriction that all markets clear at all times. The preference for Walrasian analysis to non-Walrasian analysis finds its roots in the comparison of welfare positions. Non-Walrasian analysis has the severe drawback that the welfare level heavily depends on

---

1. This excerpt (Keynes [1973, p. 297]) is taken from a letter by John Maynard Keynes to Roy F. Harrod, dated July 4, 1938, in which Keynes discusses Tinbergen's work on business cycles.

the *ad hoc* rigidities and is therefore not suitable as a tool for the evaluation of resource allocations. However, I should stress that the Walrasian tool of analysis is not useful at all times. As Friedman [1955, p. 909] put it:

> *"A person is not likely to be a good economist who does not have a firm command of Walrasian economics; equally, he is not likely to be a good economist if he knows nothing else".*

Macroeconomic systems pose questions which are too complex to be analysed by means of a Marshallian approach. The use of the condition 'ceteris paribus' can lead to misleading conclusions under certain circumstances. One cannot analyse the problem of demographic change by keeping other things constant. The channels through which changes in demography affect the economy are too diverse and should therefore be studied simultaneously.

This introductory chapter describes the elements of a theory, which will be used extensively in later chapters; these elements refer to the maximum principle underlying economic choice, social welfare and the treatment of future generations. Finally, these elements are taken together in an attempt to illustrate the dynamics of economic growth. Necessarily, the discussion of the elements is of a limited nature, but the references in the text should guide the reader to more thorough analyses.

2.1 MAXIMUM PRINCIPLE OF CHOICE

One of the central economic problems in modern history of economic thought has been the optimal allocation of scarce resources at a point in time *and* over time. The determination of an optimal allocation involves static as well as dynamic optimisation. Classical authors solved the problem analytically by static optimisation, leaving the questions of changes over time to sweeping theories of 'magnificent dynamics'. The fulfillment of conditions of static optimality, however, does not automatically ensure dynamic optimality. As shown by Dorfman *et al.* [1958], different static optimal programmes trace out different intertemporal paths which are not all dynamically efficient. With the introduction of methods of dynamic optimisation the questions of optimisation over time could finally be studied. The methods of calculus of variation, dynamic programming and optimal control theory are the methods of dynamic optimisation most widely known in the toolbox of a present day economist. The calculus of variations, as applied in, e.g., Ramsey [1928], has its limitations, such as its failure to yield an equilibrium when the solution is at the boundary of the space of feasible solutions. It is therefore that I restrict my attention to the method of optimal control theory, as initiated by Pontryagin *et al.* [1964].

The models presented in this thesis are all based on the assumption of rational expectations. In a completely deterministic environment, rational expectations boil down to perfect foresight. The critics of rational expectations often associate this assumption of rationality with models of an Arrow-Debreu mode, as used in New Classical contributions[2]; such models are characterised by dynamic efficiency. However, it should be pointed out that rational expectations are not a sufficient condition for obtaining a Pareto-efficient allocation. Competitive equilibria can just as well be suboptimal if one of the assumptions of a dynamic Arrow-Debreu

---

2. For a review of New Classical models one is referred to Hoover [1988].

model is violated, which concerns markets and the form of preferences, endowments and technology. Models of overlapping generations (Samuelson [1958]), dynamic models that give rise to erratic time series (Benhabib and Day [1982]) and models that capture aspects of employment coordination failure (Roberts [1987]) or failures in the saving-intermediation coordination (Diamond and Dybvig [1983]), are all models that use rational expectations but they still illustrate competitive inefficiencies.

THE MAXIMUM PRINCIPLE

The object of optimal resource allocation is to lay down rules of a choice of instrument values $v(t)$, which establish that scarce resources are allocated to different productive uses and consumption in an efficient manner. The state of an economic system in which agents interact or in which one representative agent does all the calculative work, is described by a finite dimensional vector $x(t)$. The state of an economic system might suitably be represented by the amount of physical and human capital and financial claims and liabilities. The development of the economic system is described by the transition equation,

$$(2.1) \quad \dot{x} \equiv dx/dt = G[x(t),v(t),t]$$

Time t enters the transition equation to account for any non-stationarities in the economic environment over time, such as technical change, population growth, preference drift or other exogenous factors. Given the initial state of the system, x_0, and the choice of instruments $v(t)$, the system is determined. The problem is now to choose exactly one path of instruments which maximises a criterion function, usually defined as utility U. The arguments which enter this welfare function are again the same arguments as in equation (2.1), since they are intimately related.

(2.2) $U = U[x(t),v(t),t]$

The utility function offers the means to express preferences between different histories of the economic system. To avoid valuation problems to the state ('scrap value') at the finite end of the transition process, we will continue our discussion in terms of infinite horizons. To make things even more simple than they are, it will be assumed that the welfare function is additive over time, i.e. at each moment in time t, there is a return of felicity $U(.)$ which depends only on the values of the state variables and instruments at time t, such that the utility of a whole history is the integral of the values of the felicities at each moment in time.

(2.3) $$\int_0^\infty \beta(t)U[x(t),v(t),t]\ dt$$

A discount factor $\beta(t)$ (where β is a decreasing function of time) has been added to ensure that the integral (2.3) converges. In finite time this factor is not necessary since in that case the cumulative utility value is a finite number. Assuming that a policy leads to a constant utility value the integral (2.3) will converge. This is tantamount to the condition that the summation of the discount factor over time:

(2.4) $$\int_0^\infty \beta(t)\ dt \quad \text{converges.}$$

This convergence requirement is satisfied for $\beta(t) = e^{-\rho t}$ with the rate of time preference $\rho > 0$.

We are now ready to state the optimal resource allocation in more definite terms. For an optimal policy to exist, it is necessary to state conditions for a converging utility functional. A discussion of the non-existence of an optimal path can be found in Koopmans [1965, pp. 251-253] and will not be repeated here.

The necessity and sufficiency conditions of Pontryagin's [1964] Maximum Principle are listed here to guide our thoughts[3].

PROPOSITION 1: NECESSITY CONDITIONS

Let $v^*(t)$ be a choice of control variables ($t \geq 0$) which maximises $\{\int_0^\infty \beta(t)U[x(t),v(t),t]\ dt\}$ subject to the conditions of transition of the system or state:

(2.5) $\dot{x} = G[x(t),v(t),t]$,

a set of constraints:

(2.6) $F[x(t),v(t),t] \geq 0$

involving the control variables and possibly the state variables, initial conditions on the state variables, and the non-negativity conditions:

---

3. Proofs of the following propositions are not given here but can be found in textbooks such as Intriligator [1971], Tu [1984] and Seierstad and Sydsæter [1987].

(2.7) $x(t) \geq 0$

on the state variables. If the constraint qualification (i.e. condition (2.6)) holds, then there exist costate variables $\lambda(t)$ and multipliers $q(t)$ and $\mu(t)$ for each t satisfying the conditions that,

(2.8) $v^*(t)$ maximises the Hamiltonian $H(x,v,\lambda,t)$

subject to $F[x,v,t] \geq 0$ and the additional constraints $G_i(x,v,t) \geq 0$ for all i for which $x_i(t) = 0$ and where the current-value Hamiltonian is $H(x,v,\lambda,t) = U(x,v,t) + \lambda \cdot G(x,v,t)$; the development over time of the shadow price, $\lambda(t)$,

(2.9) $\dot{\lambda}_i = \rho(t)\lambda_i(t) - \partial L/\partial x_i(t)$,

evaluated at $x = x(t)$, $v = v^*(t)$, $\lambda = \lambda(t)$, $q = q(t)$ and $\mu = \mu(t)$ (i.e. the multiplier associated with the constraint $G_i \geq 0$), where

(2.10) $\rho(t) = - \dot{\beta}/\beta(t)$,

and where the Lagrangean is defined as,

(2.11) $L(x,v,\lambda,q,\mu,t)= H(x,v,\lambda,t) + q \cdot F(x,v,t) +$

$$+ \mu \cdot G(x,v,t)$$

The Lagrangean multipliers q and μ are such that,

(2.12) $\partial L/\partial v = 0$ for $x = x(t)$, $v = v^*(t)$, $\lambda = \lambda(t)$,

$q(t) \geq 0$, $q(t) \cdot F[x(t),v^*(t),t] = 0$, $\mu(t) \geq 0$,

$\mu(t) \cdot x(t) = 0$ and $\mu(t) \cdot G[x(t),v^*(t),t] = 0$

PROPOSITION 2: NECESSITY AND SUFFICIENCY CONDITIONS

If $H^0(x,\lambda,t)$ (i.e. Max $H(x,v,\lambda,t)$ with respect to v, where the maximisation is over an infinite horizon) is a concave function of x for given λ and t, then any policy satisfying the conditions of proposition 1 and the transversality conditions:

(2.13) $\lim\limits_{t \to \infty} \beta(t)\lambda(t) \geq 0$ and $\lim\limits_{t \to \infty} \beta(t)\lambda(t)x(t) = 0$

is an optimal policy.

As a word of warning, in later chapters the attention will mainly be focussed on interior solutions and not so much the entire plethora of boundary solutions.

In an endeavour to discover some economic interpretation of the Hamiltonian system, we see that the current-value Hamiltonian H multiplied by a certain interval Δ represents the total utility enjoyed during this interval, plus the accumulation of capital during the interval valued at its shadow price λ. The maximum principle of economic policy is to choose the control variable v during the current interval so as to make H as large as possible. Of course, the planner cannot maximise H with respect to the state variable x, since x is not an instrument variable. But from equation (2.9) we can see that the planner is well advised to choose the time paths of v and λ such that the resultant values of x make the sum of utility enjoyed and the increment value of capital as large as possible in every short time interval.

It is often assumed that the underlying conditions of the optimisation are of a stationary nature which helps rephrasing the model after some simple normalisations. The most general formulation of 'stationarity' is that all functions involved in the optimisation, $U(.)$, $F(.)$, $G(.)$ and $\rho(.)$, are independent of time. A steady state is defined as the equilibrium path where

$$(2.14) \quad \dot{\lambda} = \dot{x} = 0$$

We are in fact looking for the ultimate equilibrium where all motion ceases. The ease of handling a set of equations is however not the prime reason for concentrating on steady states. Steady state situations are often found useful because they provide a well-defined reference point. The system of equations describing the steady state are essentially the trend of business cycles. Lucas [1977] viewed business cycle regularities as "comovements of the deviations from trend in different aggregative time series". The business cycle itself is defined by Lucas as the "movements about trend in gross national product". Kydland and Prescott [1990] point out that Lucas does not define the term 'trend' and in their opinion the most natural concept of trend can be found in the steady state of the neoclassical growth model. One can quite easily derive the underlying parameters of long-run economic growth. However, the study of steady states intermingles with short-run phenomena as soon as the data of the economic system are of a non-stationary nature. Population growth is a case in point. As the intro- ductory chapter made clear, population growth can only be seen as a stationary time series with out-of-focus vision. This thesis will look at a particular kind of non-stationarity, viz. a non-stable world population.

If one agrees that one can model planning questions and competitive economies *mathematically*, one should also be aware of the idiosyncracies of optimal control processes, which mainly amount to questions of uniqueness and stability. In order to focus on questions of stability, it is often convenient to summarise a dynamical system only in terms of state and costate variables. The differential equation system, better known as a Modified Dynamic Hamiltonian System, is then described by the following system of equations, assuming an interior solution:

$$(2.15a) \quad \dot{\lambda}_i = \rho\lambda_i - \frac{\partial H(\lambda_i, x_i)}{\partial x_i}$$

$$\text{where} \quad H(\lambda, x) \equiv \max_{\dot{x}} \{U(x, \dot{x}) + \lambda\dot{x}\}$$

$$(2.15b) \quad \dot{x}_i = \frac{\partial H(\lambda_i, x_i)}{\partial \lambda_i}$$

If we interpret x_i as the stock of capital good i and λ_i as the price of capital good i, we may interpret the Hamiltonian H as the current value of national income evaluated at prices λ. A solution of the time path $\{\lambda(t), x(t)\}_{t=0}^{\infty}$ can only be called optimal if state $x(t)$ is the solution $\psi(t)$ to the problem:

$$(2.16) \quad \text{Max} \int_0^{\infty} e^{-\rho t} U[x(t), \dot{x}(t)] \, dt$$

$$\text{subject to } x(0) = x_0$$

where ρ is the constant rate of time preference.

The stability problem is the question whether growth paths converge to a steady state or not. Research has been devoted to finding sufficient conditions on optimal solutions $\psi(t)$ such that, as time approaches infinity, the optimal solution settles down to a steady state: $\psi(t) \rightarrow (\bar{\lambda}, \bar{x})$ as $t \rightarrow \infty$. In addition to this question one also tries to find sufficient conditions such that the steady state is independent of initial conditions. The branch of mathematics that examines these questions is known as *stability theory*. It generally concentrates on the local behaviour of (2.15), in the neighbourhood of a steady state and the global behaviour of solutions $\psi(t)$. Local stability analysis studies a linear approximation of (2.15) around a steady state allocation. Results on global stability are less general than the local stability analysis, which is quite understandable since systems may recover quite easily from small perturbations. Large shocks may not establish a convergence to a steady state $(\bar{\lambda}, \bar{x})$. For instance, global stability in an economy with a convex-concave production function (as in Skiba [1978]) is not guaranteed, since agents may 'eat up' their entire capital stock below a certain threshold level of (λ, k). Sufficient conditions for global stability of the system can be given for a system linearised around a steady state:

$$(2.17) \quad \dot{z}_1 = F_1(z_1, z_2)$$

$$(2.18) \quad \dot{z}_2 = F_2(z_1, z_2)$$

where $z_1 = \lambda(t) - \bar{\lambda}$, $z_2 = x(t) - \bar{x}$, $F_1(z) \equiv -H_2[z + (\bar{\lambda}, \bar{x})] + \rho(z_1 + \bar{\lambda})$; $F_2(z) \equiv H_1[z + (\bar{\lambda}, \bar{x})]$ and $H_1 = \partial H/\partial x$ and $H_2 = \partial H/\partial \lambda$. Stability analysis boils down to inspection of the curvature matrix $Q(z)$:

$$(2.19) \quad Q(z) = \begin{bmatrix} -H_{11}(z) & \frac{1}{2}\rho I \\ \frac{1}{2}\rho I & H_{22}(z) \end{bmatrix}$$

where $H_{11}(z) \equiv (\partial H_1/\partial z_1)[z + (\bar{\lambda}, \bar{x})]$, $H_{22} \equiv (\partial H_2/\partial z_2)[z + (\bar{\lambda}, \bar{x})]$ and I is the $n \times n$ identity matrix (where n is the dimension of x and λ). Some of the technical jargon can be translated into economic content. The Hamiltonian $H(\lambda, x)$ can be interpreted as the current value of national income[4] when $\lambda(t)$ is the shadow price of investment, $x(t)$ is the capital stock, and utility is used as the numéraire. The derivative $\partial H/\partial \lambda$ can then be interpreted as the optimum investment level and $\partial H/\partial x$ the value of the marginal product of capital. Cass and Shell [1976] interpret therefore $\partial H/\partial \lambda$ as the 'internal supply curve for investment' and $\partial H/\partial x$ as a 'Marshallian demand curve for capital services'. Thus, the second derivatives, $H_{11} = \partial^2 H/\partial \lambda^2$ and $H_{22} = \partial^2 H/\partial x^2$ are generalised slopes of supply and demand curves for investment and capital services. Just as in the static theory of supply and demand, we need some basic conditions on the curvature of these schedules in order to ascertain a stable solution. A sufficient condition for stability is that $Q(z)$ be positive definite. Scheinkman [1976] has shown that global stability of an optimal steady state holds as long as the rate of time preference ρ is near zero. It should be noted that the curvature matrix does not expose any information on the quantities H_{12} and H_{21}. The curvature matrix Q summarises some information on supply, demand and the rate of time preference ρ. A stable solution arises if the slopes of the supply curves for investment and the demand curves for capital services are large

---

4. See for a discussion of this issue Weitzman [1976].

relative to the rate of time preference ρ, and the cross terms, H_{12} and H_{21}, are small relative to own terms. The quantity H_{12} represents a shift in the internal supply curve of investment when the capital stock is increased and the increase in H_{12} could therefore be destabilising. This source of instability is not exposed by the curvature matrix.

As Benhabib and Nishimura [1981] have shown, violation of certain stability conditions can lead to chaotic situations; Drazen [1985] gives an example where optimal control solutions are history-dependent, a phenomenon better known as hysteresis. Besides the mathematical elegance of such unstable phenomena, one might wonder what the economic content of such theories is. Essentially the research questions flowing from stability theory are, e.g., "Is capitalism inherently stable or inherently unstable?", "Does speculation serve any socially useful purpose?" and "What forces determine the speed of adjustment to a steady state?" Although this thesis does not cover these kind of questions, it may be good to point out that a lot of simulations of transition paths are fraught with these kind of dynamical questions, but which are ruled out from the start, just as Samuelson's Correspondence Principle [1947], linking stability conditions with comparative dynamics, rules out unstable equilibria. As Brock [1986] points out, the dynamics of the Correspondence Principle were ad hoc and not linked to self-interested purposive behaviour by agents. In a way, the message that Brock brings across is that Samuelson implicitly assumes that the economy *is* inherently stable. Many a simulation of transition paths employs a short cut by assuming that actors start from a steady state and end up again in another steady state. The interval between these two equilibria is simply called 'transition path'. Economic theory of adaptive or learning processes has been rather poor on this score, and future research concentrating on this aspect might be considered the key to modelling so-called 'disequilibria'.

2.2 SOCIAL WELFARE AND INDIVIDUAL CHOICE

Economic policy design is primarily concerned with collective economic choice. The rationale for undertaking an activity collectively presumes knowledge about individual welfare and collective opportunities; opportunities which are beyond control of the individual. However, the role of the state may be questionable, since the degree to which individuals are represented collectively and the manner in which opportunities are secured are not as easily established as one might think at first. Clearly if one wants to evaluate economic policy, one needs to have a notion of what the ends of society are and how one should value those ends. It is at this point that economics borrows a leaf from philosophy. One way of evaluating alternative policies affecting the private allocation is the property of Pareto efficiency. A Pareto-efficient allocation is one in which no change in policies, affecting the opportunities and con-straints individuals face, can make anyone better off without making someone else worse off. Pareto efficiency is an individualistic criterion of social optimality because it is based on an individual's utility.

The theory of public economics takes as a point of departure the two fundamental theorems of welfare economics. The first of these states that a competitive equilibrium is Pareto-efficient. The second states that a centrally designed Pareto-efficient allocation can be achieved as a competitive equilibrium if prices are set appropriately and lump-sum incomes are allocated so that each individual can buy the consumption bundle given in the allocation at the prices that will prevail. However, the possibility may be raised that even though one finds oneself in a situation which is called Pareto efficient, this allocation may still be the worst of all possible worlds. One would like to go beyond the Pareto-efficiency criterion and consider different 'states of the world' resulting from different economic policies. The Pareto principle eschews interpersonal comparisons of utility (see Sen [1977]) and thus the principle cannot be used for comparing policies that generate gains for one group and losses to other groups. In the modern theory of public economics this problem is 'solved' by the construction of a Paretian social welfare function. The ease with which many social welfare functions are written down suggests that there is hardly a controversy on this point. This is indeed a false impression. If one asserts that a certain allocation is Pareto optimal, it can only be called so in the eye of the beholder. There are some intricacies involved in arriving at *a* social welfare function. First of all, it is tacitly assumed that one *can* aggregate individual preferences into a collective preference ordering. Arrow's [1950,1964] impossibility theorem has given ample proof that, by obeying the rules of a democratic voting procedure, arriving at a collective preference ordering is not that easy a task, unless, of course, everyone agrees on certain issues. Mainstream literature on questions of social welfare has circumvented some problems by the introduction of a representative agent and often a composite commodity. Perhaps this may seem reprehensible to some observers of the nitty-gritty of political life, but it helps to focus on ethical questions that matter, irrespective of the degree of heterogeneity of a society. The Paretian social welfare functions as used in this thesis are still individualistic in the sense that individual values are respected though a certain comparability across individuals is required. In the case of one

representative family in society this amounts to the property
that the social planner can compare the utility of the family
head and his/her children. The most commonly used social welfare
functions are listed in Table 2.1. The variable $C(t)$ denotes
aggregate consumption and $N(t)$ denotes the population of a
country. The fourth welfare function contains some variables. X_h
denotes some arbitrary policy instruments that yield utility for
an individual or group h ($h = 1,2...H$) and each individual or
group h is assigned a weight, ω_h, in the total welfare function.
The planning horizon in the cited welfare functions of Table 2.1
is left unspecified, but with normative questions of economic
policy it seems best to view the State of a country on a 'going
concern' basis, thus having an infinite horizon.

TABLE 2.1 SOCIAL WELFARE FUNCTIONS

---

1. $\displaystyle\int_0^T e^{-\rho t} U[C(t)/N(t)]\ dt$ Average utility criterion

2. $\displaystyle\int_0^T e^{-\rho t} N(t).U[C(t)/N(t)]\ dt$ Total utility criterion

3. $\displaystyle\int_0^T e^{p(t)} U[c(t)]\ dt$ Utility criterion with
flexible time preference

    where

$$p(t) = \left\{ - \int_0^t \rho[U(c(s))]\ ds \right\}$$

4. $\displaystyle\int_0^T \sum_h^H \omega_h(t) U_h[X_h(t)]\ dt$ Complex utility criterion

---

Ethical principles need mathematical screening to determine whether in given circumstances they are capable of implementation. There are in general three issues that deserve attention in discussing dynamic economic policy, viz.:

(1) Which should be the arguments in the utility criterion?

(2) How should one treat future generations, in other words, should the rate of time preference be positive?

(3) Should one weight the welfare of the different groups or generations in society?

The first issue depends to a large extent on the model used in describing an economy. If, for instance, one uses a macroeconomic model, which displays disequilibria and money illusion, the objectives of economic policy can be summed up as say, minimum unemployment, an equitable and efficient distribution of income and no inflation. However, in a real business cycle model there is no money illusion and labour is always fully employed, so one should concentrate on the real ends of production and exchange, viz. the individualistic ends, such as consumption and leisure, and societal ends, such as public goods with consumption and production externalities.

The second and third issues are interrelated since they apply to a society in which the population is temporally or inter-temporally heterogenous. For the remainder of this section I will discuss the social welfare functions that one may encounter in the mainstream of economic literature.

The average utility criterion (no. 1) has been ascribed to the work of John Stuart Mill and Knut Wicksell. The planner with such a welfare criterion attaches high priority to individual welfare and not so much to the number of people enjoying a certain consumption bundle. Harsanyi [1955] has argued that social welfare should be represented by the unweighted average of the utility of all individuals. He defends his position by referring to the so-called Ramsey-norm that every rational individual would endorse such a specification if he/she were absolutely uncertain with respect to his/her position in society. The issue whether the rate of time preference should be zero or positive is highly relevant here. Positive time preference is usually ascribed to 'impatience' or 'myopia'. The roots of the analysis of time preference can be found in Von Böhm-Bawerk's [1921] *Capital and Interest*. He suggests that two elements influence intertemporal choice: (i) diminishing marginal utility of consumption at any given time, where utility is an unchanging function of the amount of consumption at that time, and (ii) discounting of future versus present utility. Both elements are present in the utility functions of Table 2.1. The marginal utility function functions as a progressive tax system: $U' > 0$, $U'' < 0$. Generations that are relatively well-endowed receive a smaller weight in the marginal utility function over time. The second element of intertemporal choice is the so-called discount factor $\beta(t)$ or alternatively the rate of time preference, ρ. In case the rate of time preference is constant we can define: $\beta(t) = e^{-\rho t}$. The question whether time preference should be non-negative is an ethical question which has remained unsolved to a large extent. Ramsey [1928], on instigation of Pigou [1920/1952], was perhaps the first to reflect on this aspect of economic decision making over time and he was firmly against a positive rate of time preferences, since discounting is "ethically indefensible and arises merely from weakness of the imagination". The reason why Ramsey was against positive discounting is intuitively quite clear. If one generation, say the present, makes plans for today and tomorrow and after tomorrow the world ends, then any shifting of resources from tomorrow to the present will leave the future generation with less resources. In terms of capital theory, positive discounting will lead to consumption of part of the capital stock. Maximum consumption can only be attained if the present generation abstains from discounting. In case of a stationary environment, the use of positive discounting would be tantamount to living off one's children's endowments.

As Koopmans [1960,1964] brought out strongly, there is a fundamental difficulty with zero discounting. Koopmans started from a set of postulates about utility functions which have no explicit reference to time preference. Koopmans *et al.* [1964] go on to show that the complete preference orderings do exhibit 'time perspective'. Time perspective is derived from an analogy with the notion of perspective in space. For a more thorough understanding of the Koopmans [1960] argument the following postulates were used. If a continuous utility function exists on the space of consumption streams extending to infinity and if in addition we assume:

(i) Sensitivity, i.e. utility can be changed by changing the consumption vector in some designated period;

(ii) Limited non-complementarity of consumption levels. A particular bundle of goods consumed in the first period has no effect on the preference between alternative sequences of bundles in the remaining future; and

(iii) Stationarity, i.e. passage of time is not allowed to have an effect on preferences, then the utility of consumption according to different generations cannot be treated in the same way. The postulates set up to derive an intertemporal utility function simply *imply* impatience. In other words, one cannot reject time preference without involving oneself in a logical contradiction, in the sense of violating one of the assumptions. The surprising aspect of this result is that, while impatience used to be presented as arising from what Von Böhm-Bawerk calls "a defective telescopic faculty", impatience in Koopmans' view appears as implied in a perfectly rational preference ordering. The crucial question concerning time preference is whether we should accept the Koopmans postulates. So, if we are not persuaded on purely logical grounds we will have to fall back on the Pigou-Ramsey approach, which defines time preference as an explicit value postulate. As Chakravarty [1969] points out, one has to discuss whether the concept of timing neutrality ought to be regarded as a primary value judgement or as a derivative one. Pigou and Ramsey thought that a zero rate of time preference would serve the equity between generations best. However, the timing neutrality may not always be equitable. Certain future generations may be well off compared to present generations. The present generation can take certain actions that will affect people in the future, while the future (unborn) generations cannot do something for the present generation. It cannot be considered equitable if certain generations are 'endowed' with a living standard that is well below the standard of some future generation. In the original position one would certainly endorse a criterion that redistributes resources across time. A desirable trait of such a planning problem would be the existence of a functional relationship between the rate of time preference and technology or endowments.

The total utility criterion (no. 2), associated with the Benthamite dictum "the greatest happiness for the greatest number", pays attention to the number of people enjoying a certain welfare level. The average utility is therefore weighted by the size of a generation. If the population grows at a zero or negative rate this criterion is well-behaved. However, positive population growth is more widespread than the phenomenon of a stationary or a vanishing population. If a population grows at a constant rate, $n > 0$, then one has to restrict the rate of time preference to be larger than or equal to the rate of population growth, $\rho \geq n$, if one wants a converging welfare functional. Failing this condition, the maximisation cannot be carried through with an infinite horizon. With an arbitrary choice of a *finite* horizon, the principle feature of the optimal time path of capital accumulation completely depends on that arbitrary choice (see Koopmans [1967b] for an exposition). In case of the average utility criterion, one can think it indefensible to discount future consumption and therefore restrict the discount factor to the value one, while under conditions of the total utility criterion one has to extend the discussion to the compound discount factor, $e^{(n-\rho)t}$, and one no longer finds positive discounting indefensible. It may seem rather odd to the outsider that first one argues that it is despicable to discount future welfare and in a different setting one hears the argument that one should take account of the size of respective generations through time with *positive* discounting. The general idea in taking account of the size of generations is that the discount factor may vary rather than be constant. But if one is convinced that the total utility criterion is the right way to take account of different generations one still has to solve the question of what the rate of time preference should be. Michel [1990] argues that one should return to the undiscounted programming problem of Ramsey by setting the rate of time preference equal to the rate of population growth so that the discount factor is equal to one for each and every generation. In chapter 4 I will go into this question more extensively, since this section is merely meant to be an introduction.

The third utility criterion is a utility criterion with a flexible rate of time preference and this particular criterion can solve the problem of determining the social rate of time preference. As mentioned above, Tjalling Koopmans has been the initiator of designing such models. The utility functional no. 3, as given in table 2.1, is the form chosen by Uzawa [1968], but stems essentially from the work by Koopmans. By formulating the rate of time preference as being dependent on the current level of consumption, one can make clear why a social planner transfers resources between generations. In chapter 4 I will expand on the characteristics of this model and see what it implies for a demographically divided world. In a way the Uzawa model of optimal growth is analogous to a growth model with habit formation, like in Boyer [1978], where decisions on consumption and capital formation depend on levels of welfare from the past[5]. The trouble with habit formation is that planners may overshoot the modified golden rule state and then oscillatory approaches to the steady state become possible.

Last but not least, the complex utility criterion (no. 4 in Table 2.1) is a welfare function which is used in two related fields of research, viz. the theory of the welfare economics of

---

5. As a final note on the use of flexible rate of time preference: in a finite horizon setting, one can still restrict the rate of time preference to zero (see Buckholtz and Hartwick [1989]). This property is however lost in infinite horizon models.

cooperation and the theory of public choice. In the theory of welfare economics the welfare weights are given arbitrary values (see Buiter and Kletzer [1991] and Chari and Kehoe [1990a]) because the sole reason for performing the analysis is to examine conditions which do not violate private property rights. E.g., in an interdependent world economy the weights should be chosen such that they set to zero an excess savings function associated with a joint planning problem. As shown by Chari and Kehoe [1990a], a cooperative equilibrium that respects private ownership is a social optimum. However, this particular social optimum may still be the worst of all possible worlds.

In the theory of public choice the complex utility criterion, or *interest function* as Van Winden [1983, 1987] calls it, deals with the aggregation of heterogenous representative individuals in society. The public choice approach side-steps the *normative* problem of weighting the interests of individuals in the social welfare function. The interest function represents the general interest as it is effective for the individual involved in actual economies. The interest function is "a weighted representation of the interest functions perceived by government sector workers for the positions to which they refer [..] including their own position" (Van Winden [1987, p. 16]). Only recently, Drissen and Van Winden [1991], based on the work by Coughlin *et al.* [1990a,b], demonstrated that one can derive the welfare weights, ω_h (which includes the discount factor), attached to a particular group h in a society with a two-party system as a function of the size of the interest groups, the reputation parties have for being able to influence real economic variables, and the range of values of idiosyncratic voting behaviour. In equilibrium, each party acts as if it maximises an objective function which is a specific weighted sum of the utilities of all citizens. Still, it remains *ad hoc* what

ends society values. Estimating policy makers' preferences with
the help of optimal control techniques can be of use, such as
the empirical work by Swank [1990] shows. However, such
empirical models of public choice do not offer an insight into
the question whether public choices are efficient. The view
policymakers hold of how the world works may be inconsistent
with actual developments. A more serious drawback of models in
which policy makers pursue their own interests or general
interest as *they* perceive it (see, e.g., Swank [1990]), is that
the objective function is no longer microeconomically founded,
so a normative standard of argument is missing.

An aspect of welfare economics, which is related to the previous
discussion of welfare, is the choice of the *numerical* form of
the social welfare function. Equation (2.20) shows the iso-
elastic utility function.

$$(2.20) \quad U(c) = \frac{1}{1 - \gamma} c^{1-\gamma} \quad \text{for } \gamma \geq 0 \text{ and } \gamma \neq 1$$

$$= \log c \quad \text{for } \gamma = 1$$

The iso-elastic utility function involves a constant elasticity
of the marginal utility of consumption. The parameter γ can be
seen as an index of the egalitarian bias of the social planner:
the higher γ, the sharper is the relative rate at which marginal
utility of consumption, $\partial U/\partial c$, decreases when consumption is
going to rise in the future.

   Although sometimes one may not realise it, choosing a
functional form of a social welfare function is also a policy-
loaden choice. To take the iso-elastic functional, one can
choose generally between four parameter settings, viz. (1) the
linear, $\gamma = 0$; (2) the loglinear, $\gamma = 1$; (3) the general iso-

elastic specification, $\gamma \in (0,\infty)$ and $\gamma \neq 1$; and (4) the Rawlsian maximin criterion, i.e. parameter γ approaches infinity (i.e. $\gamma \to \infty$): the social planner maximizes the welfare of the worst-off individual. Figure 2.1 illustrates the four forms.

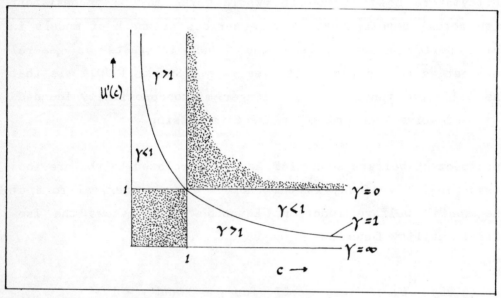

FIGURE 2.1: AN ISO-ELASTIC UTILITY FUNCTION

The linear utility function seems an improbable choice on two counts: (i) in a positive sense, it implies an intertemporal rate of substitution approaching infinity, which runs counter to empirical findings, and (ii) in a normative sense, the planner attaches equal weight (viz. one, see figure 2.1) to an extra unit of consumption, irrespective of the standard of living. The iso-elastic form is more balanced in that respect: an increase in consumption will be valued less when a country is rich than when it is poor. The loglinear form merely gives weights in a symmetric manner, as one can deduce from figure 2.1. It is often chosen for reasons of tractability. E.g., the marginal propensity to consume out of the present value of wealth is equal to the rate of time preference if the utility function is loglinear.

The iso-elastic utility function implies that the inter-temporal rate of substitution in consumption between two consecutive periods is a constant:

$$(2.21) \quad \sigma \equiv - \frac{U'(c(t))}{U''(c(t)) \cdot c(t)} = 1/\gamma > 0$$

The inverse of γ is in fact the intertemporal rate of substitution: $1/\sigma = \gamma$. The iso-elastic function has a dual role to play in economic theory. Under conditions of uncertainty, the parameter γ has an alternative interpretation, viz. the coefficient of relative risk aversion is the reciprocal of the elasticity of intertemporal substitution: $\gamma = - U''c/U'$. Aversion to risk and aversion to intertemporal substitution are however two distinctly different concepts and should be treated as such. The mechanical restriction that the two concepts are the same may lead thoughts about intertemporal decisionmaking astray. Weil [1990] therefore introduced *generalised iso-elastic preferences* which distinguish between the aforementioned attitudes. It is however outside the scope of this thesis to consider the problem of decision making under uncertainty. The distinction is nevertheless important in interpreting the empirical and theoretical results of optimal economic growth.

Substantial empirical work by, amongst others, Hall [1988] has been carried out to estimate $1/\sigma$ under the assumption that this parameter is indeed constant. The results suggest very low values of the elasticity of substitution, thereby pointing to either that consumers are not very willing to shift consumption across time in response to changing interest rates, or the possibility that consumers may be willing, but are not able to shift consumption across time. In other words, the presence of borrowing constraints may be an important factor in explaining intertemporal consumption behaviour. Deaton [1989] and Hayashi [1987] were persuaded to explain consumption behaviour in terms of the latter cause.

2.3 THE THEORY OF OPTIMAL ECONOMIC GROWTH

Debates in circles of economic policy makers give the impression that the best economic policy is one that achieves the maximum rate of economic growth. This is indeed a false description of civilised *economic* decision making. It is true that a high rate of economic growth helps to suppress certain policy issues, like cosmetics helps overcome crow's feet. The maximum rate of growth would be a good description of an ascetic society and under certain circumstances of an LDC[6] (less developed country). Take, for instance, the standard production function: $Y(t) = Z(t).F[K(t),Q(t)L(t)]$, where Z denotes the (Hicks-neutral) state of technology, Q is the labour augmenting technology and K and L denote the endogenous aggregate capital stock and labour supply. Labour supply is a composition of the hours supplied and the number of workers, $L(t) \equiv N(t)\ell(t)$. If we differentiate the production function[7] with respect to time and use a Cobb-Douglas functional form, $F(.) = K^{\beta}(Q.L)^{\alpha}$, where β and α represent the income shares of the production factors, we obtain the following equation:

---

6. Indeed, Chakravarty and Manne [1968] examined the case of optimal growth for planners with an instantaneous utility function that depends on the rate of growth of consumption.

7. A discussion of a wider variety of growth models, both exogenous and endogenous, can be found in Sala-i-Martin [1990].

$$(2.22) \quad \frac{\dot{Y}}{Y(t)} = \beta \cdot \frac{\dot{K}}{K(t)} + \alpha \left\{ \frac{\dot{L}}{L(t)} + \frac{\dot{Q}}{Q(t)} \right\} + \frac{\dot{Z}}{Z(t)}$$

Labour supply $L(t)$ and capital investment are both endogenous and they develop according to the following differential equations:

$$(2.23) \quad \dot{L}/L(t) = \dot{N}/N(t) + \dot{\ell}/\ell(t)$$

$$(2.24) \quad \dot{K} = I(t) - \delta K(t)$$

Aggregate labour supply grows according to the exogenous rate of population growth and the endogenous growth rate of work effort. This last rate can only vary temporarily, since a day has only 24 hours. Physical capital accumulates as long as gross investment, $I(t)$, exceeds the rate at which capital depreciates, $\delta K(t)$.

A maximum rate of economic growth would imply devoting all income to capital accumulation (and hence no consumption), working 24 hours a day and hoping for mannah from heaven (i.e. increasing returns to scale, $\alpha + \beta > 1$, and a positive rate of technical progress). The public finance problem of ageing is sometimes approached by the calculation of growth rates necessary to cover the increases in public expenditure (see, e.g. OECD [1988, p. 39]). This approach leaves out the possibility that the phenomenon at the core of the policy problem, ageing, has an dynamic structure entirely of its own. The calculation of 'should be' growth rates is going to be a futile excercise when the 'would be' growth rates have a life of their own. The interaction of age structure and the rate of technical progress are essential for understanding such questions. To understand the economic consequences of non-stationary population growth one should therefore not only look at this growth rate but one should also examine the consequences of technology shocks (i.e. shocks in Z and δ). In the various chapters of this thesis I will keep technology and population growth separate, without assuming some ad hoc interrelationship.

To illustrate how aspects of technology, time preference and endowments interact in the determination of the optimal time path of investment and consumption, I will construct in this section a simple one-sector optimal growth model. The point of view taken in this section is a normative one, since the remaining chapters are concerned with questions of economic policy and do not describe competitive economies. The equivalence between competitive allocations and centrally planned allocations is well-known ever since the work of Arrow [1951] and Debreu [1954]. The strategy of turning optimal growth models into competitive market models and borrowing results from optimal growth theory is at the heart of modern macroeconomics, and what has become known as models of real business cycles. The adjective 'real' is added not for reasons of realism. 'Real' refers to the non-monetary propagation mechanisms which generate fluctuations in economic activity over time. For some purposes it is helpful to reflect on the positive questions of economic growth. There is indeed a thin line between normative and positive analysis, since one cannot construct credible policies that are based on unrealistic models of economies. In that respect there is always a positivistic tone in economic policy. Although Barro [1989a, p. 228] ascribes the property of describing how an economic system does *not* work to normative models ("..one that fits the data badly"), I think this statement is a contradiction in terms. If we replace the King-Philosopher of normative analysis by the Robinson Crusoe of positive analysis the model would suddenly be a description of how a competitive economic system *does* work. The opposite proposition, there is always a normative tone in positive economics, is however not true. One can dispense with a normative tone in positive analyses, since the objective of such an analysis is the explanation or the prediction of a certain outcome. Only when the prediction or explanation is *used*, one encounters questions of normative economics.

In the first section the standard neoclassical growth model is set up and some properties are studied. In the second section the comparative statics of this economy are examined and I conclude this chapter with the main elements that play a central role in this thesis.

2.3.1 THE MODEL

THE REPRESENTATIVE FIRM

The way in which the national product is produced is often modelled as generated by the efforts of a representative firm or producer. For a macroeconomic theory of economic fluctuations this is perhaps the most tractable foundation on microeconomic principles. A theory of production is concerned with the behaviour of firms in hiring and combining productive inputs to supply commodities at appropriate prices. The transformation of inputs into outputs involves two sets of issues: the technical constraints which limit the range of feasible productive processes and the institutional aspect of production, namely the characteristics of the market where commodities and inputs are exchanged. The markets on which producers compete for production factors are assumed to be perfectly competitive. Of course, other settings are imaginable, but then one has to completely spell out the rules of the *game*. The assumption of one representative firm producing under competitive conditions, is short-hand for the modelling of macroeconomic outcomes as Nash equilibria of decisions of a large number of identical producers.

In the subsequent analysis I will use the following production function $Y(t)$ with constant returns to scale:

$$(2.25) \quad Y(t) = Z.F[K(t),Q.L(t)] \equiv Z.N(t).f[k(t),Q.\ell(t)]$$

or

$$(2.25') \quad y(t) \equiv Y(t)/N(t) = Zf[k(t),Q.\ell(t)]$$

with the following Inada-conditions:

A.1 $f: R_+ \rightarrow R_+$ with $\partial f/\partial k$, $\partial f/\partial \ell > 0$, $\partial^2 f/\partial k^2$, $\partial^2 f/\partial \ell^2 < 0$

and $\partial^2 f/\partial k \partial \ell > 0$, $(\partial^2 f/\partial k^2)(\partial^2 f/\partial \ell^2) - (\partial^2 f/\partial k \partial \ell)^2 \geq 0$

no 'free lunch': $f(k,0) = f(0,\ell) = 0$ and

$\lim_{s \to 0} f'(s) = \infty$ and $\lim_{s \to \infty} f'(s) = 0$ for $s = k,\ell$

The implication of this assumption is that there exists a maximum sustainable amount of capital k^{max}, with $0 < f(k^{max}) = k^{max} < \infty$. The total labour force effort, $L(t)$, consists of the population $N(t)$ times the numbers of hours worked, $\ell(t)$. The population grows exponentially at the constant rate n. The scalar Z represents the level of disembodied technology and is time dependent. Although this conventional neoclassical growth model does not explain all endowment flows, it does stress two important factors of production, viz. *capital* and *labour*. Both capital and labour have a dual interpretation. The physical capital stock is accumulated 'consumption foregone' and labour supplied is 'leisure foregone'. This close interconnection between the two factors of production and well-being made the use of the representative consumer/producer a widespread phenomenon in modern neo (and New or Neo-neo) classical macroeconomics. In the remaining analysis I will model the entire optimal growth question as being answered by a social planner, who represents the consumer/producer perfectly.

THE MAXIMISATION PROBLEM

The social planner maximises the present value of utility of the representative or average consumer's bundle of consumption and leisure:

$$(2.26) \quad V_0 = \int_0^\infty e^{-\rho t} U[c(t), x(t)] \, dt$$

where ρ is the rate of time preference, $c(t)$ is consumption per capita and $x(t)$ is the amount of leisure as a percentage of the individual agent's total time endowment (which is normalised to one). The welfare function exhibits the following properties:

A.2: $U: R_+ \to R$ with $\partial U/\partial i > 0$, $\partial^2 U/\partial i^2 < 0$, $\partial^2 U/\partial i \partial j > 0$ and

$(\partial^2 U/\partial c^2)(\partial^2 U/\partial x^2) - (\partial^2 U/\partial i \partial j)^2 \geq 0$ for $i, j = c, x$ and $i \neq j$

$\lim_{i \to 0} \partial U/\partial i = \infty$ and $\lim_{i \to \infty} \partial U/\partial i = 0$

The premise that the utility functional is additively separable in time implies that there is absolutely no complementarity between levels of consumption in different periods. Although economic life might be characterised by some form of interdependence, like habit formation, for most analyses it suffices to use the additively separable form. As Samuelson [1937] once argued utility functions that incorporate full complementarity between different periods become so general that it makes the analysis unnecessarily complex and the model vacuous. Indeed if a utility functional does not rule anything out, it will be consistent with almost any type of behaviour and the economist will remain with those famous words "it all depends...".

The problem of optimal economic growth is to choose a consumption/leisure path $\{c(t),x(t)\}_0^\infty$ out of many alternative paths, that maximises the utility functional (2.26). The problem is of a dynamic nature since the representative planner has the choice either to consume the good today, or to save the bifunctional good and accumulate a capital stock k, which enables one to produce with the existing production technology $f(.)$ and consume at a later date. In addition, the planner can vary the hours worked over time. Labour or human capital forms a productive coalition with physical capital. Neither factor can be productive without the efforts of the other. Furthermore, there is no such thing as a free lunch in this economy: zero labour effort or capital yields zero production. The maximisation problem is subject to the budget constraint (2.27) and a time constraint of the representative agent (2.28):

$$(2.27) \quad c(t) + \dot{k} \leq Zf[k(t),Q.\ell(t)] - (\delta + n)k(t)$$

$$(2.28) \quad x(t) + \ell(t) \leq 1$$

(2.29) $c(t) \geq 0 \ \forall \ t$

(2.30) $k(0) = k_0$

where δ denotes the rate of capital depreciation, $k(t)$ the physical capital/labour ratio and $\ell(t)$ labour supply (in hours). The path $\{c(t), x(t), k(t)\}$ which satisfies (2.27) and (2.28) is called a *feasible* path. Condition (2.29) simply rules out negative values of consumption and condition (2.30) states that the planner starts planning with a given initial capital stock. We can formulate the current-value Hamiltonian as follows:

(2.31) $H(c,x,k,\lambda) =$

$$U[c(t),x(t)] + \lambda(t)[y(t) - c(t) - (\delta + n)k(t)]$$

The necessary and sufficient conditions for the *optimal time path* can be summarised by the following set of equations:

(2.32) $\dfrac{\partial H}{\partial c(t)} = 0 = U_c(.t) - \lambda(t)$

(2.33) $\dfrac{\partial H}{\partial x(t)} = 0 = U_x(.t) - \lambda(t)y_1(.t)$

where y_1, U_c and U_x denote the partial derivatives $\partial y/\partial \ell$, $\partial U/\partial c$ and $\partial U/\partial x$. The law of motion of shadow price of investment is described by,

$$(2.34) \quad \dot{\lambda} = \rho\lambda(t) - \frac{\partial H}{\partial k(t)} = \{\rho + \delta + n - y_k(.t)\}\lambda(t)$$

or

$$(2.34') \quad y_k(.t) = \rho + \delta + n - \frac{\dot{\lambda}}{\lambda(t)}$$

where the shadow price of investment $\lambda(t)$ is equal to the marginal utility of consumption U_c as one can deduce from (2.32). Equation (2.34') is simply the non-stationary golden rule of capital accumulation. By differentiating the shadow price, as given in (2.32), with respect to time we obtain an expression in terms of consumption:

$$(2.35) \quad \dot{\lambda} = U_{cc}\dot{c} + U_{cx}\dot{x}$$

For the Cobb-Douglas utility function $U(.) = c^{\eta}x^{1-\eta}$ (where $0 < \eta < 1$), we can write out the optimal time path of capital accumulation:

$$(2.36) \quad y_k(.t) = \rho + \delta + n - (1 - \eta)\left\{\frac{\dot{x}}{x(t)} - \frac{\dot{c}}{c(t)}\right\}$$

This optimality condition asserts that along such a path, the rate of consumption and leisure at each moment in time must be chosen so that the marginal productivity of physical capital equals the sum of: (1) the rate of time preference, (2) the rate of depreciation, (3) the rate of population growth and (4) the percentage rate at which the psychic cost of saving diminishes through time. This last term can be seen by noting that the psychic cost of saving at any time is U_c. Its time rate of change is $U_{cc} dc/dt + U_{cx} dx/dt$ (where U_{cx} represents a cross effect on the demand for leisure), and its percentage time rate of change is then the fourth term on the right-hand side of (2.36). In conjunction with the other first order conditions, (2.32) and (2.33), the national resource constraint and the transversality conditions, one can trace the optimal time path for consumption, leisure and investment.

Alternatively, one could have used the first order condition for the labour supply as a starting point. For the Cobb-Douglas form of utility and production function, the optimal time path of capital accumulation becomes:

$$(2.37) \quad y_k\,(.t) = \rho + \delta + n + \eta\left\{\frac{\dot{x}}{x(t)} - \frac{\dot{c}}{c(t)}\right\} + \beta\left\{\frac{\dot{k}}{k(t)} - \frac{\dot{\ell}}{\ell(t)}\right\}$$

The last two terms between brackets represent the percentage rate at which the psychic and physical cost of leisure, respectively, diminish through time. Leisure plays a dual role in this growth model. If one increases leisure time, one automatically decreases one's labour supply with its subsequent effects on the rate of capital accumulation.

The infinite horizon endpoint condition is given in (2.38). The consumer starts with some given capital stock, k_0, and as time approaches infinity, the present value of the capital stock is zero. This end-point condition rules out the possibility of the agent increasing current consumption without the penalty of a reduction in consumption at some point in the future.

(2.38) $\lim_{t \to \infty} e^{-\rho t}\lambda(t)k(t) = 0$ and $\lim_{t \to \infty} e^{-\rho t}\lambda(t) \geq 0$

Simulations for a similar model (with utility-separability in consumption and leisure) are given in King *et al.* [1988a,1988b]. A stationary optimal allocation of resources, in the absence of technical progress, is defined by the following conditions:

(2.39) $\dot{k} = \dot{c} = \dot{x} = \dot{\lambda} = 0$

The steady state allocation is hence given by the aggregate resource constraint, consumption/leisure rule and the investment rule, respectively:

(2.40) $Zf[k,Q.\ell] - c - (\delta + n)k = 0$

(2.41) $\dfrac{U_x}{U_c} = y_1$

(2.42) $y_k = \rho + \delta + n$

Equation (2.41) gives the trade-off between leisure and consumption: the marginal rate of substitution between leisure and consumption should be equal to the marginal rate of the transformation of a unit of leisure into a unit of productive labour, in other words the wage rate. This condition holds, of course, also outside the steady state. Equation (2.42) is the modified Golden Rule of capital accumulation. In a steady state the planner should accumulate capital up to the point where the marginal productivity of capital equals the sum of the rate of population growth, the rate of depreciation and the rate of time preference. If we do not discount future consumption we are back in the ordinary Golden Rule state, as examined by Phelps [1961] and others[8]. With $\rho = 0$ one obtains a truly Golden Age since consumption per capita is at a maximum. The positive rate of time preference reflects the attitude of the planner, who reckons it not such a good deal to reduce current consumption in order to reach a higher Golden Rule level of consumption. The Golden Rule (2.42) is important for understanding long-run movements in economic activity since it implies that the real interest rate is ultimately determined by the rate of population growth, the rate of depreciation and the social rate of time preference.

An explicit solution for the amount of leisure demanded, or its complement the amount of labour supplied, can be obtained for the case where the Cobb-Douglas production function, $f(.) = k^{\beta}(Q\ell)^{1-\beta}$, applies. The time spent on leisure in the steady state is:

$$(2.43) \quad x = \frac{1}{1 + S^{-1}}$$

---

8. Samuelson [1965] draws attention to those 'others' by referring to the golden year 1962-63 for Golden Rules of Capital Accumulation at M.I.T. "In the seminar of Robert Solow and Edmund Phelps (visiting from Yale), Christian von Weizsäcker (of Basel, Hamburg and Berlin), Christopher Bliss (of Cambridge), and others proved all kinds of theorems. Professor Phelps reminds me that Weizsäcker and T. Koopmans had independently developed this device, as did S. Chakravarty (of Delhi) during his 1963-64 stay at M.I.T." Other authors than the ones mentioned here should however also be credited for their contribution, viz. Allais, Desrousseaux, Malinvaud, Joan Robinson, Swan and Srinivasan.

$$\text{where } S = \left\{ \frac{(n + \delta)(1 - \beta) + \rho}{(\rho + \delta + n)} \right\} \cdot \frac{(1 - \eta)}{\eta(1 - \beta)Q} > 0$$

One can see that the steady state demand for leisure is independent of the disembodied state of technology, Z and the time endowment constraint is always satisfied, i.e. $0 < x < 1$.

2.3.2 COMPARATIVE STATICS

The study of comparative statics tries to establish how endogenous variables react to shocks in one of the parameters. The full derivation is presented in appendix 2A to this chapter.

Table 2.2 summarises the reaction signs of the three endogenous variables to changes in parameters. Comparative statics point out that a population growth decline can be a mixed blessing. The steady state leisure time increases unambiguously, since the wage rate increases with a falling real rate of interest. However, consumption per capita need not increase (see appendix 2A for a description of the symbols):

$$\frac{dc}{dn} = - \frac{(A_{21}\rho + A_{31})B_{13}}{A_{11}} + \rho B_{23} - k \gtrless 0 \text{ for } \rho > 0$$

Only in case that the planner does not discount future utility the effect of a population decline on consumption will be positive. This effect is the standard capital dilution effect of population growth as stressed by Solow [1956]. The only unambiguous welfare improving change can be found in a positive shock in the Hicks-neutral technology scalar, Z. It leaves the time spent on leisure unaffected and consumption per capita is positively affected. The labour-augmenting technology scalar, Q, affects consumption positively but at the same time it leads to

TABLE 2.2: COMPARATIVE STATICS FOR THE ONE-SECTOR GROWTH MODEL

| Utility | Shocks in: | | | | |
| | Technology | | Time Preference | Population | |
	Z	Q	ρ	Growth Rate n^a	share η
Physical Capital	+	+/–	–	+/–	+
Leisure	0	–	+	–	–
Consumption per Capita	+	+	–	+/–[b]	+

a) The comparative statics for the changes in the rate of depreciation coincide with those of changes in population growth.
b) $dc/dn = dc/d\delta < 0$ if $\rho = 0$.

a decline in leisure. The effect is asymptotically bounded by the following limits:

$$(2.47) \qquad \lim_{Q \downarrow 0} x = 1 \qquad \lim_{Q \to \infty} x = 0 \qquad \text{for } Q > 0$$

These boundaries point out that it is no use working when thehours worked are not effectively used in production, whereas if one unit of labour is magnified into an enormous amount of effective labour, one does not sit idle about if one can earn gold by moving a fingertip.

TABLE 2.3: STEADY STATE ALLOCATIONS FOR THE ONE-SECTOR GROWTH MODEL

For the parameter values: $\rho = 0.02$, $n = 0.01$, $\delta = 0.05$, $Z = 3.0$, $Q = 1.0$, $\beta = 0.25$ and $\eta = 0.5$ we calculate the benchmark case:

	c	x	k	y	c/y
Benchmark	2.73	0.52	9.49	3.04	81.2%
$\beta = 0.10$	1.57	0.51	2.13	1.70	92.4%
$= 0.40$	6.00	0.53	42.88	8.58	70.0%
$= 0.50$	15.47	0.56	154.69	24.75	62.5%
$\eta = 0.10$	0.46	0.91	1.78	0.57	81.2%
$= 0.25$	1.23	0.76	4.74	1.52	81.1%
$= 0.60$	2.98	0.42	11.47	3.67	81.2%
$\rho = 0.00$	2.61	0.50	14.50	3.48	75.0%
$= 0.05$	2.26	0.54	5.95	2.62	86.4%
$= 0.12$	1.99	0.55	3.02	2.17	91.6%
$Z = 1.0$	0.57	0.52	2.19	0.70	81.5%
$= 2.0$	1.44	0.52	5.53	1.77	81.2%
$= 5.0$	4.87	0.52	18.75	6.00	81.2%
$n = -0.01$	2.73	0.53	13.63	3.27	83.4%
$= 0.00$	2.61	0.52	11.34	3.17	82.3%
$= 0.02$	2.35	0.52	8.11	2.92	80.5%
$Q = 0.75$	1.58	0.59	6.08	1.94	81.5%
$= 1.50$	4.47	0.42	17.20	5.50	81.3%
$= 3.00$	10.39	0.27	43.29	13.85	75.0%

To see what kind of steady state allocations result from this model, I have also calculated a benchmark allocation, as well as some alternative allocations. Table 2.3 must be seen as a complement to Table 2.2. One can clearly see that an increase in the rate of time preference is a hedonistic act: leisure time increases and the level of consumption moves further away from the maximum steady state consumption (i.e. the case of $\rho = 0$). A number of the parameters are based on empirical findings. Kula [1984] estimated the social rates of time preference for the U.S.A. and Canada. His estimates are 0.03 and 0.02 respectively, which seem quite reasonable. One would at least expect the social rate of time preference to be lower than the individual rate of time preference. Viscusi and Moore [1989] find an individual rate of time preference of 0.11, although this rate of time preference decreases with the level of education. The rate of depreciation of physical capital can only be gathered tentatively. Hendershott and Hu [1980, p. 332] show that this rate for the U.S. economy lies in the range of 0.02 and 0.04 for housing, 0.13 and 0.16 for equipment and 0.03 and 0.06 for structures. The aggregate rate of population growth of 0.01 seems to reflect post-world war II development of the population. As one can see from Table 2.3 the outcomes are quite sensitive to the parameter value of capital's share in total income, β. This outcome is even more surprising if one considers the effect of a change in the state of technology, Z. One of the stylised facts of market economies is that the share β tends to fall over time towards some steady state value, although Kaldor [1961] asserted that one of his stylised facts was a constant capital share in total income *at all times*. Table 2.4 presents some long-run tendencies of the capital income share in a few industrialised countries. The empirical models of economic growth restrict *a priori* the sum of shares of production factors in total income to one. However, models of economic development may have the production property of an S-curve: initially increasing returns to scale, and as time progresses economies

TABLE 2.4 CAPITAL INCOME SHARES

Country	Interval	Capital Income share (%)	Reference
Japan	1913-1938	40	Ohkawa and Rosovsky
	1954-1964	31	[1973]
Germany	1850	26	Helmstädter [1973]
	1874	23	
	1913	30	
U.K.	1856-1873	41	Matthews, Feinstein
	1873-1913	43	and Odling-Smee
	1913-1951	33	[1982]
	1951-1973	27	
U.S.A.	1899-1919	35	Kendrick [1961]
	1919-1953	25	
	1929-1953	29	Kendrick [1973]

move to a production technology of constant returns to scale. Threshold levels of capital and labour supply may be important under those circumstances (see Dechert and Nishimura [1983]) for understanding the dynamics of economic development.

2.4 SUMMARY

Models of economic growth and business cycles are constructed to make the dynamics of human action transparent. The statement that actual economies are complex is a proposition that needs no proof. Still, it is tempting to use all those megabytes to construct a 1000-equation model that 'really' mimics actual economies. Economic theory and economic policy go astray the moment such goals are pursued. The art of economics is to choose good simplifications; simplifications that highlight the issues at stake and that use assumptions which generate robust results. The economist's objective of research is to maximise the realism of a model under the restriction that principles and mechanisms remain transparent. The shadow price of investment in realism implies generally a loss in tractability.

The present chapter has presented some elements of a theory of economic policy which will be used in the remainder of this thesis. Each element involves a choice in abstraction and ethics. For instance, the choice of the method of dynamic optimisation may appear to some as a mere 'technicality'. Nothing could be further from the truth. To model time as continuous, runs counter to the experience that some decisions are made at discrete points in time. To endow a planner with an infinite lifetime is an act which may well be wishful thinking for some developing countries. And to impose a transversality condition that, e.g., all debts will be repaid, is again a property which runs counter to the experience of the international debt problem. These choices, albeit unrealistic for studying such real world problems as the international debt crisis, are realistic when framing the issue of non-stable population structures. Non-stable populations involve dynamic, interdependent, and to a large extent, deterministic questions of economic policy.

The second choice discussed in section 2.2 is of an ethical nature: what constitutes social welfare? In many economics texts one has to read between the lines to discover by what measure certain economists[9] judge economic development. Only few take the trouble to articulate their choice. In section 2.2 I have presented the most commonly used welfare criteria and their numerical form. The most fundamental difference of opinions in economic policy can be found in the use of the total versus the average utility criterion. It is a debate which is still very much alive (see, e.g., Ng [1989] and Nerlove [1988]) and not easily solved. In the remainder of this thesis I will use the average utility criterion as I am persuaded by the argument that people are led by a mixture of egoistic and altruistic motives, but when it comes to the question which factor predominates, I would say that egoism prevails. The average principle of utility is the ethic of a single rational individual who tries to maximise his own utility whereas the classical principle of total utility is the ethic of perfect altruists (see Rawls [1972, pp. 150-192]). One could, of course, build a bridge between these two principles and one would certainly arrive at a compromise. It is, however, good to know what extrema lie behind such a compromise.

In the last section of this introductory chapter I have shown how a central planner, endowed with an infinite horizon and perfect foresight, makes decisions on attaining maximum utility of consumption and leisure. The theory of optimal economic growth is a useful piece of analysis for judging economic development. It is so because it has a nice market analogue. Resource allocations are usually effectuated through the market in which the price mechanism acts as the auctioneer. There are, however, two more resource allocation mechanisms which play a

---

9. E.g., Robert Solow [1970, p. 81] introduces in his eloquent discussion of growth theory and economic policy a Benthamite social welfare function as if it is the only function around.

role in economic policy debates, viz. the public budget mechanism and the family. In the theory of optimal growth, the government perfectly represents the family, and in its endeavour to effectuate its policy it faces a perfectly competitive factor market. However, through time, certain goods and services change position with respect to the allocation mechanism through which they are provided. Social security was traditionally a family affair, but following the German Bismarck republic in 1891, industrialised countries took responsibility in providing a vast expanding social security programme. The difficulty which a government encounters in a mixed economy is that it generally has to use policy instruments that distort private decisions. Policy is no longer first best, but second best. In a first-best world the government has access to instruments which do not distort individual decisionmaking, such as lump-sum taxes. In a second-best world the government has to take the reactions of individuals with respect to the policy instruments into account if it does not want to fall into the Lucas [1976] Trap of economic policy design. In the first half of this thesis one does not encounter such problems, since the policy design problem is set in a world with a commitment technology and one decision maker, who represents the private sector perfectly. In the second half of this thesis the distinction between a private and public sector becomes quite important.

APPENDIX 2A: COMPARATIVE STATICS FOR THE ONE-SECTOR GROWTH MODEL

The comparative statics are derived from the golden rules (2.41) and (2.42), the steady state aggregate resource constraint (2.40), the production function $y = Z.k^\beta (Q\ell)^{1-\beta}$ and the utility function, $U = c^\eta x^{1-\eta}$. Since the optimal amount of time spent on leisure is stated explicitly in terms of the parameters of the system in equation (2.43), we have to start from this equation and work backwards to the optimal amount of physical capital and consumption per capita. Total differentiation of these three equations yields the following system of equations:

(A.2.1)

$$\frac{1}{(1-x)^2} dx = -C\frac{(1-\beta)Q}{[\eta Q(1-\beta)]^2} d\eta - C\frac{(1-\eta)\eta(1-\beta)}{[\eta Q(1-\beta)]^2} dQ-$$

$$-\frac{(1-\eta)\beta\rho}{\eta(1-\beta)Q(\rho+n+\delta)^2}(dn+d\delta) + \frac{(1-\eta)\beta(\delta+n)}{\eta(1-\beta)Q(\rho+n+\delta)^2} d\rho$$

where $C = \left\{\dfrac{(n+\delta)(1-\beta)+\rho}{(\rho+\delta+n)}\right\}.$

(A.2.2)

$$dk + Ddx = \frac{1}{\beta-1}.D^{2-\beta}\frac{\ell}{\beta ZQ^{1-\beta}}(dn+d\rho+d\delta) +$$

$$-\frac{1}{\beta-1}.D^{2-\beta}\frac{\ell(\rho+\delta+n)\beta Q^{1-\beta}}{(\beta ZQ^{1-\beta})^2}dZ - D^{2-\beta}\frac{\ell(\rho+\delta+n)\beta ZQ^{-\beta}}{(\beta ZQ^{1-\beta})^2}dQ$$

where $D = \left\{ \dfrac{n + \delta + \rho}{\beta Z Q^{1-\beta}} \right\}^{1/(\beta-1)}$

(A.2.3)

$$dc - \rho dk + (1 - \beta)ZQk^{\beta}(Q\ell)^{-\beta}dx = -kd\delta - kdn +$$

$$+ k^{\beta}(Q\ell)^{1-\beta}dZ + Z(1 - \beta)\ell k^{\beta}(Q\ell)^{-\beta}dQ$$

In matrix notation:

(A.2.4)

$$
\begin{bmatrix} A_{11} & 0 & 0 \\ A_{21} & 1 & 0 \\ A_{31} & -\rho & 1 \end{bmatrix}
\begin{bmatrix} dx \\ dk \\ dc \end{bmatrix}
=
\begin{bmatrix} B_{11} & B_{12} & B_{13} & B_{14} & B_{15} & 0 \\ 0 & B_{22} & B_{23} & B_{24} & B_{25} & B_{26} \\ 0 & B_{32} & -k & -k & 0 & B_{36} \end{bmatrix}
\begin{bmatrix} d\eta \\ dQ \\ dn \\ d\delta \\ d\rho \\ dZ \end{bmatrix}
$$

where:

$A_{11} = 1/(1 - x)^2 > 0$

$A_{21} = [(\rho + \delta + n)/(\beta.Z.Q^{1-\beta})]^{1/(\beta-1)} > 0$

$A_{31} = (1 - \beta)Z.Q.k^{\beta}(Q.\ell)^{-\beta} > 0$

$Det = A_{11}$

$B_{11} = -C(1 - \beta)Q/[\eta Q(1 - \beta)]^2 < 0$

$B_{12} = -C(1 - \eta)\eta(1 - \beta)/[\eta Q(1 - \beta)]^2 < 0$

$B_{13} = B_{14} = -(1 - \eta)\beta\rho/[\eta(1 - \beta)Q(\rho + n + \delta)^2] < 0$

$B_{15} = (1 - \eta)\beta(\delta + n)/[\eta(1 - \beta)Q(\rho + n + \delta)^2] > 0$

$B_{22} = -[D^{2-\beta}\ell(\rho + \delta + n)\beta ZQ^{-\beta}]/(\beta ZQ^{1-\beta})^2 < 0$

$B_{23} = B_{24} = B_{25} = [D^{2-\beta} \cdot \ell]/[(\beta - 1)\beta Z Q^{1-\beta}] < 0$

$B_{26} = (\ell(\rho + \delta + n)\beta Q^{1-\beta} D^{2-\beta})/[(\beta - 1)(\beta Z Q^{1-\beta})^2] > 0$

$B_{32} = Z(1 - \beta)\ell k^\beta (Q\ell)^{-\beta} > 0$

$B_{36} = k^\beta (Q\ell)^{1-\beta} > 0$

The inverse matrix A^{-1} can be calculated as:

$$\frac{1}{\text{Det}} \begin{bmatrix} 1 & 0 & 0 \\ -A_{21} & A_{11} & 0 \\ -(A_{21}\rho + A_{31}) & A_{11}\rho & A_{11} \end{bmatrix}$$

The comparative statics can now be derived by multiplying the inverse matrix A^{-1} with the matrix B (see system (A.2.4)). Table 2.2 summarises the signs of the comparative statics.

CHAPTER 3: OPTIMAL ECONOMIC GROWTH IN A DEMOGRAPHICALLY DIVIDED
WORLD

The economic consequences of a divergence in positive population
growth rates seem to amount to a bleak future for the world as a
whole: widespread poverty amidst negligible plenty. Many
developing countries are expected to fall into the demographic
trap of a return to the first phase of demographic development,
with high birth and death rates, instead of completing the
demographic transition to the phase of low birth and death
rates. African countries in particular have gone well beyond the
carrying capacity of their ecological system. Of course, one
must not adopt the Malthusian stance that a positive rate of
population growth is *always* 'bad' by ruling out technical
progress and environmental resilience. However, the
straightforward calculation of the interaction between
population growth, ecological constraints and economic
development[1] shows more than clearly the prospect for a number
of developing countries is that the people must live on the
subsistence level of consumption (see Brown and Jacobson
[1986]). It has therefore been argued at various occasions that
development planning and family planning should go hand in hand.
However, the stance in development 'planning' in the developed
world is, to put it bluntly: transfer 1½% of your national
income to the developing world and all is well. It does not come
as a surprise to the armchair development economist that this
state of affairs has not led to a better world. As I will argue
in this chapter, the fact that population developments diverge

---

1. See for the issue of sustainability of economic development
Pezzey [1989].

leads to untenable or repugnant policy conclusions. More
seriously, the practice of development aid is bound to be well
meant but futile. Being a Good Samaritan is not enough.
Development efforts should at least lead to a convergence of
population growth rates and preferably to a convergence of
technology levels. To clarify my points on questions of
development planning, and more generally on optimal resource
allocation, I will construct a model of optimal growth in a two-
region world economy to show the straightforward consequences
and difficulties of a demographically divided world (section
3.1). It is used to contrast the analysis of later chapters. The
comparative statics of this model are derived in section 3.2.
The general conclusion which one may deduce from the standard
model of optimal growth is that there is no time like the
present for carrying out population policies directed at
lowering the population growth rate in developing countries. Or
in a more formal tone of voice: the sooner the population growth
rate of the developing countries converges to that of the
developed world the better.

Section 3.3 discusses the use of development planning in a
more or less 'decentralised' setting. Development aid is
inspired by the care of the developed world for people living in
the developing world at a lower living standard. Interdependence
of utility in a demographically divided world leads again to a
modified repugnant conclusion if population growth is exogenous
and if the planners take the average principle of utility as
their policy objective: if the size of the population of the
developing world becomes too large compared to the population of
the developed world, the developed world will not offer any aid,
or in case of an exogenous difference in population growth rates
it will stop transferring resources to the developing world at a
certain point in time. If, however, the planners use the total

utility principle of welfare as their objective, the developing world will generally receive help, although in per capita terms the help may be negligible.

3.1 THE TWO-REGION MODEL

The question of optimal economic growth is set in an extended version of the Koopmans [1965]-Cass [1965] model of capital theory. The policy problem at hand, optimal growth in a demographically divided world, is rather complex and to keep things simple, I will use a global social planner as the central decisionmaker. The problem can be seen as a policy problem of two planners, who agree to cooperate and maximise a global social objective function. Under quite general conditions the use of international transfers between agents alive at one moment in time is necessary. The planner (e.g., the United Nations) determines the optimal resource allocation between two regions with the restriction that consumption per capita in both countries is always positive. The regions differ with respect to the level of production technology and the rate of population growth: the country which is technologically superior is characterised by a relatively low population growth rate[2]. It is assumed that the populations in the two countries grow at a constant exponential rate, n_h:

$$(3.1) \qquad \dot{L}_h = n_h L_h(t) \quad \text{for } h = 1,2$$

---

2. This state of affairs can be explained within a growth model where population growth depends on the level of consumption (see, e.g., Van Marrewijk and Verbeek [1991]).

There is no *a priori* reason for considering different utility functions, but for matters of generality I will start off with differences in utilities. The weights attached to the welfare of citizens in the two regions are their population share of the total world population[3], hence we are dealing with the Millian objective of *average* world welfare. Labour is assumed to be immobile, since complete mobility of labour in a world characterised by differences in technology would imply an exodus from the technologically inferior to the technologically superior country (i.e. concentration of production in the technologically superior country, see Galor and Stark [1991]).

The optimal growth problem for the social planner can be summarised as follows:

$$(3.2) \qquad \underset{c_h, i_h}{\text{Max}} \; V_0 = \int_0^{\infty} e^{-\rho t} \left\{ U_1 [c_1] \theta(t) + U_2 [c_2] (1 - \theta(t)) \right\} dt$$

where the population shares are denoted as $\theta(t) = L_1(t)/[L_1(t) + L_2(t)]$ and the maximisation problem is subject to the differential equations (for $h = 1,2$):

$$(3.3) \qquad \dot{k}_h = i_h(t) - (n_h + \delta_h) k_h(t)$$

$$(3.4) \qquad k_h(0) = k_{h0}$$

---

3. To use a more general utility function with population shares as utility parameters gives rise to questions of time-dependent utility interdependence: $V = (U_1)^{\theta} \cdot (U_2)^{1-\theta}$. This Cobb-Douglas function and related functions (e.g. $V = [U_1 \theta]^{\alpha} \cdot [U_2 \cdot (1-\theta)]^{1-\alpha}$) are however not suitable for welfare questions in a world of diverging population growth, since first and second derivatives violate concavity assumptions in the long-run.

the non-negativity constraints:

(3.5) $c_h(t) \geq 0$, $i_h(t) \geq 0$,

and the temporal world resource constraint:

(3.6) $\theta(t)[y_1(.) - c_1(t) - i_1(t)] +$

$$+ (1 - \theta(t))[y_2(.) - c_2(t) - i_2(t)] = 0$$

The utility function is described by the following assumptions:

$U_h'(c_h) > 0$ for $0 \leq c_h \leq f_h(k_h)$,

$U_h''(c_h) < 0$ for $0 \leq c_h \leq f_h(k_h)$, and

$\lim_{c \to 0} U_h'(c) = \infty$

The latter assumption is convenient in excluding the boundary case in which all output is saved. The production function, y_h, satisfies the conventional Inada-conditions:

$y_h' > 0$, $y_h'' < 0$ for $k_h > 0$ and $\lim_{k \to \infty} y_h' = 0$, $\lim_{k \to 0} y_h' = \infty$

In the present set-up, one can make clear the shifting of resources from one region to the other. The current-value Hamiltonian and Lagrangean (or generalised Hamiltonian) for optimal growth problem (3.2) are defined as[4]:

$$(3.7) \quad H = \theta U_1(c_1) + (1 - \theta)U_2(c_2) + \lambda_1[i_1 - (\delta_1 + n_1)k_1] +$$

$$+ \lambda_2[i_2 - (\delta_2 + n_2)k_2] +$$

$$+ \lambda_3[\theta(y_1 - c_1 - i_1) + (1 - \theta)(y_2 - c_2 - i_2)]$$

$$(3.8) \quad L = H + \mu_1 c_1 + \mu_2 c_2 + \mu_3 i_1 + \mu_4 i_2$$

The necessary and sufficient conditions for an optimal solution are:

$$(3.9) \quad \partial L/\partial c_1 = U_1'(c_1)\theta - \lambda_3\theta + \mu_1 = 0, \ \mu_1 c_1 = 0, \ \mu_1 \geq 0$$

$$(3.10) \quad \partial L/\partial c_2 = U_2'(c_2)(1 - \theta) - \lambda_3(1 - \theta) + \mu_2 = 0,$$
$$\mu_2 c_2 = 0, \ \mu_2 \geq 0$$

$$(3.11) \quad \partial L/\partial i_1 = \lambda_1 - \lambda_3\theta + \mu_3 = 0, \ \mu_3 i_1 = 0, \ \mu_3 \geq 0$$

$$(3.12) \quad \partial L/\partial i_2 = \lambda_2 - \lambda_3(1 - \theta) + \mu_4 = 0, \ \mu_4 i_2 = 0, \ \mu_4 \geq 0$$

We also know that the shadow prices λ_1 and λ_2 are continuous on $t \in (0,\infty)$ and satisfy the differential equations and transversality conditions, respectively,

$$(3.13) \quad \dot{\lambda}_1 = \rho\lambda_1 - \frac{\partial L}{\partial k_1} = \lambda_1(\delta_1 + n_1 + \rho) - y_1'\lambda_3\theta$$

---

4. For notational convenience I will drop time indicators where no confusion can arise.

$$(3.14) \quad \dot{\lambda}_2 = \rho\lambda_2 - \frac{\partial L}{\partial k_2} = \lambda_2(\delta_2 + n_2 + \rho) - y_2'\lambda_3(1 - \theta)$$

$$(3.15) \quad \lim_{t \to \infty} e^{-\rho t}\lambda_1(t)k_1(t) = 0 \text{ and } \lim_{t \to \infty} e^{-\rho t}\lambda_2(t)k_2(t) = 0$$

Throughout the rest of the analysis I will concentrate on interior solutions. The following can be deduced from conditions (3.9)-(3.12), given that the non-negativity constraints are satisfied ($\mu_i = 0$ for $i = 1,2$):

$$(3.16) \quad \lambda_3 = U_1'(c_1) = U_2'(c_2)$$

$$(3.17) \quad \lambda_1 = \lambda_3\theta \quad \text{and} \quad \lambda_2 = \lambda_3(1 - \theta)$$

Condition (3.16) amounts to distributing resources in such a fashion that the marginal utility of consumption in country 1 is equal to the marginal utility of country 2. Condition (3.17) describes the equality of the shadow price of investment in country h to the marginal utility of consumption of that country, weighted for the relative population share, L_h/L. The differentiation of equation (3.17) with respect to time yields:

$$(3.18) \quad \dot{\lambda}_1 = \dot{\lambda}_3\theta + \lambda_1(n_1 - n(t))$$

$$(3.19) \quad \dot{\lambda}_2 = \dot{\lambda}_3(1 - \theta) + \lambda_2(n_2 - n(t))$$

where $n(t) = n_1\theta(t) + n_2(1 - \theta(t))$. Rewriting these two equations in terms of λ_3 and combining them with equations

(3.13), (3.14) and (3.17) gives us the temporal equilibrium
condition:

$$(3.20) \qquad y_1' - \delta_1 = y_2' - \delta_2$$

The shadow price of world resource constraint develops according
to the following differential equation:

$$(3.21) \qquad \dot{\lambda}_3 = \lambda_3 (\rho + n(t) + \delta_h - y_h') \qquad \text{for } h = 1,2$$

The next question in this demographically divided world is: does
a steady state exist? A steady state is defined by constant per
capita levels of capital, i.e. $dk_h/dt = 0$ (for $h = 1,2$) and:

$$(3.22) \qquad \dot{\lambda}_3 = \dot{\lambda}_1 = \dot{\lambda}_2 = 0$$

Condition (3.22) can be satisfied only if population growth
rates are identical: $n_1 = n_2$. But what kind of policy rules
should be followed when this steady state condition does not
apply? The optimal resource allocation is determined by the two
arbitrage conditions (3.16) and (3.20), the world resource
constraint and the non-stationary investment rule (3.21). A
simple investment rule can be obtained in this world economy if
the utility function is linear in consumption, $U(c_h) = c_h$, which
boils down to the property of an elasticity of intertemporal
substitution in consumption which approaches infinity. Another
interpretation of the linear utility function is that the
planner values all changes in consumption at the same rate, no
matter whether the consumer is rich or poor. If we take this
numerical description of the social welfare function as our

objective functional, the modified *Global Golden Rules* for a demographically divided world are:

(3.23) $y_1' - \delta_1 = \rho + n(t)$

(3.24) $y_2' - \delta_2 = \rho + n(t)$

The social planner should adhere to the Global Golden Rule during the demographic transition and accumulate capital up to the point where the net marginal product of capital, $y_h' - \delta_h$, is equal to the rate of time preference and the non-stationary *world* population growth rate. Only when the population growth rates coincide, one obtains a steady state. At this point I should stress the peculiar nature of these golden rules. First of all, the investment rules are time dependent, since in a demographically divided world the world population growth rate will increase and as time approaches infinity the world population will grow at the highest population growth rate (see Keyfitz [1977]). The novelty of time dependent golden rules can be found in Van Imhoff and Ritzen[5] [1988]. The novelty of this section is that *non-stationary* population growth is based on *stationary* region-specific growth rates. Besides this extension, I have made explicit the circumstances under which the Van Imhoff/Ritzen-result applies, viz. the linear utility function, $U(c) = c$.

An issue that looms in the aisles and that has caused quite some confusion amongst economists is the ethical question which

---

5. One should add that the novelty of the golden rule for non-stationary population growth was presented in a paper by Ritzen and Van Praag [1985].

principle would an individual endorse if he is uncertain as to his position on earth. Take the original position as the standpoint from which to decide on a principle of allocation and assume that parties aim to advance their own interests, but they are uncertain as to their abilities and the country of residence. Assume furthermore that the preferences are the same (i.e. $U_h = U$) in the two countries and that the Millian planner does not discount future well-being. This is implied by the uncertainty as to the place in time where individuals are born. A zero discount rate would satisfy the requirement of a planner who does not discriminate between present and future generations. In the Benthamite case one has to impose a positive discount rate if populations grow at a positive rate, $n_h > 0$. Given the 'veil of ignorance', which social planner would an individual endorse: the Benthamite planner with the total utility principle or the Millian planner with the average utility principle?

To a certain extent the problem is unsolvable, since one has to attach different rates of time preference to the planning problems. For the case of the Millian planner, we know that one of the rules of allocation is the equalisation of marginal utilities of consumption (see eq. (3.16)). Given the equality of preferences, this condition amounts to equal consumption per capita for both countries.

If we compare this solution to the welfare maximisation problem of the Benthamite planner, we can write down the following problem (where $n_1 \neq n_2$):

$$(3.25) \quad \underset{c_h, i_h}{\text{Max }} V_0 = \int_0^\infty e^{-\rho t} \left\{ \sum_{h=1}^{2} \exp(n_h \cdot t) L_{0h} U_h [c_h] \right\} dt$$

subject to the fundamental differential equations (3.3) and the aggregate world resource constraint:

$$(3.26) \quad L_1(t)[y_1(.) - c_1(t) - i_1(t)] +$$

$$+ L_2(t)[y_2(.) - c_2(t) - i_2(t)] = 0$$

One can check that most of the steady state conditions go through, except the capital accumulation rule. This rule amounts to:

$$(3.27) \quad y_h' - \delta_h = \rho$$

Hence, a steady state exists despite differences in population growth. However, through the golden rules of capital accumulation the amount of capital accumulated will be lower in the case of total utility than in the case of average utility, since the constant rate of time preference has to exceed the global rate of population growth in order to establish a converging utility functional. In the long run this condition would amount to a rate of time preference that exceeds the highest rate of population growth.

The comparison of ethical principles of justice brings to the foreground that one needs a more general principle to cope with differences in population growth or non-stationary population growth. Neither of the welfare function is entirely satisfactory. Michel [1990] prefers to use the undiscounted optimal growth setting, as studied by Ramsey [1928]. In the Millian case this would amount to a zero rate of time preference. In the Benthamite case of welfare maximisation, the undiscounted optimal growth objective function is obtained by setting the social discount rate equal to the rate of population growth. In the two-region world this would amount to a rate of time preference that coincides with the world population growth rate. The solution offered by Michel is to a certain extent artificial: both the welfare criteria are mathematically identical just as they would have been if the rates of population growth were zero. The criteria are only distinct in their interpretation but not in the effects of their implementation (see Koopmans [1967a, p. 573]): countries with a high rate of population growth should also choose a high rate of discount in order to obtain the Golden Rule level of consumption. Whereas the Benthamite planner first thought it important to take account of the size of the generations, with the choice of time preference, as forwarded by Michel [1990], we are now back in the unweighted welfare case of the Millian planner with a zero rate of time preference.

3.2 COMPARATIVE STATICS

In this section I derive the comparative statics in order to examine the steady state effects of shocks in one of the parameters of the two regions. The general equilibrium effects are calculated for general utility functions[6] $U_h(c)$ belonging to the Millian planner and the production function $y_h = Z_h f_h(k_h)$ where Z_h is a scalar representing the disembodied state of technology. The steady state is defined by the condition: $dk_h/dt = 0$. This implies the equality of population growth rates: $n_1 =$

---

6. In the case of the linear utility function, it would be a matter of indifference to make a distinction between one world consumption level or two country consumption levels, since the social planner would take the weighted sum of per capita consumption: $c = c_1 \theta + c_2 (1 - \theta)$.

$n_2 = n$.

Totally differentiating one of the golden rules of capital accumulation plus the arbitrage conditions of equating the marginal utilities and productivity of capital, (3.16) and (3.20), the differential equations (3.3) and the world resource constraint (3.6) one can derive the comparative statics effects.

(3.28) $$Z_1 f_1' \, dk_1 = d\rho + dn + d\delta_1 - f_1' \, dZ_1$$

(3.29) $$Z_1 f_1' \, dk_1 - Z_2 f_2' \, dk_2 = d\delta_1 - d\delta_2 - f_1' \, dZ_1 + f_2' \, dZ_2$$

(3.30) $$U_1' \, dc_1 - U_2' \, dc_2 = 0$$

(3.31) $$di_h - (\delta_h + n) \, dk_h = k_h \, d\delta_h + k_h \, dn \text{ for } h = 1,2$$

(3.32) $$\theta Z_1 f_1' \, dk_1 - \theta \, di_1 - \theta \, dc_1 + (1 - \theta) Z_2 f_2' \, dk_2 +$$

$$- (1 - \theta) \, di_2 - (1 - \theta) \, dc_2 = -\{(Z_1 f_1(k_1) - c_1 - i_1)$$

$$- (Z_2 f_2(k_2) - c_2 - i_2)\} \, d\theta - \theta f_1(k_1) \, dZ_1 +$$

$$- (1 - \theta) f_2(k_2) \, dZ_2$$

$$(3.33) \quad \begin{bmatrix} dk_1 \\ dk_2 \\ di_1 \\ di_2 \\ dc_1 \\ dc_2 \end{bmatrix} = A^{-1}.B. \begin{bmatrix} d\rho \\ dn \\ d\theta \\ d\delta_1 \\ d\delta_2 \\ dZ_1 \\ dZ_2 \end{bmatrix}$$

where

$$A^{-1} = \frac{1}{Det} \times$$

$$\begin{bmatrix} Z_2 f_2''Q & 0 & 0 & 0 & 0 & 0 \\ Z_2 f_2''Q & -Z_1 f_1''Q & 0 & 0 & 0 & 0 \\ Z_2 f_2''(n + \delta_1)Q & 0 & 0 & Det & 0 & 0 \\ Z_1 f_1''(n + \delta_2)Q & -Z_1 f_1''(n + \delta_2)Q & 0 & 0 & Det & 0 \\ \rho U_2''P & Z_1 f_1''(1-\theta)\rho U_2'' & (1-\theta)M & -\theta U_2''M & -(1-\theta)MU_2'' & -U_2''M \\ -\rho U_1''P & -Z_1 f_1''(1-\theta)\rho U_1'' & -\theta M & -\theta U_1''M & -(1-\theta)MU_1'' & -U_1''M \end{bmatrix}$$

$Det = M.Q < 0$

where $M = Z_1 f_1''Z_2 f_2''$

$Q = [U_1''(1-\theta) + U_2''\theta]$

$P = [Z_1 f_1''(1-\theta) + Z_2 f_2''\theta]$

$$B = \begin{bmatrix} 1 & 1 & 0 & 1 & 0 & -f_1' & 0 \\ 0 & 0 & 0 & 1 & -1 & -f_1' & f_2' \\ 0 & 0 & 0 & 0 & 0 & 0 & 0 \\ 0 & k_1 & 0 & k_1 & 0 & 0 & 0 \\ 0 & k_2 & 0 & 0 & k_2 & 0 & 0 \\ 0 & 0 & S & 0 & 0 & -\theta f_1 & -(1-\theta)f_2 \end{bmatrix}$$

where $S = -\{(Z_1 f_1(k_1) - c_1 - i_1) - (Z_2 f_2(k_2) - c_2 - i_2)\}$, i.e. the shifting of resources across countries. Without going through the complete list of comparative statics effects (as summarised in Table 3.1) I will concentrate on the most

TABLE 3.1: COMPARATIVE STATICS IN A TWO-REGION WORLD

Shocks in:	Time Preference ρ	Population Growth n	Population Share $\theta = L_1/L$	Depreciation Rate δ_1	δ_2	Technology Z_1	Z_2
k_1	$-$	$-$	0	$-$	0	$+$	0
k_2	$-$	$-$	0	0	$-$	0	$+$
i_1	$-^a$	$+/-^b$	0	$+/-^b$	0	$+$	0
i_2	$-^a$	$+/-^b$	0	0	$+/-^b$	0	$+$
c_1	$-$	$-$	$+^c$	$-$	$-$	$+$	$+$
c_2	$-$	$-$	$+^c$	$-$	$-$	$+$	$+$

a) if $n + \delta > 0$.
b) $di_h/dn = di_h/d\delta_h = \{(n + \delta_h)/Z_h y_h''\} + k_h \gtrless 0$ for $h = 1,2$.
c) For the case $Z_1 > Z_2$ and $f_1 = f_2$

important effects, although some of the most interesting effects are swept under the carpet of steady state conditions. For instance the parameters θ and n interact by definition, but in this steady state analysis they are by definition not related. If one could somehow model the difference in population growth one might obtain a strikingly asymmetric effect of population growth. A decrease in population growth in the developing countries is always welfare improving, while a similar change in the developed world may not always be welfare improving.

The most interesting effect is to be found in the steady state effect of a shift in the population share of the two countries. It stresses that as long as the developed world (i.e. the relatively technological advanced region) increases its share in the world population, the average welfare will increase. An increase in population growth is, however, detrimental to the average world utility as a consequence of the capital dilution effect of a population growth increase. Note that the problem becomes a trivial one if production technologies are identical in the two countries.

3.3 DEVELOPMENT AID IN A DEMOGRAPHICALLY DIVIDED WORLD

The previous sections have illustrated the long-run consequences of a demographically divided world in which the population of the developing world grows at a faster rate than that of the developed world. We arrived at the rather repugnant conclusion that in the long-run we all 'enjoy' the welfare level of the technologically inferior country. As a contrast to the previous sections in which decisions were made by one central planner, I would like to consider in the present section a resource allocation problem in a more decentralised fashion. It would seem like a reasonable assumption that the developed region cares about the people living in the developing region. This section might enhance understanding as to why donor countries are hesitant as to transferring resources to the Third World. Table 3.2 gives an impression of the size of official development aid by a number of OECD countries. Of course, the remittance of private and public debt should be included to give a more accurate description of the size of transfers. But as to this moment, remittance of debts has not been a widespread practice.

To approximate real world decision making I will replace the Utopian social planner of section 3.1 by two social planners who

TABLE 3.2: OFFICIAL DEVELOPMENT ASSISTANCE FROM OECD COUNTRIES (as a percentage of donor GNP)

	1965	1975	1985
Canada	0.19	0.54	0.49
France	0.76	0.62	0.79
Germany	0.40	0.40	0.47
Netherlands	0.36	0.75	0.91
United Kingdom	0.47	0.39	0.33
U.S.A.	0.58	0.27	0.24
Japan	0.27	0.23	0.29

Source: Worldbank [1987, p. 242]

make decisions independently, but whose welfare depends, besides their own consumption, on the welfare of the neighbouring country. I would like to examine the conditions under which the developed world transfers resources to the developing world. To make the examination fair, I will compare the Millian planner with the objective of average utility with the behaviour of the Benthamite planner with the total utility criterion. The national resource constraints of the two countries of section 3.1 are modified for the development aid offered and received, respectively.

A MILLIAN SOCIAL PLANNER

The following value function for country 1 (i.e. the technologically superior country, $Z_1 > Z_2$, where $f_1 = f_2$) is maximised:

$$(3.34) \quad \max_{c_1,m} V_0 = \int_0^\infty e^{-\rho t} U_1 \left\{ c_1(t), U_2 \{c_2(t)\} \right\} dt$$

subject to:

$$(3.35) \quad \dot{k}_1 = Z_1 f[k_1(t)] - [\delta_1 + n_1] k_1(t) - c_1(t) - m(t)$$

$$(3.36) \quad m(t) \geq 0, \ k(0) = k_0$$

Consumption per capita in the donor country amount to the following equation:

$$(3.37) \quad c_2 = Z_2 f[k_2] - [\delta_2 + n_2] k_2 + m.L_1/L_2 - \dot{k}_2$$

and $\partial U_h/\partial c_h$, $\partial U_h/\partial n_h > 0$, $\partial^2 U_h/\partial c_h^2$, $\partial^2 U_h/\partial n_h^2 < 0$, $\partial U_h/\partial U_j \gtrless 0$ if $c_h \gtrless c_j$ for $h \neq j$. If $\partial U_h/\partial U_j = 0$ for both agents we are back in the standard neoclassical growth model. Consumption in country 2 is augmented with the development aid corrected for the relative population sizes: $m.L_1/L_2$. In this section I will restrict my attention to one-way patterns of redistributions of resources[7]. Development aid m will flow from rich to poor countries and the size of aid is determined by the rich country. The development aid can only be used as an instrument to enhance consumption in the developing countries. The current-value Hamiltonian for the rich economy is:

(3.38) $H_1 = U_1[c_1,U_2^*] +$

$$+ \lambda_1 \{Z_1 f[k_1] - [\delta_1 + n_1]k_1 - c_1 - m\}$$

and for the poor country,

(3.39) $H_2 = U_2[c_2,U_1^*] +$

$$+ \lambda_2 \{Z_2 f[k_2] - [\delta_2 + n_2]k_2 - c_2 + m.L_1/L_2\}$$

where an asterisk denotes the foreign utility that the planners of the recipient and donor country take into account in determining their own welfare level. To rule out a 'hall of mirrors'-effect, the foreign utility that both planners take into account depends only on the level of consumption per capita of their neighbour.

Necessary and sufficient conditions for an *interior* optimal solution in country h ($h = 1,2$) are:

---

7. The procedure is in some ways similar to the approach introduced by Hochman and Rodgers [1969], although their approach justifies redistributive activities without a social welfare function that makes interpersonal comparisons.

$$(3.40) \quad \frac{\partial H_h}{\partial c_h} = \frac{\partial U_h}{\partial c_h} - \lambda_h = 0$$

$$(3.41) \quad \frac{\partial H_1}{\partial m} = \frac{\partial U_1}{\partial U_2} \frac{\partial U_2}{\partial c_2^*} \frac{L_1}{L_2} - \lambda_1 = 0$$

$$(3.42) \quad \dot{\lambda}_h = \rho_h \lambda_h - \frac{\partial H_h}{\partial k_h} = \lambda_h [\rho_h + \delta_h + n_h - Z_h f_h']$$

$$(3.43) \quad \lim_{t \to \infty} = \lambda_h(t) e^{-\rho t} k_h(t) = 0$$

A steady state allocation (k_h, c_h, m) for countries h (for $h = 1,2$) is described by the following equations:

$$(3.44) \quad Z_h \partial f / \partial k_h = \rho_h + \delta_h + n_h$$

$$(3.45) \quad \dot{k}_1 = 0 = Z_1 f[k_1] - [\delta_1 + n_1] k_1 - c_1 - m$$

$$(3.46) \quad \dot{k}_2 = 0 = Z_2 f[k_2] - [\delta_2 + n_2] k_2 - c_2 + m.L_1/L_2$$

$$(3.47) \quad \frac{\partial U_1}{\partial c_1} = \frac{\partial U_1}{\partial U_2} \frac{\partial U_2}{\partial c_2^*} \frac{L_1}{L_2}$$

Development aid, m, affects the developing country by increasing consumption per capita in the developing world by the amount $m.L_1/L_2$.

A steady state is defined by the conditions $dk_h = 0$ for $h = 1,2$. This need not imply that the steady state is characterised by an equality of population growth rates. To see this consider the steady state condition (3.47). To get an impression of this condition I will use the following numerical form:

$$(3.48) \qquad U_1 = c_1^\omega c_2^{(1-\omega)}$$

If we write out condition (3.48) we obtain the following condition:

$$(3.49) \qquad \omega.c_2.L_2 = (1 - \omega)c_1.L_1$$

Equation (3.49) makes clear that, although the developed world cares about the *per capita* level of consumption in the developing world, the developed world compares in effect *total* consumption levels. The total consumption levels are corrected for the parameter of altruism (ω), c.q. egoism. If an interior solution exists, the developed world will shift m between countries until condition (3.49) is satisfied. The existence of an interior solution at all times is, however, doubtful. The exact condition for this inequality-constrained control problem is given below in condition (3.50).

$$(3.50) \qquad \frac{\partial H_1}{\partial m} \le 0 \text{ then } \begin{cases} m = 0 \\ m > 0 \end{cases}$$

One of the general conclusions one can draw about this condition, is that the closer the levels of consumption are the less aid is offered. One can see that a steady state with a positive level of development aid can never be obtained if differences in population growth rates exist. The factor accounting for relative population sizes changes continuously and thereby the development aid received. One can see this element more clearly by substituting the budget constraints (3.45) and (3.46) in condition (3.49). The following expression for development aid can then be used:

$$(3.51) \qquad m = (1 - \omega)s_1 - \omega s_2 \, \frac{L_2}{L_1}$$

where s_h denote the excess savings, $Z_h f[k_h] - [\delta_h + n_h]k_h - c_h$, for country h.

The previous exercises highlight the aspect that a sacrifice by the developed world in the form of development aid can lead to a better world. If transfers come about, the average standard of well-being in case of altruism will exceed the average welfare level of two countries in isolation. The reason simply being that the developed world will feel better because the standard of living rises in the developing world and the envy in the developed world decreases because the standard of living decreases by the amount of the transfer.

A BENTHAMITE SOCIAL PLANNER

Without going through the whole exercise again we can write down the utility criterion of the Benthamite social planner. The average utility across time is weighted by the size of the generations:

$$(3.52) \qquad \underset{c_1, m}{\text{Max }} V_0 = \int_0^\infty e^{-\rho t} \, L_1(t) U_1 \left\{ c_1(t), \frac{L_2(t)}{L_1(t)} U_2\{c_2(t)\} \right\} dt$$

subject to conditions (3.35)-(3.37). The current-value

Hamiltonian can be formulated for the rich country as follows:

(3.53) $H_1 = U_1[c_1, L_2/L_1 U_2^*] +$

$+ \lambda_1 \{Z_1 f[k_1] - [\delta_1 + n_1]k_1 - c_1 - m\}$

and for the poor country,

(3.54) $H_2 = U_2[c_2, L_1/L_2 U_1^*] +$

$+ \lambda_2 \{Z_2 f[k_2] - [\delta_2 + n_2]k_2 - c_2 + m.L_1/L_2\}$

Necessary and sufficient conditions for an *interior* optimal solution in country h ($h = 1,2$) are:

(3.55) $\dfrac{\partial H_h}{\partial c_h} = \dfrac{\partial U_h}{\partial c_h} - \lambda_h = 0$

(3.56) $\dfrac{\partial H_1}{\partial m} = \dfrac{\partial U_1}{\partial U_2}\dfrac{\partial U_2}{\partial c_2^*} - \lambda_1 = 0$

(3.57) $\dot{\lambda}_h = (\rho_h - n_h)\lambda_h - \dfrac{\partial H_h}{\partial k_h} = \lambda_h[\rho_h + \delta_h - Z_h f_h']$

and the usual transversality conditions (3.43). If we take the same numerical utility function (3.48) we can find the equilibrium condition for development aid:

(3.58) $c_2 = \dfrac{(1 - \omega)}{\omega} c_1$

and condition (3.49) changes to

(3.59) $m = [(1 - \omega)s_1 - \omega s_2]/Q$

where $Q = 1 - \omega + \omega.L_1/L_2$. As one can see from condition (3.59) the Benthamite planner who cares about total utility compares average welfare levels across the two countries. However, if the planner cares a lot about its own welfare (i.e. $\frac{1}{2} < \omega < 1$) and consumption levels do not differ very much, the situation might arise that the planner of the rich country does not offer any help. Another characteristic of the solution presented is that the Benthamite planner hardly has to offer any help when the rich become extremely numerous compared to the number of poor (i.e. $L_1/L_2 \to \infty$).

The lesson that we can draw from the comparison of the two types of planners - Benthamite versus Millian - is that both can incline to transfer no aid to the developing world. The Millian planner will stop sooner than the Benthamite planner because the aid offered may not become effective. If the developed world becomes small compared to the developing world (i.e. $L_1/L_2 \to 0$), the aid 'evaporates' in per capita terms the moment it arrives in the developing world. The Benthamite planner does not care about average welfare and as long as it can make one person happy in the developing world it will transfer resources. The real altruist can therefore be considered the Benthamite planner, if the act of *giving* is considered the yardstick of altruism. But at the same time, one must conclude that the Benthamite planner is quite naive: the transfer may make one person happy while millions of people are living on a subsistence level. As long as it makes one additional person happy, all is well. In that respect, the Millian planner is more realistic (but harsh) since he cares about the entire developing world. Only if the planner can improve the well-being of the collective nation he will transfer resources, otherwise he will abstain from such a benevolent action.

As a final remark, the two principles of welfare coincide if the rates of population growth are zero and the population sizes are identical.

3.4 SUMMARY

The conclusions from these exercises in optimal economic growth in a demographically divided world are simple though revealing. The sooner the population growth rate of developing countries (i.e. technologically inferior) converges to the growth rate of the developed world (technologically superior), the better.

One of the theoretical novelties of this chapter is that if population growth rates differ and the welfare function is characterised by a linear utility function (i.e. a function with an elasticity of intertemporal substitution in consumption approaching infinity), capital in each region should be accumulated according to the Global Golden Rule: the marginal product of capital, net of the rate of depreciation, should equal the sum of the rate of time preference and the non-stationary world population growth rate. This setting makes quite clear that differences in population growth, as they exist today, will lead to a level of consumption which decreases for ever. For more general utility functions one would have to think in terms of world lifetime wealth. Differences in population growth will lead to an ever decreasing contribution of industrialised countries to world wealth. The sooner this development is stopped the better.

In the second part of this chapter I have examined the question of who is the real altruist: the Benthamite or the Millian social planner? For the Millian condition for development aid to come about, it is required that the developing world does not become too large compared to the developed world. This reveals quite a harsh attitude, if this condition does not materialise: the developed world cares about the developing world but it does not give a dime to the poor, because they are too numerous. It is, however, an aspect of the real world which should not be neglected: at present the population of the developing world is roughly four times the size of that of the developed world. The Benthamite planner is, on the contrary, the real altruist since this planner will keep on giving resources to the developing world as long as it can make an extra person happy. The Benthamite planner is, however, to a certain extent naive, because he may give help that may not enhance average well-being under certain circumstances, viz. when the population of the donor country is very small compared to the recipient country.

The main lesson one should draw from this chapter is that if one assumes a world economy with different population growth rates and/or population sizes, the design of the optimal allocation of resources can lead to the unacceptable or repugnant conclusions. It would seem that repugnant conclusions should not be a trait of ethical measuring rods.

CHAPTER 4: INTERNATIONAL DEBT IN A DEMOGRAPHICALLY DIVIDED WORLD

In research on closed and open economies, fluctuations in economic activity triggered off by productivity shocks figure prominently (see Kydland and Prescott [1982], Cantor and Mark [1987] and Clarida [1990]). A much neglected determinant of economic fluctuations is the change in the demography of a country. Van Imhoff [1989a] has shown for a closed economy that a permanent demographic shock can trigger off real business cycles. This finding may be more attractive to the student of (real) business cycles than the finding by King et al. [1988a], who find that recurrent technology shocks are needed to generate economic fluctuations in a standard neoclassical growth model. Only recently Becker and Barro [1988,1989] have stressed the need for dynamic general equilibrium models with endogenous population growth. This chapter will not go as far as to endogenise fertility choice or migration but instead it will look to the question of how (exogenous) demographic shocks are transmitted to production, consumption, capital and debt accumulation.

In this chapter a deterministic, perfect foresight model of two interdependent countries is presented, each inhabited by a social planner with an infinite planning horizon. The interdependence of the two countries is made explicit by international goods and capital markets. Fluctuations in economic aggregates such as production and consumption, are brought about by changes in demography.

The question examined in this chapter is the grand question of optimal economic growth: *how much* should a country consume today and save for the future in order to enjoy the maximum amount of welfare over its planning horizon? The well-known Golden Rule of Capital Accumulation, as derived by Koopmans [1965] and Cass [1965], offers us a guiding principle for closed economies. In a competitive world economy characterised by perfect capital mobility, the central question of the theory of optimal economic growth should be extended to include another question, viz. *where* should a country invest its savings? The present chapter addresses this question extensively for a world in which population growth rates and rates of time preference differ across countries. Indeed, the normative standpoint may be of great importance since directors of funded pension programmes in industrialised countries increasingly become aware of the possibility that investing all their savings domestically may prove inefficient. Investing part of their savings abroad is the logical alternative.

This chapter points, however, to another normative question, viz. should social planners in an interdependent world economy use an individualistic utility criterion, i.e. the objective defined in per capita terms, or should the planners take the total utility into account, by weighting the average utility by the size of the present and future generations? If planners use the average utility criterion, the problem of optimal economic growth in a world of diverging populations shows some similarities with the case of lending and borrowing between agents with differences in impatience. The most patient household will accumulate assets infinitely, while the less patient households are all net debtors living eventually at a subsistence level. The ultimate question is whether such a pattern is desirable.

The chapter is organised as follows. First, I will set up the world model (section 4.1) with the help of the standard neoclassical Koopmans-Cass model as a basis for the maximisation problem. Section 4.2 offers an insight into the direction of capital flows in an interdependent world economy when one of the two countries encounters demographic shocks. As will become apparent, the standard one-sector model has its drawbacks in the analysis of steady state optimal allocations in a world economy characterised by (constant) different population growth rates. Section 4.3 therefore shows how resources are allocated intertemporally when the rate of time preference is endogenous. In the last section (4.4) I will sum up the findings.

4.1 THE TWO-COUNTRY WORLD MODEL

The world consists of two countries, each inhabited by a social planner with an infinite planning horizon. The two countries differ with respect to the population growth path, the rate of time preference and production technologies. There is only one good which can be used as a consumption good as well as a capital good. I assume that no migration of labour takes place and both countries engage in transactions on perfect international markets for capital and commodities. Perfect capital mobility is assumed throughout the analysis.

Each social planner aims at maximising the instantaneous utility of consumption per capita[1], i.e. $U(C_h/L_h)$, over an infinite horizon and these welfare functions are identical across the two countries. The maximisation problem for the social planner in country h ($h = 1,2$) can be formalised by the following time additive utility functional,

_____

1. Variables stated in capital letters denote aggregates whereas the corresponding lower case letters denote variables in per capita terms. A dot over a variable denotes its derivative with respect to time.

(4.1) $\underset{c_h, i_h}{\text{Maximise}} \int_0^\infty \beta_h(t)U[c_h(t)]\, dt$

where $\beta_h(t) = \exp(-\rho_h.t)$. In their endeavour to realise optimal welfare, the planners have to choose between investing part of their production in their own country, earning the marginal product of capital, on the one hand, and borrowing (or lending) a certain fraction abroad, earning the world real interest rate $r(t)$, on the other hand. Country h chooses an optimal sequence of $\{c_h(t), i_h(t)\}_{t=0}^\infty$ and any divergence between savings and investment is covered by borrowing or lending abroad at the world capital market at the interest rate $r(t)$. The planner encounters no adjustment costs in investment. Borrowing and lending are performed on the international capital market with the ulterior motive to smooth consumption. An alternative formulation would be productively allocated foreign assets, as in Ruffin [1979], in a perfect competitive capital market. Together with the assumption of complete mobility of capital this *implies* that at every point in time interest rates $r(t)$ are equalised,

$$f_1'[a_1(t) - d(t)] = f_2'[a_2(t) + d(t).L_1/L_2] = r(t)$$

The term a_i denotes the capital per capita *owned* by the labour force in country i. Capital moves across country boundaries to equate rates of return, hence country 1 *locates* d units of its capital stock abroad so that the capital-labour ratio in country 1 is $a_1 - d$. The capital-labour ratio located in country 2 is $a_2 + d.L_1/L_2$. Interest equalisation under conditions of identical production technologies implies that at every moment in time the capital-labour ratios located in the two countries are identical. This particular formulation has, however, one interesting implication for optimal growth paths, viz. the *optimal foreign debt is indeterminate* (i.e. it cannot be ascribed a unique value, independent of the initial state). In a model of heterogenous households a similar finding was reported by Becker [1980] and Becker and Foias [1987].

The current account deficit is equal to spending on consumption, investment and interest payments abroad in excess of domestic output. By separating the savings and investment decision we can show more clearly their dynamics. To formulate this more formally: the social planner must value increases in physical capital and foreign debt against the alternative of consumption. The current account imbalance is equal to the change in foreign assets: dD_h/dt. A current account deficit is defined as the difference between the interest payments of foreign debt minus the trade surplus, $X_h - M_h$, i.e. the net exports of goods:

$$(4.2) \qquad \dot{D}_h = r(t)D_h(t) - (X_h - M_h)$$

or in per capita terms:

$$(4.2') \qquad \dot{d}_h = r(t)d_h(t) - (x_h - m_h) - n_h d_h(t)$$

The types of assets develop according to the following differential equations:

$$(4.3) \qquad \dot{K}_h(t) = I_h(t) - \delta_h K_h(t)$$

$$(4.4) \qquad \dot{D}_h(t) = Z_h F_h[K_h(t), L_h(t)] - C_h(t) - I_h(t) +$$

$$+ r(t) D_h(t)$$

The labour force coincides with the population and in each country the labour force grows at the exogenous rate n_h:

$$(4.5) \qquad \dot{L}_h(t) = n_h L_h(t)$$

Rephrasing all equations in per capita terms, we arrive at the following current-value Hamiltonian:

$$(4.6) \qquad H_h(c, i, k, d, \lambda, \mu) = U[c_h(t)] +$$

$$+ \lambda_h(t)\{i_h(t) - (\delta_h + n_h)k_h(t)\} +$$

$$+ \mu_h(t)\{Z_h f_h[k_h(t)] - c_h(t) - i_h(t) +$$

$$+ (r(t) - n_h)d_h(t)\}$$

The production function $Z_h f_h(.)$ is written in the labour-intensive form. It represents the well-known neoclassical production function and it suffices to state that it produces the composite commodity under conditions of constant returns to scale and that it is well behaved ($\partial f/\partial k > 0$ and $\partial^2 f/\partial k^2 < 0$). The scalar Z_h accounts for the state of technology in country h. Since this scalar is constant across time, it automatically implies that there is *no technical progress* in this world economy.

Necessary and sufficient conditions for an interior solution are summarised by the following set of equations:

$$(4.7) \qquad \frac{\partial H_h}{\partial c_h} = 0 = U'[c_h(t)] - \mu_h(t)$$

$$(4.8) \qquad \frac{\partial H_h}{\partial i_h} = 0 = \lambda_h(t) - \mu_h(t)$$

The law of motion of shadow prices is described by,

$$(4.9) \qquad \dot{\lambda}_h = \rho_h \lambda_h(t) - \frac{\partial H_h}{\partial k_h} = \lambda_h(t)(\rho_h + \delta_h + n_h) +$$

$$- \mu_h Z_h f'_h[k_h(t)]$$

$$(4.10) \qquad \dot{\mu}_h = \rho_h \mu_h(t) - \frac{\partial H_h}{\partial d_h} = \{\rho_h + n_h - r(t)\}\mu_h(t)$$

where the shadow price of investment $\lambda_h(t)$ is equal to the marginal utility of consumption $U'[c_h(t)]$ as one can deduce from (4.7) and (4.8). From equations (4.8)-(4.10) one can immediately deduce the investment rule in an open economy: one should accumulate capital up to the point where the net marginal productivity of capital equals the world interest rate, $r(t)$:

$$(4.11) \qquad Z_h f'_h[k_h(t)] - \delta_h = r(t)$$

In this world we need a condition that prevents countries from choosing a path with exploding debt relative to the size of the population. The transversality condition (4.12), better known as the No-Ponzi-game condition, requires that the present value of a country's wealth, arbitrarily far in the future, be non-negative. In other words, the country's per capita wealth should not increase asymptotically faster than the interest rate net of population growth, $(r(t) - n_h)$:

(4.12) $\lim\limits_{t \to \infty} d_h(t)R_h(t) \geq 0$

where the short term discount factor $R_h(t)$ is given by,

$$R_h(t) = \exp\left\{-\int_0^t [r(s) - n_h]\ ds\right\}.$$

A Ponzi-game situation might arise if one of the social planners borrows until the marginal utility of consumption is equal to zero and then borrows further to meet interest payments on the debt outstanding. This can be illustrated by substituting the foreign assets in the utility function:

(4.13) $U[Z_h f_h[k_h(t)] - i_h(t) + (r(t) - n_h)d_h(t) - \dot{d}_h]$

One can easily see that the change in foreign assets should not asymptotically increase faster than the interest rate net of population growth, $(r(t) - n_h)$:

$$\dot{d}_h/d_h(t) \leq r(t) - n_h$$

It is unlikely that the lending party would be willing to continue lending if the country's only means of paying off its debt were to borrow more. Accordingly, the No-Ponzi-game condition (4.12) should be stated with equality. The property of a finite number of decision makers is enough to rule out the occurrence of a rational Ponzi game (see proposition 2 of O'Connell and Zeldes [1988]). Only if the number of traders is infinite (i.e., $h \to \infty$) this kind of rationality is possible.

The conventional transversality condition (4.14) boils down to the condition that the limit value of optimal capital stocks and foreign assets is zero:

$$(4.14a) \quad \lim_{t \to \infty} \; \beta_h(t) \lambda_h(t) k_h(t) = 0$$

$$(4.14b) \quad \lim_{t \to \infty} \; \beta_h(t) \mu_h(t) d_h(t) = 0$$

Finally, equation (4.15) states that countries start off with a given capital stock and external debt position. Equation (4.16) restricts consumption and investment choices to non-negative values.

$$(4.15) \quad k_h(0) = k_0^h \quad \text{and} \quad d_h(0) = d_0^h$$

$$(4.16) \quad c_h(t), \; i_h(t) \geq 0$$

If we differentiate the shadow price of investment, as given in (4.7), with respect to time we obtain an expression in terms of consumption:

$$(4.17) \quad \dot{\mu}_h = U''[c_h(t)]\dot{c}_h$$

By defining the elasticity of the marginal utility of consumption as $\sigma(c_h) = - [c_h U'']/U'$ we can write down the differential equation for consumption,

$$(4.18) \quad \dot{c}_h = \frac{c_h(t)}{\sigma_h(t)} \left[Z_h f_h'[k_h(t)] - \rho_h - n_h(t) - \delta_h \right]$$

One can see why one cannot tilt or depress consumption permanently in a small open economy. Given the fact that one wants to smooth consumption over time ($\sigma_h > 0$), a divergence in the rate of return to savings $r(t)$ and the rate of time preference (assuming for the moment that the rates of population growth are identical) would imply that if $r(t) < \rho_h + n$ for country h, then it would keep on accumulating debt and decreasing its consumption level (i.e. $dc/dt < 0$) until it approaches its boundary value of zero. A divergence in population growth (assuming identical rates of time preference) and the rate of return would even lead to the dismal situation that in the long run a negligible part of the world enjoys a very high level of consumption and the rest of the world population lives on the subsistence level of consumption at some date T ($T < \infty$). This setting is very similar to the one examined by Becker [1980] for a model with heterogenous households with respect to time preference. He analyses an economy in which households have additive utility functionals but different constant rates of time preference. In the long-run all capital is owned by the most patient household, whereas the less patient households are all net debtors, consuming their fixed endowment in the steady state. This is an undesirable outcome of a model of optimal economic growth and it has led many authors to assume this difficulty away. For instance, Arrow and Kurz [1969] impose some boundedness assumptions on equilibrium allocations in infinite horizon models. The relevant boundedness assumptions are summarized below and one can check that these assumptions restrict the infinite horizon problem of social planners in a demographically divided world to a particular world economy setting.

Boundedness assumption 1:

The magnitude $r(t)$ converges to a positive finite limit r_∞ and,

$$\left| \int_0^\infty [r(t) - r_\infty] dt \right| < \infty$$

Boundedness assumption 2:

The magnitude $w(t)$ converges to a positive finite limit w_∞.

Boundedness assumption 3:

The optimal consumption policy of individual h, $c_h(t)$, converges to a positive finite limit c_∞ and dc_h/dt approaches zero.

One of these restrictions is that one must define the entire population growth paths with *converging* rates in the steady state. Throughout the remaining analysis I will use this property and allowing for time dependent population growth rates: $n_1(t) \neq n_2(t)$ and $n_1(\infty) = n_2(\infty) = n$.

By integrating the labour-intensive current account equation (4.4), and using the No-Ponzi-game condition (4.12), we obtain the level of consumption:

$$(4.19) \qquad \int_0^\infty c_h(t)R_h(t)dt = \int_0^\infty \{Z_h f[k_h(t)] - i_h(t)\}R_h(t)dt + d_{h0}$$

$$= v_{h0}$$

The present value of consumption is equal to net wealth at time 0, v_{h0}: the present value of net output plus the initial level of foreign assets. For a given value of initial consumption c_0 we can integrate equation (4.18) forward to obtain (assuming for simplicity that $\sigma_1(t) = \sigma_2(t) = \sigma$),

$$(4.20) \qquad c_h(t) = c_{h0} \, \exp\left\{ \int_0^t \sigma^{-1}[r(s) - n_h(s) - \rho_h] ds \right\}$$

If we replace expression (4.20) in the intertemporal budget constraint (4.19), we obtain a consumption function linear in wealth[2]:

$$(4.21) \qquad c_{h0} = p_c \cdot v_{h0}$$

where the propensity to consume out of wealth, p_c, depends on the expected path of interest rates:

$$(4.22) \qquad p_c^{-1} =$$

$$= \left(\int_0^\infty \exp\left\{ \int_0^t \{(\sigma^{-1} - 1)[r(s) - n_h(s)] - \rho_h \sigma^{-1}\} ds \right\} dt \right)$$

Since this type of consumption function depends to a large extent on the future path of interest rates, I will restrict the remaining analysis to the more simple Friedmanite consumption function. This logarithmic utility function, $U[c_h(t)] = \log c_h(t)$ from which $\sigma = 1$, is independent of the time path of interest rates. It has an attractive analytical property: the propensity to consume out of wealth is equal to the rate of time

---

2. Note that if one assumes $r(t) = \rho + n(t)$ for all t one can proceed the analysis with the convenient consumption property that consumption is constant: $c_h(t) = c_{h0}$. This may be a suitable assumption for a small open economy.

preference, ρ_h, since the elasticity of intertemporal subsitution in consumption, $\sigma^{-1} = 1$. Under these conditions initial consumption is:

(4.23) $c_{h0} = \rho_h v_{h0}$

The consumption at time 0 is equal to the marginal propensity to consume out of wealth, ρ, times the net wealth of the consumer. The change in consumption is given by differential equation (4.18).

Market clearing in this particular model boils down to determining the path of intertemporal terms of trade, $r(t)$. An exogenous interest rate is a satisfactory approximation of a small open economy, though it is unrealistic in a two-country world. World interest rates should clear two markets; first, the international capital market condition (4.24):

(4.24) $D_1(t) + D_2(t) \equiv 0$

which amounts to the condition that an equilibrium in a two-country world is only feasible if there exists a net lender and a net borrower. The second market that needs to be cleared is the world goods market, as summed up below:

(4.25) $\displaystyle\sum_{h=1}^{2} \left\{ (Z_h f_h [k_h(t)] - c_h(t) - i_h(t)) \frac{L_h(t)}{\sum\limits_h L_h(t)} \right\} \equiv 0$

World interest rates must then vary to equilibrate net current account surpluses and deficits. As shown by Cantor and Mark

[1987], an explicit interest rate solution with different production technologies is quite complicated in an infinite horizon model. In order to gain insight in the development of the current account dynamics we need to unravel the current account components a bit further. In this interdependent world economy domestic saving, $s_h(t)$, and investment need not be equal at each point in time. The current account deficit net of population growth is equal to investment minus saving (i.e.- $dD_h/dt \equiv I_h(t) - S_h(t)$ where $(dD_h/dt)/L_h(t) = dd_h/dt + n_h d_h(t))$. Current saving (or dissaving) in the two countries is defined as the difference between the gross national product (i.e. GNP = GDP + rd_h) and consumption:

(4.26a) $s_1(t) = Z_1 f_1[k_1(t)] + r(t)d_1(t) - c_1(t)$

(4.26b) $s_2(t) = Z_2 f_2[k_2(t)] + r(t)d_2(t) - c_2(t)$

By multiplying both equations by their relative population shares, $\theta = L_1/L$, adding equations (4.26) and using the capital market restriction, $d_1\theta + d_2(1 - \theta) = 0$, one arrives again at the goods market identity (4.25). Given the consumption relation (4.23) and the fact that playing of Ponzi games is not permitted, we can rephrase equation (4.26) in present value terms and arrive at an intertemporal world market identity:

$$(4.27) \quad \sum_{h=1}^{2} \left[Z_h f_h[k_h(t)] - i_h(t) \right] \frac{L_h(t)}{L(t)} +$$

$$+ \sum_{h=1}^{2} P_h(t) \left\{ \rho_h \int_0^\infty \left[\{Z_h f_h[k_h(t)] - i_h(t)\}R(t) \right] \frac{L_h(t)}{L(t)} dt \right\} = 0$$

where $P_h(t) = \exp\left\{\int_0^t [r(s) - n_h(s) - \rho_h]ds\right\}$

The *present* world net output should equal present world consumption, $c_1(t).\theta + c_2(t).(1 - \theta)$, which is equal to the propensity to consume out of wealth times the *future* net output. Note that the model collapses to the closed economy version of optimal growth if one of the two countries is extremely large, for instance: if $L_1/L \rightarrow 0$ we can restrict our attention to the closed economy of country 2. Saving and investment in a closed economy can no longer diverge simply because there is no external party willing to cover the difference. It is outside the scope of this paper to examine the comparative dynamics of shocks in technology in great detail. The reader is again referred to Cantor and Mark [1987] for the intricacies of such shocks.

STEADY STATE

In a steady state (i.e. $dk/dt = dd/dt = 0$) the following investment rule should be used as a guideline for maximising consumption per capita:

(4.28) $Z_h f'_h(k^*_h) - \delta_h = \rho_h + n_h$ for $h = 1,2$

(4.29) $Z_1 f'_1(k^*_1) - \delta_1 = Z_2 f'_2(k^*_2) - \delta_2$

These open economy golden rules of investment (4.28) and (4.29) tell us: (i) to accumulate capital up to the point where the *net* marginal product of capital (i.e. net of depreciation) equals the sum of the rate of time preference and population growth rate of the country in question; and (ii) to invest at home and abroad up to the point where the net marginal productivity of capital is equal in the two countries. If we assume that the function describing production y_h is of a Cobb-Douglas form:

$$(4.30) \quad y_h(t) = Z_h k_h(t)^\alpha$$

we can express capital and consumption as a function of final steady state parameters (for $h = 1,2$):

$$(4.31) \quad k_h^* = \left\{ \frac{\rho_h + n_h + \delta_h}{Z_h \cdot \alpha} \right\}^{1/(\alpha-1)}$$

$$(4.32) \quad y_h^* = Z_h k_h^{*\alpha}$$

$$(4.33) \quad c_h^* = y_h^* - (\delta_h + n)k_h^* + \rho_h d_h^*$$

where $\theta d_1^* + (1 - \theta)d_2^* \equiv 0$. In the steady state, the current account should be balanced and trade surpluses should cover the interest payments on foreign debt, corrected for the rate of population growth:

$$(4.34) \quad x_h^* - m_h^* = (r^* - n_h)d_h^*$$

Given the fact that the real interest rate is equal to the net marginal productivity of capital, the interest rate on the steady state foreign assets is equal to the rate of time preference.

It must be obvious that a steady state in this two-country world with planners using unweighted per capita social welfare as their criterion of investment is only possible if and only if:

(4.35) $\quad \rho_1 + n_1 = \rho_2 + n_2$

It would be very bold to say that this is a stylised fact of the world economy of today. However, to assume differences in population growth rates and rates of time preference which do not satisfy condition (4.35) does not make the interdependent world economy model completely worthless. The standard model of optimal economic growth is only of use when converging population growth paths and rates of time preference are defined over time. In the next section, I will use the property of converging population growth rates, and in section 4.3 the interaction between population growth and time preference will be modelled.

4.2 DEMOGRAPHIC SHOCKS AND OPTIMAL CAPITAL FLOWS

This section tries to establish how shocks in population growth are transmitted. The study is similar in nature to the analysis of comparative dynamics performed by Cantor and Mark [1987], who examine the transmission of technology shocks in a two-country world and the analysis by Van Imhoff and Ritzen [1988], who examine the transmission of a permanent demographic shock in a closed economy. The distinction between transient and permanent shocks of population growth n is defined as follows. A transient shock amounts to:

$$(4.36) \quad n(t) = \begin{cases} n & t = (-\infty, 0) \\ n^* & t \in [0, T) \\ n & t \in [T, \infty) \end{cases}$$

and a permanent shock:

$$(4.37) \quad n(t) = \begin{cases} n^* & t = (-\infty, 0) \\ n^{**} & t \in [0, T) \\ n & t \in [T, \infty) \end{cases}$$

where $n^* > n^{**} > n$ (or $n^* < n^{**} < n$). I will use the terminology of demography by defining a transient shock $n^* > n$ as a baby boom and $n^* < n$ as a baby bust. A permanent shock, as defined by $n^* > n^{**} > n$, is generally known as a demographic transition. Furthermore, it is assumed that both countries start and end with identical population growth rates. This assumption does not rid the analysis of interesting time paths. The *timing* of demographic transition is just as important as the transition itself. The economic consequences of differences in time preference in a two-country world of overlapping generations can be found in Buiter [1981] and are not repeated here. Throughout the analysis I will restrict my attention to identical rates of time preference: $\rho_1 = \rho_2 = \rho$.

4.2.1 TRANSITORY SHOCKS

The transitory shock that we examine in this section is a sudden decline in one of the population growth rates. As time goes by, the population growth rate returns to its original level. We assume that this shock occurs in the developing world, i.e. the country with the relatively inferior production technology.

One of the basic aspects of a transitory shock is that it does not affect the steady state capital stock. The only variable it does affect is the aggregate population size and the relative population shares in the total world population. This simple observation has far-reaching consequences. A transitory shock can have a permanent effect on the future pool of per capita asset accumulation.

The sudden and unexpected decline in population growth leads to a sudden increase in the capital-labour ratio, with its immediate consequences for the world interest rate and international capital flows. The world interest rate will drop due to the pool of savings which is larger than normal. In a closed economy this shock would have led to a sharper fall since there would be no external party engaging in trade. International lending and borrowing will however dampen the interest rate movement. Foreign assets flow, under the assumed circumstances, from the developing world to the developed world. The windfall gain originating in the developing country is partly consumed, partly invested in domestic production and still another part is invested in international bonds by the social planner of the developing country. The current wealth of the two countries increases because of the lower interest rates and higher output levels that prevail during the transition to the steady state. Since the production in the developed world at the time of the shock, t_0, does not change, the increase in consumption and investment is entirely financed by international borrowing. Consumption in both countries increases and decreases in line with each other. One can see this by employing the interest equalisation condition and equation (4.18). From (4.18) one obtains the following equality (note that utility functions are identical):

$$(4.38) \qquad n_1 - n_2 = \left\{ \frac{\dot{c}_2}{c_2} - \frac{\dot{c}_1}{c_1} \right\} \sigma$$

If $n_1 - n_2 > 0$ and the elasticity σ is a constant, consumption in country 2 will grow at a higher rate than the consumption in country 1. If population growth rates are identical and shocks in technology occur, one could derive that the consumption growth rates in both countries are identical (as in Cantor and Mark [1987]). In the developing country net output starts above the consumption level and the difference between these two variables is invested abroad. As the population growth rate returns to normal, the developing economy can run a permanent trade deficit since it receives interest payments on foreign assets.

The magnitude of these capital flows depends primarily on the levels of technology, Z_1 and Z_2, and the initial population shares, θ, of the two countries in the world population. In general, it will make a difference if the demographic shock occurs in the developing country or in the developed country. However, the economic consequences of such shocks might be equivalent for a certain configuration of parameters. The equivalence of shocks is quite understandable. E.g., the developing world is roughly three to four times the size of the developed world. The states of technology are unknown, but one can well imagine that the developed world establishes higher production levels than the developing world with the same capital/labour ratio. Despite the smaller share in the world population, the developed world may generate a larger sum of savings due to a superior state of technology.

4.2.2 PERMANENT SHOCKS

To model a permanent shock in a two-country world is quite complex. Both the population growth rates have to converge at some date and it would seem that two (unexpected) shocks are necessary to analyse such a case. One can, however, also focus on the timing of the demographic transition. If the shocks are expected but the timing of these shocks is unexpected, one can restrict one's attention to only one shock. The demographic transition is assumed to occur first in the developed world with the developing world lagging behind in the demographic transition. Although demographic transition does not necessarily imply that the initial population growth rate differs from the new steady state population growth, I will model the new steady state growth rate as being lower than its initial rate. If the lagging behind of developing countries is unexpected, the developing world will experience a higher population growth than planned and consequently a lower capital-labour ratio. Production in the developing world is fixed at time t_0 of the shock. The ex ante interest rate in the developing world is higher than the interest rate in the developed world. Capital therefore flows from the developed to the developing world. The developed world runs a current account deficit which is balanced, after the demographic transition is completed, with a sequence of future current account surpluses. The new steady state is characterised by higher levels of consumption in both countries. The steady state foreign debt is non-zero in general. The current account is balanced in the steady state and net output in the developing country must rise sufficiently so that the trade balance shows a surplus; a surplus which is compensated for by the interest payments (corrected for the rate of population growth) on foreign debt. The ultimate debt positions are therefore determined by the initial debt position and the source of the demographic shock. If we assume that the initial foreign debt is zero, $d(0) = 0$, the case of a delayed demographic transition will result in the developing world becoming a net debtor and the developed world a net creditor.

There are, however, a number of important aspects of the demographic transition. As long as the population growth rates differ and the demographic transition is not completed, the world population will be non-stable and the aggregate per capita level of consumption will fall. The delay in demographic transition causes the developing world to accumulate more foreign debt. The share of the developing country in the world population will increase and consequently the world pool of savings will decrease. The sooner the demographic transition is completed (i.e. population growth convergence), the better. The per capita present value of consumption is then unambiguously higher than in the case of a delayed demographic transition. The longer the delay in the transition, the higher the steady state foreign debt, which in turn has to be covered by future trade surpluses. Future net output should therefore exceed the steady state level of consumption. A higher debt implies a lower steady state consumption level, otherwise the planner cannot create such necessary trade surpluses. A practical drawback of a delayed demographic transition is the amount of debt that will be accumulated. In an infinite horizon model the steady state debt level does not matter very much since it can be rolled over indefinitely, and with positive discounting a social planner does not care much about the debt position far into the future. In practice the debt level does bring about credibility problems which are absent in the present model (see, e.g., Kletzer [1988] for a discussion of credibility and Bardhan [1967] for an analysis, where the interest rate depends on the level of foreign indebtedness).

In conclusion, the previous sections 4.1 and 4.2 have brought forward two determinants of international lending and borrowing:

consumption *smoothing* and consumption *tilting*. These motives are implicit in the golden rule of capital accumulation. The motive of consumption smoothing is relevant when there are fluctuations in endowments. In a conventional growth model the fluctuations can only be found in the exogenous labour force growth rate. The motive of consumption tilting is relevant when there are differences in time preference. The third motive of international lending and borrowing (see Frenkel and Razin [1987, ch. 5]) is consumption augmenting. This last motive is better known as the *gains from trade*. The most simple case to consider is the shifting of capital from the country that overinvests in physical capital to the country that underinvests in physical capital (see Buiter [1981]). Along the optimal growth path in a stationary world economy there are no gains from trade. As made clear by Srinivasan [1989], it is a mistake to compare steady state welfare levels, since it is the discounted sum of the difference in welfare levels (free trade versus autarky) that induces countries to engage in trade. Therefore the gains in the model presented here must be seen in terms of a smoother consumption path, yielding a higher welfare level. Real gains, such as increased factor productivity, cannot be established in this model.

4.3 ENDOGENOUS TIME PREFERENCE

Standard models of optimal growth employ intertemporal social welfare functions, where future utilities are discounted by a rate which is kept constant, independent of the time profile of the utility stream associated with each consumption schedule. In the last two sections we saw that a steady state equilibrium should eventually be characterised by an equality of golden rule parameters; an equality which at first sight seems rather improbable or ad hoc. Of course, there must be more to international lending and borrowing for agents with an infinite horizon than imposing the 'transversality' condition of identical population growth rates (or for that matter identical rates of time preference). This difficulty has led many authors to back away from the problems of divergences in time preference or population growth. Indeed, Ramsey [1928, p. 559] himself conjectured[3] that under conditions of a divergence in rates of time preference:

> "...*equilibrium would be attained by a division of society into two classes, the thrifty enjoying bliss and the improvident at the subsistence level*"

One could, however, imagine well that at every point in time the equality $\rho_1 + n_1 = \rho_2 + n_2$ holds by some explicit relationship between either time preference and consumption or population growth[4] and consumption. A similar assumption has been made by Becker and Barro [1988, p. 14]. They *assume* for a model of endogenous fertility that the degree of altruism toward children (which functions as the rate of time preference in their model) depends negatively on the number of children. In this section I will show that time preference and changes in population growth are negatively related. I will therefore employ a general utility function as constructed by Uzawa [1968].

Similar work concerning the endogeneity of time preference is

---

3. This conjecture was proven by Becker [1980]. For an overview of the literature on optimal growth and the role of (endogenous) time preference see Becker and Majumdar [1989] and Obstfeld [1990].

4. In a two-country overlapping generations model of international lending and borrowing the endogeneity of fertility is analysed by Kondo [1989a].

found in Epstein and Hynes [1983] and Epstein [1987]. They extend and generalise the work by Uzawa [1968] and Becker [1980]. The present analysis concentrates on the derivation of a proposition concerning international lending and borrowing by paying attention to differences in population growth. In an international setting Pitchford [1989] used the Uzawa-model to examine the current account dynamics of permanent and transitory (exogenous) income fluctuations for a small open economy. One of the main results was that when discount rates are endogenous one needs to know whether an income shock is permanent or temporary before the economic consequences of income fluctuations can be established. In the present setting, the world economy consists of two interdependent countries engaging in international lending and borrowing.

4.3.1 THE UZAWA MODEL OF TIME PREFERENCE

As a prelude to the infinite horizon model I will first explain in rather general terms the idea of endogenous time preference, as forwarded by Uzawa [1968, pp. 486-490]. The rate of time preference can be defined as the rate, $p_{0,t}$ (extending over various time periods $t = 0,1...T$), by which future utility is discounted to the present, summarizing the preference structure of an individual decisionmaking unit with regard to present and future consumption. If the level of present utility U describes the preference structure of the planner in question, we can define time preference, $p_{0,t}$, as:

$$(4.39) \quad U = u_0 + \frac{u_1}{1 + p_{0,1}} + \ldots + \frac{u_T}{1 + p_{0,T}}$$

The rate of time preference is the rate by which future utility is discounted to make it comparable with present utility. The rate of time preference depends upon the entire time profile of the utility stream:

$$(4.40) \quad p_{0,t} = p_{0,t}(u_0, u_1, \ldots u_T) \qquad t = 1, 2, \ldots T$$

Uzawa [1968] applied questions of intertemporal decision making to a concept of time preference that satisfies three postulates:

1. The rate of time preference $p_{0,t}$ for utility at time t is independent of utility levels beyond time t, i.e. $p_{s,t}$ for $s < t$ may be specified as:

$$(4.41) \quad p_{s,t} = p_{s,t}(u_s, \ldots u_t) \qquad s < t$$

2. The discounting procedure based on time preference function (4.41) is independent of the manner in which it is done; in particular it is required that:

$$(4.42) \quad 1 + p_{0,t} = (1 + p_{0,s})(1 + p_{s,t}) \quad \text{for } 0 < s < t < T$$

Relation (4.42) yields (for $0 < t < T$):

$$(4.43) \quad \frac{1 + p_{0,t}(u_0, \ldots u_t)}{1 + p_{0,t-1}(u_0, \ldots u_{t-1})} = 1 + p_{t-1,t}(u_{t-1}, u_t)$$

The logarithmic increase in the rate of time preference (plus one) depends on the utility levels for consumption at time $t-1$ and time t.

3. The structure of time preference remains invariant through time, i.e. $p_{t-1,t}$ in (4.43) is some function $\rho(.)$ independent of time:

$$(4.44) \quad \frac{1 + p_{0,t}(u_0,\ldots.u_t)}{1 + p_{0,t-1}(u_0,\ldots.u_{t-1})} = 1 + \rho(u_{t-1},u_t)$$

Now if we move on to the infinite horizon planning problem of optimal growth we can consider the following utility functional as suggested by Uzawa [1968]:

$$(4.45) \quad V_0 = \int_0^\infty U[c(t)]\ e^{-p(t)}\ dt$$

where $p(t) = \left\{ \int_0^t \rho[U(c(s))]\ ds \right\}$

where U is a well-defined concave utility function ($U' > 0$, $U'' < 0$) and the rate of time preference $p(t)$ depends upon the time profile of a continuous utility stream $U(.t)$ and relation (4.43) becomes:

$$(4.46) \quad \dot{p} = \rho[U(c(t))]$$

A number of conditions are needed to guarantee a stable solution. The following Uzawa-conditions should be satisfied:

$$(4.47) \quad \rho(U) > 0,\ \rho'(U) > 0,\ \rho''(U) > 0 \quad \text{for all } U > 0, \text{ and}$$

$$(4.48) \quad \rho(U) - \rho'(U)U > 0$$

The relationship between the instantaneous rate of time preference and current utility is positive and the first and second derivatives of time preference with respect to utility are also positive. A higher level of consumption at time s increases the discount factor applied to utility at and after s (i.e. the second assumption in condition (4.47)). Condition (4.48) ensures that between two stationary consumption paths the one with the higher level of instantaneous utility is preferred.

4.3.2 A TWO-COUNTRY WORLD ECONOMY

To simplify the analysis I will assume that utility functions and time preference functions are identical. The planners of country h (for $h = 1,2$) maximise (4.45) subject to the following differential equations:

$$(4.49) \quad \dot{k}_h = i_h(t) - (\delta_h + n_h)k_h(t)$$

$$(4.50) \quad \dot{d}_h = Z_h f_h[k_h(t)] - c_h(t) - i_h(t) + (r(t) - n_h)d_h(t)$$

and the development of time preference as described by equation (4.46). To simplify the optimisation problem one should first transform the time variable t into one in terms of which the rate of time preference becomes a constant. If, following Uzawa [1968, p. 491], we take p as the independent variable instead of t in the maximand we can obtain the following maximand:

$$(4.51) \quad \int_0^\infty U\, e^{-p}\, dt = \int_0^\infty \frac{U}{\rho(U)}\, e^{-p}\, dp$$

while the differential equations can be reformulated in a similar fashion:

(4.52) $dk_h/dp_h = [i_h - (\delta_h + n_h)k_h]/p_h\,(U)$

(4.53) $dd_h/dp_h = [Z_h f_h[k_h] - c_h - i_h + (r - n_h)d_h]/p_h\,(U)$

The *current-value* Hamiltonian is given in (4.54),

(4.54) $H_h\,(c,i,k,d,\lambda,\mu) = U[c_h\,(t)] +$

$+ \lambda_h\,(t)\{i_h\,(t) - (\delta_h + n_h\,(t))k_h\,(t)\}$

$+ \mu_h\,(t)\{Z_h f_h[k_h\,(t)] - c_h\,(t) - i_h\,(t)$

$+ (r - n_h\,(t))d_h\,(t)\}$

and it can be rewritten in *present value* terms. The present value of the imputed national income H is to be discounted at the rate of time preference $\rho[U(.)]$, and is given by:

(4.55) $\dfrac{H}{\rho[U(.)]}\ e^{-p(t)}$

The optimum consumption level, c_h, is determined at the level at which the present value (4.55) of imputed income is maximised. Necessary and sufficient conditions for an interior solution are:

(4.56) $\dfrac{\partial H_h}{\partial c_h} = [U'(c_h) - \mu_h] +$

$$-\frac{\rho'(.).U'(c_h)}{\rho[U(c_h)]}[U(c_h) + \lambda_h \dot{k}_h + \mu_h \dot{d}_h] = 0$$

(4.57) $\dfrac{\partial H_h}{\partial i_h} = \mu_h - \lambda_h = 0$

(4.58) $\dot{\lambda}_h = \lambda_h \{\rho[U(c_h)] + \delta_h + n_h\} - \mu_h Z_h f_h'$

(4.59) $\dot{\mu}_h = \mu_h \{\rho[U(c_h)] + n_h - r\}$

(4.60) $\lim\limits_{t \to \infty} e^{-P(t)} \mu_h(t) d_h(t) = 0$

(4.61) $\lim\limits_{t \to \infty} e^{-P(t)} \lambda_h(t) k_h(t) = 0$

To understand condition (4.56) we can rewrite it as follows:

(4.62) $U'(c_h) = \mu_h + \dfrac{\rho'(.).U'(c_h)}{\rho[U(c_h)]} H_h$

This condition points out that the planner should equal the marginal utility of consumption (i.e. the LHS) to the sum of the imputed value of borrowing and lending on the international capital market, μ_h, and the marginal increase in the present value of the imputed income due to a marginal decrease in the rate of time preference. If the rate of time preference, $\rho(.)$, is constant this relation reduces to the condition $U'(c_h) = \mu_h$ of the Ramsey model in section 4.1.

For the remainder of this section I will concentrate on

steady states, since this was the main problem of the earlier section. A steady state allocation in a two-country world (i.e. $dk_h/dt = dd_h/dt = 0$ for $h = 1,2$) can be defined as the allocation that is consistent with the following set of equations:

$$(4.63) \quad Z_h f_h'(k_h^*) = \rho[U(c_h^*)] + \delta_h + n_h$$

$$(4.64) \quad r^* = Z_1 f_1'(k_1^*) - \delta_1 = Z_2 f_2'(k_2^*) - \delta_2$$

$$(4.65) \quad c_h^* = Z_h f_h(k_h^*) - (\delta_h + n_h)k_h^* + (r^* - n_h)d_h^*$$

Equation (4.63) is the modified golden rule of capital accumulation. If each of the social planners treats the interest rate parametrically, there exists a unique steady state. One interesting observation that can be made at this stage is about the steady state consumption and distribution of wealth in a demographically divided world: if all countries have the same discount rate function and production technologies, but different rates of population growth, then all countries have the same steady state capital-labour ratio but the country with the lowest (highest) population growth will have the highest (lowest) steady state consumption level. If the discount functions differ, steady state distributions will be more complex. What is most puzzling about the present formulation of optimal economic growth, is that in the standard growth model, patience was a virtue in obtaining wealth and it enabled one to enjoy a higher level of consumption, whereas in the Uzawa-formulation the wealthy are characterised by a high rate of impatience. Perhaps the last interpretation is not quite correct, since 'patience' depends on the level of consumption, hence each individual lives within his/her means. The relatively wealthy are therefore those countries or persons that can shift relatively more resources from the future to the present. In this way one can circumvent the postponed splurge in consumption which arises in case the planner is of a Benthamite persuasion with a finite horizon and the population growth rate exceeds the rate of time preference. A property of the optimal growth model which Koopmans [1967a,1976] found undesirable. The model seems to embody the feeling that is inherent to intertemporal planning and expressed vividly by Solow [1974, p.9]: "We have actually done quite well at the hands of our ancestors. Given how poor they were and how rich we are, they might properly have saved less and consumed more". However, the model seems to have some implications that run counter to plain observation. The rich (i.e. the country with the superior production technology) turn out to be net debtors in the steady state and the poor are net creditors in the long-run. At present it would seem like a fair description to say that the developed world can be seen as a net creditor and the developing world as the net debtor. The implicit assumption was that countries have identical preferences and, of course, countries can have different utility and time preference functions which give rise to more real-to-life descriptions. But then one has to study the relationship between how preferences develop in response to technology and endowments. Such a study exceeds the scope of this chapter.

The ability of the present model to generate time paths in spite of a divergence in population growth rates must not be underestimated. The early literature on optimal capital accumulation takes the view (e.g. Inada [1968], p. 324) that it is irrelevant to treat countries with different growth rates. For instance, Inada examines the consequences of different population growth rates and asserts that identical population growth rates are not a severe limitation to international growth models because "[i]f the population growth rate in one country is greater than in the other country, after a sufficiently long period the former economy becomes overwhelmingly large compared with the latter economy.." and "[the] capital accumulation process in [the former economy] under free trade is described approximately by the same model as in the no-trade situation". In the long run this assertion is certainly true, but in a medium term context the divergence of population growth rates must be of influence on international capital flows and consumption behaviour. Dixit [1981, p.283] draws attention to the difficulties involved in the treatment of different growth rates in the trading countries. E.g. "during the course of the supposed steady state, trading prices must change from the autarky prices of one country to those of the other". These consequences of different growth rates are "inconsistent with the logic of a steady state". The present model is quite elegant when it comes to the transition of a world economy with two interdependent countries to a world economy in which one country, the high population growth country, acts as if it is a closed economy and the low population growth country has become so small that it faces a world interest rate, determined by the high population growth country.

In the subsequent analysis I will perform the analysis of comparative statics for an interdependent world economy with diverging population developments.

4.3.3 COMPARATIVE STATICS

If we totally differentiate the set of equations (4.63)-(4.65) we have six equations explaining variables c_h, r, d and k_h (for $h = 1,2$). In the appendix 4A the full derivation is given of the comparative statics. At this point I will restrict myself to discussing the qualitative outcomes of the comparative statics.

First of all, it must be said that some of the standard results of neoclassical capital theory still stand. What does differ from standard theory are the international spillover effects. For instance, the effect of a population growth decline on consumption per capita is always positive for the country where the population shock occurs but the effect abroad depends on the sign of $(\rho'U'a_h - 1)$. In effect, the influence of a population growth shock on capital accumulation, foreign assets, the world interest rate and consumption abroad depend on the sign of $(\rho'U'a_h - 1)$. In Table 4.1 I have presented the effects with the restriction that $\rho'U'a_h < 1$ (for $h = 1,2$). This is mainly done to keep the model within bounds of plausibility,

TABLE 4.1: COMPARATIVE STATICS FOR THE MODEL OF ENDOGENOUS TIME PREFERENCE FORMATION

Shocks in:	Population growth rate		Depreciation rate		Technology	
	n_1	n_2	δ_1	δ_2	z_1	z_2
k_1	$-$[a]	$+$[b]	$-$[c]	$+$	$+/-$	$-$
k_2	$+$[a]	$-$[b]	$+$	$-$[c]	$-$	$+/-$
r	$+$[a]	$+$[b]	$-$	$-$	$+$	$+$
d	$-$[a]	$-$[b]	$+$	$+$	$-$	$-$
c_1	$-$	$+$[b]	$-$	$-$	$+$	$+$
c_2	$+$[a]	$-$	$-$	$-$	$+$	$+$

a) if $\rho'U'a_1 < 1$, where $a_1 = k_1 + d$.
b) if $\rho'U'a_2 < 1$, where $a_2 = k_2 - d.L_1/L_2$.
c) if $\rho'U'k_h < 1$ for $h = 1,2$.

i.e. it does not give rise to exploding debt situations and it remains comparable to the existing body of optimal growth models. To proceed with the comparative statics, the effects of technology (δ_h, Z_h) are unambiguous to a large extent. Positive technology shocks, Z_h, give rise to an increase in consumption and thereby to the rate of time preference, *irrespective* of the country where the shock occurred. It does, however, have an ambiguous effect on the rate of capital accumulation at home (i.e. $dk_h/dZ_h \gtrless 0$). E.g., a positive shock in the state of technology occuring in country 1 leads to a rise in the world interest rate as a consequence of the rise in the rate of time preference ($\rho[U_1]$). The increase in interest rate leads to a fall in capital accumulation in country 2, but the effect on k_1 is ambiguous because, on the one hand, the need to accumulate more capital has increased (see equation 4.63) and on the other hand the planner feels the need to consume part of this newly acquired wealth and increase the rate of time preference.

There is, however, a difficulty when differences in population growth arise. As long as a divergence in population growth rates exists, the country with the relatively high rate of population growth will have a negligible amount of interest (corrected for the rate of population growth) to pay since:

$$(4.66) \qquad \lim_{t \to \infty} (r - n_2)d.L_1/L_2 = 0$$

In the steady state, the high population growth country accumulates assets *as if* it is a closed economy. The low population growth country becomes a small open economy under those circumstances and the social planner receives interest payments on its foreign assets.

The normative significance of the present section is of

considerable importance. The way in which we value living standards in the world of today is bound to fall into one of the two extreme welfare criterions: total utility criterion $L.U[C/L]$, as proposed by Meade [1955], or the average utility criterion, $U[C/L]$. The total utility (or Benthamite) criterion is bound to imply a Vatican stance in questions of population policy, whereas the average utility criterion leads to a Malthusian attitude: the less, the merrier. As recognised by Ng [1989], when numbers differ, both principles are unsatisfactory policy devices if one has to make a judgement over the value of life (as represented by living standards). Ng [1989] 'solves' the problem by introducing an ad hoc compromise: maximisation of number-dampened total utility, $q(L).U[C/L]$ where $q' > 0$, $q'' < 0$ and $q(.)$ is bounded from above, i.e. the function q never reaches infinity, even if L goes to infinity. This function which establishes a compromise has no economic or ethic content at all. The value attached to the first person exceeds all values attached to other persons in the economy.

Another solution is offered by Michel [1990] who opts for the ethical stance in which the social rate of time preference equals the growth rate of population. This would indeed solve the problem of a demographically divided world, but it remains *ad hoc* in that it is merely a translation of the undiscounted average utility case to the conditions of undiscounted total utility. It is the rather unhappy implication that the planners of relatively fast growing populations may use a higher discount rate than the planners representing slower growing populations. The analysis of the present section avoids the ad hocery of Ng [1989] and Michel [1990] and, in fact, endogenises the care for future generations. Endogenous time preference formation establishes a compromise between the average utility criterion and the total utility criterion. The welfare theoretical interpretation is that, in an *interdependent* world economy, social planners of countries with fast growing populations should relatively care more about future generations than planners of slow growing populations. Each social planner has to take into account the domestic and foreign rate of population growth.

Summarising, the interdependent nature of the world economy of this section is apparent. Whether a change in tastes, endowments or technology occurs at home or abroad, it always affects consumption, investment and factor prices in both countries.

4.4 SUMMARY

The central aim of this chapter was to explore the question how shocks in the population growth rate of a country affect international lending and borrowing, production and consumption and investment in an interdependent world economy. Empirically, investment fluctuations appear to be an important determinant of current account fluctuations (Sachs [1981]). However, many authors (Sachs [1982], and Obstfeld [1983]) abstract from investment by the use of the partial equilibrium framework of a small open economy. Interdependent economies with endogenous investment turn out to be extremely complicated as Bovenberg [1989] and Cantor and Mark [1987] show, but still it brings to the fore how foreign actions and endowments affect domestic actions. However, a simple one-sector model of optimal growth of a two-country world economy allows only a limited number of population growth paths to be studied that are non-repugnant. In an infinite horizon model, convergence of population growth rates is a necessary condition for patterns of international lending and borrowing to be a viable solution, without ending up with a repugnant conclusion. Optimal capital flows during a (delayed) demographic transition should be directed from the relatively low population growth country to the higher population growth country. The country with the temporarily higher population growth rate runs a current account deficit, to be compensated for by a permanent current account surplus after the demographic transition is completed. In the steady state the trade balance consists only of the interest payments on steady state foreign assets.

When time preference is endogenous and depends on the utility of current consumption streams, a divergence in population growth rates will be offset by the rate of time preference. A low population growth country will therefore have a high(er) rate of time preference and the opposite proposition applies to the high population growth country. The model is more flexible since it can trace the entire time path of asset accumulation in a permanently demographically divided world economy. The long-run consequences of a divergence in population growth rates are however trivial: the high population growth country accumulates capital as if it is a closed economy and the low population growth country accumulates assets as a small open economy facing a perfectly competitive international capital market, represented by the economy of the high population growth country.

The present chapter has addressed a question that numerous authors have neglected[5] or considered unimportant. The issue of

---

5. E.g., Bardhan [1965], Oniki and Uzawa [1965] and Inada [1968] all play down the difficulties of using different growth rates in models of international lending and borrowing. The only exception to this rule is Deardorff [1985,1987] who considers the economic consequences of a world of diverging populations in

diverging population growth developments is, however, from a theoretical and from practical point of view interesting.

On the theoretical side different population developments in a world economy add a piece of reality to the Ramsey-model that would have gone unnoticed if we conveniently assumed population growth rates constant and equal to one another. With an increasing use of the Koopmans-Cass model of capital accumulation in normative and positive analyses (such as the real business cycle strand of literature), it seems like a worthwhile exercise to explore and elaborate on the use of this model in an international setting. The extension of endogenous time preference proved a more flexible edifice for questions of international lending and borrowing in a demographically divided world and removed somewhat the *ad hoc* restrictions of the standard growth model that are imposed in order to ensure a stable foreign asset accumulation.

On the practical side, the normative question of optimal economic growth may indeed be of some importance for studying development problems of LDCs and ageing problems of developed countries hand in hand, since it is one of the stylised facts and forecasts that the present day world economy is demographically divided (see e.g. Brown and Jacobson [1986]).

---

a model analogous to Pasinetti's two-class growth model.

APPENDIX 4A: COMPARATIVE STATICS FOR THE MODEL WITH ENDOGENOUS
TIME PREFERENCE FORMATION

The following set of equations is sufficient to derive the
steady state general equilibrium effects of changes in
parameters (for $h = 1,2$):

(4.A.1) $\quad Z_h f_h' = \rho[U(c_h)] + n_h + \delta_h$

(4.A.2) $\quad r = Z_h f_h' - \delta_h$

(4.A.3) $\quad c_1 = Z_1 f(k_1) - (\delta_1 + n_1)k_1 + (r - n_1)d$

(4.A.4) $\quad c_2 = Z_2 f(k_2) - (\delta_2 + n_2)k_2 - (r - n_2)d.L_1/L_2$

If $n_1 < n_2$ one can use the limit property of the long-run
population size ratio:

(4.A.5) $\quad \lim_{t \to \infty} L_1(t)/L_2(t) = 0$

Totally differentiating these equations we obtain in matrix
notation:

$$(4.A.6) \quad \begin{bmatrix} dk_1 \\ dk_2 \\ dr \\ dd \\ dc_1 \\ dc_2 \end{bmatrix} = A^{-1} . B . \begin{bmatrix} dn_1 \\ dn_2 \\ d\delta_1 \\ d\delta_2 \\ dZ_1 \\ dZ_2 \end{bmatrix}$$

where

$$B = \begin{bmatrix} 1 & 0 & 1 & 0 & -f_1' & 0 \\ 0 & 1 & 0 & 1 & 0 & -f_2' \\ 0 & 0 & -1 & 0 & f_1' & 0 \\ 0 & 0 & 0 & -1 & 0 & f_2' \\ -a_1 & 0 & -k_1 & 0 & f_1(k_1) & 0 \\ 0 & -a_2 & 0 & -k_2 & 0 & f_2(k_2) \end{bmatrix}$$

where $a_1 = k_1 + d$ and $a_2 = k_2 - d.L_1/L_2$, and[6]

$$A^{-1} = \frac{1}{Det} \begin{bmatrix} A_{11} & A_{21} & A_{31} & A_{41} & A_{51} & A_{61} \\ A_{12} & A_{22} & A_{32} & A_{42} & A_{52} & A_{62} \\ A_{13} & A_{23} & A_{33} & A_{43} & A_{53} & A_{63} \\ A_{14} & A_{24} & A_{34} & A_{44} & A_{54} & A_{64} \\ A_{15} & A_{25} & A_{35} & A_{45} & A_{55} & A_{65} \\ A_{16} & A_{26} & A_{36} & A_{46} & A_{56} & A_{66} \end{bmatrix}$$

$$Det = y_1''y_2''\rho_2'(r - n_2)\frac{L_1}{L_2} - \rho_1'\left\{ y_1''y_2''(-(r - n_1) + \rho_2'd(n_1 - n_2)\frac{L_1}{L_2}\right\}$$

$$+ y_2''\rho_2'(r - n_2)\rho_1\frac{L_1}{L_2} + y_1''\rho_2'(r - n_1)\rho_2 \right\} > 0$$

---

6. To shorten notation and derivatives, production is denoted by $y_h = Z_h f_h(.)$ and ρ_h' denotes $(\partial\rho/\partial U).(\partial U/\partial c_h)$, where a subscript h is added to indicate the consumption in country h.

$$A_{11} = \rho'_2 y'_2{}' (r - n_2) L_1/L_2 < 0$$

$$A_{12} = \rho'_2 y'_1{}' (r - n_2) L_1/L_2 < 0$$

$$A_{13} = y'_1{}' y'_2{}' \rho'_2 (r - n_2) L_1/L_2 > 0$$

$$A_{14} = -y'_1{}' y'_2{}' - \rho'_2 [y'_1{}' y'_2{}' dL_1/L_2 - y'_1{}' \rho_2] < 0$$

$$A_{15} = -y'_1{}' y'_2{}' \rho_1 - \rho'_2 [y'_1{}' y'_2{}' d(n_2 - n_1) L_1/L_2 - y'_1{}' (r - n_1) \rho_2] +$$
$$+ \rho'_2 y'_2{}' \rho_1 (r - n_1) L_1/L_2 < 0$$

$$A_{16} = y'_1{}' y'_2{}' (r - n_2) L_1/L_2 > 0$$

$$A_{21} = \rho'_1 y'_2{}' (r - n_1) < 0$$

$$A_{22} = \rho'_1 y'_1{}' (r - n_1) < 0$$

$$A_{23} = \rho'_1 y'_1{}' y'_2{}' (r - n_1) > 0$$

$$A_{24} = y'_1{}' y'_2{}' - \rho'_1 [y'_1{}' y'_2{}' d + y'_2{}' \rho_1] \ ?$$

$$A_{25} = y'_1{}' y'_2{}' (r - n_1) > 0$$

$$A_{26} = -y'_1{}' y'_2{}' (r - n_2) L_1/L_2 - \rho'_1 [y'_1{}' y'_2{}' d(n_2 - n_1) L_1/L_2 - y'_1{}' \rho_1 \rho_2$$
$$- y'_2{}' \rho_1 \rho_2 L_1/L_2] < 0$$

$$A_{31} = \rho'_1 [-y'_2{}' (r - n_1) - \rho'_2 y'_2{}' d(n_2 - n_1) L_1/L_2 + \rho'_2 \rho_1 \rho_2] > 0$$

$$A_{32} = y'_1{}' \rho'_2 (r - n_2) L_1/L_2 - \rho'_1 \rho'_2 \rho_1 \rho_2 L_1/L_2 < 0$$

$$A_{33} = \rho'_2 y'_2{}' \rho_2 L_1/L_2 [y'_1{}' - \rho_1 \rho'_1] > 0$$

$$A_{34} = -y'_1{}' y'_2{}' - \rho'_2 y'_1{}' [y'_2{}' dL_1/L_2 - \rho_2] + \rho'_1 y'_2{}' \rho_1 +$$
$$+ \rho'_1 \rho'_2 \rho_1 d . y'_2{}' L_1/L_2 - \rho'_1 \rho'_2 \rho_1 \rho_2 < 0$$

$$A_{35} = -y'_1{}' y'_2{}' \rho_1 - y'_1{}' y'_2{}' \rho'_2 d(n_2 - n_1) L_1/L_2 + y'_1{}' \rho'_2 \rho_1 \rho_2 < 0$$

$$A_{36} = y'_2{}' \rho_2 L_1/L_2 [y'_1{}' - \rho_1 \rho'_1] > 0$$

$$A_{41} = \rho_1 \rho'_1 [y'_2{}' - \rho_2 \rho'_2] < 0$$

$$A_{42} = -y'_1{}' \rho_2 \rho'_2 L_1/L_2 + \rho'_1 \rho'_2 [y'_1{}' d(n_1 - n_2) L_1/L_2 + \rho_1 \rho_2 L_1/L_2] > 0$$

$$A_{43} = \rho_1 \rho'_1 y'_1{}' [y'_2{}' - \rho_2 \rho'_2] > 0$$

$$A_{44} = y'_1{}' y'_2{}' - y'_1{}' \rho'_2 \rho_2 - \rho'_1 y'_2{}' [y'_1{}' d + \rho_1] + \rho'_1 \rho'_2 \rho_2 [y'_1{}' d + \rho_1] \ ?$$

$$A_{45} = y'_1{}' y'_2{}' \rho_1 - \rho_2 \rho_1 \rho'_2 y'_1{}' > 0$$

$$A_{46} = -y'_1{}' y'_2{}' \rho_2 L_1/L_2 + \rho'_1 y'_2{}' [y'_1{}' d(n_1 - n_2) L_1/L_2 + \rho_1 \rho_2 L_1/L_2] < 0$$

$$A_{51} = \rho'_1 \rho'_2 \rho_2 y'_2{}' L_1/L_2 < 0$$

$$A_{52} = \rho'_1 \rho'_2 \rho_2 y'_1{}' L_1/L_2 < 0$$

$$A_{53} = \rho'_1 \rho'_2 \rho_2 y'_1{}' y'_2{}' L_1/L_2 > 0$$

$$A_{54} = -y'_1{}' y'_2{}' \rho'_1 + \rho'_1 \rho'_2 y'_1{}' [\rho_2 - y'_2{}' dL_1/L_2] < 0$$

$$A_{55} = y'_1{}' y'_2{}' \rho'_2 \rho_2 L_1/L_2 > 0$$

$$A_{56} = y_1' 'y_2' '\rho_1' \rho_2 L_1 / L_2 > 0$$

$$A_{61} = \rho_1' \rho_2' \rho_1 y_2' ' < 0$$

$$A_{62} = \rho_1' \rho_2' \rho_1 y_1' ' < 0$$

$$A_{63} = \rho_1' \rho_2' \rho_1 y_1' 'y_2' ' > 0$$

$$A_{64} = y_2' '[y_1' '\rho_2' - \rho_1' \rho_2' [y_1' 'd + \rho_1]] \ ?$$

$$A_{65} = y_1' 'y_2' '\rho_2' \rho_1 > 0$$

$$A_{66} = y_1' 'y_2' '\rho_1' \rho_1 > 0.$$

CHAPTER 5: INTERNATIONAL MIGRATION, ECONOMIC POLICY AND HUMAN
CAPITAL ACCUMULATION

Economies with ageing populations consider more often selective
immigration as a policy alternative to alleviate domestic labour
market pressures. The reason for considering this alternative is
quite obvious. By attracting skilled labour from abroad,
sacrifices can be avoided which are inherent to the stimulation
of national welfare by means of investment in education.

This chapter examines the question whether the easy way out-
a selective immigration policy and immigration in general - is
indeed beneficial for all parties concerned, viz. the host and
the source country. The welfare point of view taken in this
chapter boils down to the following principle of optimality[1]: a
migration flow between countries can only be considered a merit
if it enhances welfare in *at least* one country, without
deteriorating the welfare in other countries. The opinion of the
man-in-the-street would be that a brain drain is always
beneficial to the country of immigration and detrimental to the
welfare of the country of emigration. The reason why this is
only one side of the story is the preoccupation with the
training costs and the negligence of the capital requirements
involved by a changing population growth rate. An increase in
the aggregate population growth rate makes a country relatively
labour abundant, so that the general equilibrium effect is a
decrease in the capital/labour ratio with a negative effect on

---

1. See for a discussion of the welfare criteria and consequences
of the brain drain, Quibria [1990], Bhagwati and Rodriguez
[1976] and Rodriguez [1976].

production and consumption per capita. The reverse applies to the case of a decline in the population growth rate. This effect is better known as the capital dilution effect. These two effects on welfare - the free rider effect of education and the capital dilution effect - are of opposite signs and imply that countries face a trade-off. Experience shows that most countries restrict the flow of migrants. An asymmetry in the treatment of migrants exists. Emigration is a basic human right established by the United Nations Universal Declaration of Human Rights (it states: "Everyone has the right to leave any country, including his own, and to return to his country"). The right of immigration into a country is however not recognised by international law. Examination of the welfare consequences of international migration can therefore shed some light on positive questions of public choice: why are migration flows often restricted by governments? and why are immigrants more likely to be restricted to move than emigrants? To examine merely the positive question in which direction migration patterns will evolve, is likely to be a trivial question in a world economy with different production technologies[2], since a migrant's economic motives are simply inspired by the prospect of improving his or her living standard. When the standard of living in one country is permanently higher than the standard of living of the neighbouring country, the country with a lower standard of living will experience an exodus (as remarked by Galor and Stark [1991]). It would therefore seem an approach more worthwile to explain why and when governments *restrict* migration. A two-country general equilibrium model is

---

2. The past few years, we have witnessed an increase in general equilibrium analyses of international migration. See, e.g., Ethier [1985], Galor [1986], Tu [1988] and Kondo [1989b].

constructed to examine this question. A composite commodity is produced by means of physical capital, skilled and unskilled labour. International lending and borrowing are excluded as means to finance investment. Capital is assumed to be restricted to domestic production. Immigration is assumed to be controlled by the social planners, whereas they have no control over emigration.

The outline of this chapter is as follows. First, we will show in section 5.1, as a matter of acquaintance, the mechanics of the human capital model in autarky, which later on will serve as a standard of argument in tackling the question whether countries should engage in an international labour market. Section 5.2 derives the comparative statics of the autarkic economic system. Section 5.3 then discusses the welfare consequences of immigration policies in a demographically divided world economy. Section 5.4 offers the reader a steady state simulation of the economic consequences of the brain drain for a variety of economies. Finally, section 5.5 sums up the conclusions.

5.1 HUMAN CAPITAL ACCUMULATION IN AUTARKY

The following analysis of human capital accumulation is set in a continuous time version of the neoclassical model. The optimal resource allocation problem for a social planner can be given in the following terms. A social planner has as a policy objective the maximisation of the instantaneous utility of consumption per capita, i.e. $U[C(t)/L(t)]$, by means of the investment rate in physical capital, $s(t)$, and the investment rate in human capital at time t, $v(t)$:

(5.1)   Maximise $V_0 = \int_0^\infty e^{-\rho t} U[c(t)]\ dt$
$\quad\quad\quad s,v$

where ρ denotes the rate of time preference. The instantaneous utility function satisfies the following conditions (where: $R_+ = [0,\infty)$),

Assumption 1: $U: R_+ \to R$ with $U' > 0$, $U'' < 0$ and

$$\lim_{c \to 0} U'(c) = +\infty \text{ and } \lim_{c \to \infty} U'(c) = 0$$

Investment in physical and human capital take up a part of the national product $Y(t)$. When rewriting the national income identity we obtain an expression for consumption per capita:

(5.2) $C(t) \equiv [1 - s(t) - v(t)]Y(t)$

where $v(t)$ is the investment ratio in human capital. The technology describing production $y(t)$ per unit of labour (= Y/L) is represented by the standard neoclassical production function $Zf(.)$. The production function $f(.)$ is homogeneous of degree 1 in terms of physical capital ($k \equiv K/L$) and the two types of human capital: untrained or "raw" labour (as a fraction of the population: $h^u \equiv H^u/L$) and trained or skilled labour h^s (= H^s/L). A country has to produce by means of both types of labour, it cannot completely specialize in either 'skilled labour' intensive or 'unskilled labour' intensive production. The reason for educating the labour force is quite straightforward: the marginal productivity of skilled labour is higher than that of unskilled labour. The present analysis abstracts from the time that is needed to educate the labour force. Although this might seem like a blatant refutation of reality, the abstraction of 'schooling time' helps to focus on the most direct aspects of migration. A model that distinguishes two types of labour but also "time to build" human capital is presented in Van Imhoff [1989a, chapter 6.2]. The production technology is described by the following Inada-assumptions,

Assumption 2:

$f\colon R_+ \to R_+$ with $\partial f/\partial x_i > 0$, $\partial^2 f/\partial x_i^2 < 0$, $\partial^2 f/\partial x_i \partial x_j > 0$,

$(\partial^2 f/\partial x_i^2)(\partial^2 f/\partial x_j^2) - (\partial^2 f/\partial x_i \partial x_j)^2 > 0$ for $i \neq j$ and $x =$

(k, h^s, h^u). No 'free lunch': $f(0, h^s, h^u) = f(k, 0, 1) =$

$f(k, 1, 0) = 0$, $\lim_{k \to 0} \partial f/\partial k = \infty$ and $\lim_{k \to \infty} \partial f/\partial k = 0$,

$\lim_{h_s \to 0} \partial f/\partial h^s$ and $\lim_{h_s \to 1} \partial f/\partial h^s \in (0,1)$

In deciding upon the investment rates the social planner has to value the increase of an extra unit of physical and human capital. The prime distinction between human and physical capital is that when an individual dies, the human capital is lost at once, but the accumulated physical capital stock is kept in use. To incorporate the aspect of mortality I assume that the aggregate rate of population growth is $n = b - \gamma$, where b denotes the (constant) rate of fertility and γ the (constant) mortality rate. We can express the development of the capital assets by the following differential equations:

(5.3) $\dot{K} = s(t)Y(t) - \delta_K K(t)$

(5.4) $\dot{H}^s = v(t)Y(t)/\eta - \delta_H H^s - \gamma H^s$

or in labour intensive terms:

$$(5.3') \qquad \dot{k} = s(t)y(t) - (\delta_K + n)k(t)$$

$$(5.4') \qquad \dot{h}^s = v(t)y(t)/\eta - (\delta_H + n + \gamma)h^s(t)$$

$$(5.5) \qquad \dot{h}^u = - \dot{h}^s$$

Following Ritzen [1977, ch. 3] human capital is accumulated through an educational process which involves training costs of η, to be associated with the training of a unit of unskilled labour to the level of skilled labour. The formation of human capital uses up part (v) of the national product. Physical capital depreciates through the use of capital in the production process. Human capital depreciates through the deterioration of health and erosion (i.e. forgetfullness) or obsolescence of skills. The depreciation rate of human capital, δ_H, will generally differ from the depreciation rate of physical capital, δ_K. The constraints on the state variables amount to:

$$(5.6) \qquad H^s(t) + H^u(t) = L(t)$$

or in labour intensive terms:

$$(5.6') \qquad h^s(t) + h^u(t) = 1$$

$$(5.7) \qquad k(t) \geq 0 \quad \text{and} \quad 0 \leq h^s(t), \ h^u(t) \leq 1$$

When differentiating constraint (5.6) with respect to time, we can see that the growth rate of the labour force is divided up in a weighted sum of skilled and unskilled labour force growth:

$$(5.8) \qquad n \equiv \frac{\overset{\bullet}{H^s}}{H^s(t)}.h^s(t) + \frac{\overset{\bullet}{H^u}}{H^u(t)}.h^u(t)$$

The restriction on the control variables amounts to:

$$(5.9) \qquad 0 \le v(t) + s(t) \le 1$$

The optimisation problem will be solved by means of Pontryagin's Maximum Principle. The corresponding current-value Hamiltonian can be formulated as follows:

$$(5.10) \qquad H(s,v,k,h^s,\lambda,\mu) = U[c(t)] +$$

$$+ \lambda(t)[s(t)y(t) - (\delta_K + n)k(t)]$$

$$+ \mu(t)[v(t)y(t)/\eta - (\delta_H + n + \gamma)h^s(t)]$$

In general, if an investment policy (s,v) and the associated accumulation path (k,h^s) are to be optimal, the following differential equations must be satisfied:

$$(5.11) \qquad \overset{\bullet}{k} = sy - (\delta_K + n)k$$

$$(5.12) \qquad \overset{\bullet}{h^s} = vy/\eta - (\delta_H + n + \gamma)h^s$$

$$(5.13) \quad \dot{\lambda} = -[U'(c).(1 - s - v) + \lambda s + \frac{\mu v}{\eta}]f_k' + \lambda(\delta_K + n + \rho)$$

$$(5.14) \quad \dot{\mu} = -[U'(c).(1 - s - v) + \lambda s + \frac{\mu v}{\eta}]\Delta w$$

$$+ \mu(\delta_H + n + \rho + \gamma)$$

$$(5.15) \quad \lim_{t \to \infty} e^{-\rho t} U'[c(t)]k(t) = 0$$

$$(5.16) \quad \lim_{t \to \infty} e^{-\rho t} \eta U'[c(t)]h^s(t) = 0$$

where $\Delta w = w^s - w^u = \partial y/\partial h^s - \partial y/\partial h^u$. A necessary condition (Kuhn-Tucker) for an inequality-constrained optimisation problem is that the control variables are chosen such that the Hamiltonian and the related Lagrangean (or generalised Hamiltonian) L are maximised at any point in time. The Lagrangean is:

$$(5.17) \quad L = H + p_1 s + p_2 v + p_3(1 - s - v)y$$

First order conditions for a maximum are:

$$(5.18) \quad \frac{\partial L}{\partial s} = (\lambda - U'[c])y + p_1 - p_3 y = 0, \ p_1 s = 0, \quad p_1 \geq 0$$

(5.19)　　$\dfrac{\partial L}{\partial v} = (\mu/\eta - U'[c])y + p_2 - p_3 y = 0, \quad p_2 v = 0, \quad p_2 \geq 0$

(5.20)　　$p_3(1 - s - v)y = 0, \quad p_3 \geq 0$

And combining (5.18) and (5.19) one obtains:

(5.21)　　$(\lambda - U'[c])y + p_1 = (\mu/\eta - U'[c])y + p_2 = p_3 y \geq 0$

When the shadow price of investing a small part of the national product exceeds the marginal utility of consuming that same part, the investment rate will be at its maximum, viz. the boundary value 1. However, given the form of the utility function, such a choice can conveniently be ruled out. The minimum boundary value of zero cannot be ruled out as an optimal choice. Combining these conditions one can compile the table of policy choices, as given in Table 5.1. Given the assumptions of the utility function, we can safely exclude the last three policy options in which all output is saved: cases E, F and G. These policies do, however, apply in the case of a linear utility function $U(.) = c(t)$.

Optimal control solutions for two-state variable problems are quite complex as demonstrated by Pitchford [1977]. The problems Pitchford discusses are restricted to independent state variables. The present problem, however, involves two *interdependent* state variables (and constrained control variables). It is therefore of some interest to know whether the steady state exists and whether it is unique. A steady state is defined by the constancy of per capita levels of capital and percentage of skilled labour:

(5.22) $\dot{k} = 0$ and $\dot{h}^s = 0$

TABLE 5.1: OPTIMAL INVESTMENT POLICIES FOR THE MODEL OF HUMAN CAPITAL FORMATION

	Controls:					Shadow prices:		
Policy:	s	v	$s + v$	$\lambda - U'[c]$	$\mu/\eta - U'[c]$	P_1	P_2	P_3
A	0	0	0	< 0	< 0	•	•	0
B	$[0,1]$	$[0,1]$	$[0,1]$	$= 0$	$= 0$	0	0	0
C	0	$[0,1]$	$[0,1]$	< 0	$= 0$	•	0	0
D	$[0,1]$	0	$[0,1]$	$= 0$	< 0	0	•	0
E	0	1	1	< 0	> 0	•	0	•
F	1	0	1	> 0	< 0	0	•	•
G	$[0,1]$	$[0,1]$	1	$\lambda > 0$	$\mu/\eta > 0$	0	0	•

Under such conditions, a Golden Age equilibrium, i.e. a resource allocation which cannot be improved by any alternative asset mix, is defined by the following conditions:

$$(5.23) \quad \frac{\partial y}{\partial k} = \rho + \delta_K + n$$

$$(5.24) \quad \Delta w/\eta = \rho + \delta_H + n + \gamma$$

Equations (5.23) and (5.24) are the modified golden rules of physical and human capital accumulation. The existence of the steady state is warranted by the Inada-conditions of the production technology: differentiate equations (5.23) and (5.24) with respect to time and one obtains the following system of equations:

$$(5.25) \qquad \begin{bmatrix} A_{11} & A_{12} \\ A_{21} & A_{22} \end{bmatrix} \begin{bmatrix} \dot{k} \\ \dot{h^s} \end{bmatrix} = 0$$

where: $A_{11} = \partial^2 y / \partial k^2 < 0$, $A_{12} = A_{21} = \partial^2 y / \partial k \partial h^s - \partial^2 y / \partial k \partial h^u > 0$ and $A_{22} = \partial^2 y / (\partial h^s)^2 + \partial^2 y / (\partial h^u)^2 - 2 . \partial^2 y / \partial h^s \partial h^u < 0$. Given these signs a steady state is possible. Uniqueness of the steady state follows from a similar kind of reasoning. If the marginal productivity terms of the golden rules are brought to the right hand side of the equations, we can conclude that the map (5.23)-(5.24) is globally univalent. This is established by strict concavity of $Zf(.)$ and the property of the Jacobian matrix: the Jacobian matrix of this system is a P-matrix: all principal minors are positive (i.e. a theorem proven by Gale and Nikaidô [1965]). We will assume that the equilibrium is stable since it is outside the scope of this paper to examine extensively the stability conditions of this optimal control problem with mixed constraints (see Seierstad and Sydsæter [1987]).

For the remainder of the analysis I will confine the (numerical) description of production, $y(t)$, to the following Cobb-Douglas function, with constant returns to scale:

$$(5.26) \qquad y = Z \cdot k^\alpha \cdot (h^s)^\beta \cdot (h^u)^{1-\alpha-\beta}, \quad 0 < \alpha + \beta < 1, \quad Z > 0$$

where α and β are the income shares of physical capital and skilled labour; Z denotes the constant level of technology. When $\eta > 0$, $\delta_H + \gamma \geq \delta_K$ and we are in a steady state situation where a country accumulates according to golden rules (5.23) and (5.24), the following equality of rates of return exists:

$$(5.27) \quad \frac{\beta}{h^s} - \frac{(1 - \alpha - \beta)}{h^u} = \eta[\alpha/k + (\delta_H + \gamma - \delta_K)/y]$$

This equality implies that the ratio of the income share of skilled labour and the stock of skilled labour is always larger than the ratio of the income share of unskilled labour and unskilled labour, unless, of course, physical capital depreciates much faster than the sum of the depreciation of human capital and the (constant) mortality rate. The golden rule of physical capital accumulation (5.23) can be expressed as a function of h^s:

$$(5.28) \quad k = \left\{ \frac{\rho + \delta_K + n}{\alpha Z h_s^\beta (1 - h_s)^{(1-\alpha-\beta)}} \right\}^{1/(\alpha-1)}$$

The golden rule of human capital accumulation (5.24) is:

$$(5.29) \quad k = \left\{ \frac{\eta(\rho + \gamma + \delta_H + n)}{Q Z h_s^\beta (1 - h_s)^{(1-\alpha-\beta)}} \right\}^{1/\alpha}$$

where $Q = \dfrac{\beta}{h^s} - \dfrac{(1 - \alpha - \beta)}{h^u}$

Equation (5.27) is also of importance in determining the range of optimal steady state values. A general analytical solution is not possible here. Only for the particular case where $\delta_K = \delta_H + \gamma$, the term expressing the equalisation of rates of return can be solved for k as a function of h^s:

$$(5.30) \quad k = \frac{\eta . \alpha . h^s (1 - h^s)}{\beta - (1 - \alpha)h^s}$$

It must be clear that the optimal human capital stock is only to be found in the interval $[0, \beta/(1-\alpha))$:

$$(5.31) \quad \lim_{h_s \uparrow \xi} k = \infty \quad \text{and} \quad \lim_{h_s \downarrow \xi} k = -\infty \quad \text{where } \xi = \beta/(1 - \alpha)$$

One can easily see that this solution is too complex to solve by hand. In simulating this particular economy (see section 5.2 and 5.4) I have therefore used an iterative procedure (viz. a Newton-Raphson algorithm).

5.2. COMPARATIVE STATICS IN AUTARKY

The aim of this section is to see how the endogenous variables react to changes in parameter values of the economy. The analysis is carried out for optimal steady states under conditions of a stable population. Five variables are of interest in this section, viz. the investment rates s and v, the physical and human capital stock, k and h^s, and consumption per capita, c. The comparative statics are derived from the golden rules (5.23) and (5.24), the optimal steady state control variables, which can be derived from the following two equations:

$$(5.32) \quad \dot{k} = 0 = sy - (\delta_K + n)k$$

(5.33) $\dot{h}^s = 0 = vy/\eta - (\delta_H + n + \gamma)h^s$

and the definition of consumption per capita:

(5.34) $c = (1 - s - v)Z.f(.)$

Total differentiation of these five equations yields the following system of equations:

$$
\begin{bmatrix}
Zf_{kk} & Zf_{kh} & 0 & 0 & 0 \\
Zf_{hk} & Zf_{hh} & 0 & 0 & 0 \\
[s.Zf_k - (\delta_K+n)] & sZf_h & Zf & 0 & 0 \\
vZf_k & [vZf_h - (\delta_H+\gamma+n)\eta] & 0 & Zf & 0 \\
-Zf_k(1-s-v) & -Zf_h(1-s-v) & Zf & Zf & 1
\end{bmatrix}
\begin{bmatrix}
dk \\
dh^s \\
ds \\
dv \\
dc
\end{bmatrix} =
$$

$$
= \begin{bmatrix}
1 & 0 & 0 & 1 & 1 & -f_k' & 0 \\
0 & \eta & \eta & \eta & \eta & -\Delta w & (\rho+\gamma+\delta_H+n) \\
k & 0 & 0 & k & 0 & -sf & 0 \\
0 & \eta h^s & \eta h^s & \eta h^s & 0 & -vf & (\delta_H+\gamma+n)h^s \\
0 & 0 & 0 & 0 & 0 & (1-s-v)f & 0
\end{bmatrix}
\begin{bmatrix}
d\delta_K \\
d\delta_H \\
d\gamma \\
dn \\
d\rho \\
dZ \\
d\eta
\end{bmatrix}
$$

where:

$f_{kk} = \partial^2 f/\partial k^2 < 0$

$f_{kh} = f_{hk} = [\partial^2 f/\partial k\partial h^s - \partial^2 f/\partial k\partial h^u] > 0$

$f_{hh} = [\partial^2 f/\partial h^{s2} + \partial^2 f/\partial h^{u2} - 2.\partial^2 f/\partial h^s \partial h^u] < 0$

The determinant D of the matrix on the left-hand side of the equality sign is always positive (i.e. a non-singular solution), hence the inverse matrix exists. Postmultiplication of the

TABLE 5.2: COMPARATIVE STATICS FOR THE MODEL OF HUMAN CAPITAL FORMATION[a]

Shocks in:	Physical Capital: Stock k	Investment Rate s	Skilled labour: Stock h^s	Investment Rate υ	Consumption per capita C/L
Depreciation Rate Physical Capital δ_K	−	+	−	+	−
Depreciation Rate Human Capital δ_H	−	+/−	−	+	−
Time Preference ρ	−	−	−	+/−	−
Population Growth Rate n	−	+	−	+	−
Mortality Rate γ	−	+/−	−	+	−
Training Costs η	−	+/−	−	+	−
Technology Z	+	+/−	+	−	+

a) To circumvent (slight) ambiguity some of the signs are calculated for a range of plausible parameters. The signs of the investment rates are particularly ambiguous for high rates of time preference.

184

inverse of this matrix by the matrix on the right-hand side of
the equality sign yields a matrix from which we can read the
comparative statics of this economic system (a complete
derivation is given in the appendix 5A to this chapter). Table
5.2 gives the reaction signs of the five endogenous variables to
changes in parameters. All signs are in line with similar
studies in this field (Van Imhoff and Ritzen [1988] and Van
Imhoff [1989b]). A fall in the level of training costs results
in a decrease in rates of investment in physical and human
capital and an increase in the physical and human capital stock.
Consumption per capita always profits from such a fall. One can
also see that changes in human and physical capital stock move
in line with the state of technology. A fall in the population
growth rate leads to an increase in the human and physical
capital stock. Investment rates can drop due to the increased
capital intensive production conditions and as a result,
consumption per capita increases. Intuitively, this result is
very appealing for considering the consequences of an economy,
making the transition from a relatively high population growth
rate to a lower growth rate. A lower growth rate amounts to
profitable conditions of investment in education and capital,
along the optimal growth path. Table 5.3 is added to gain a
quantitative insight in comparative statics.

TABLE 5.3: STEADY STATE ALLOCATIONS FOR THE MODEL OF HUMAN CAPITAL FORMATION

For the parameters: $\alpha = 0.3$, $\beta = 0.5$, $Z = 7.0$, $\eta = 12.0$, $\rho = 0.02$, $n = 0.01$, $\delta_H = 0.09$, $\gamma = 0.01$, $\delta_K = 0.05$ we calculate the benchmark:

	c	k	h^s	s	υ	y
Benchmark	11.2	58.4	68.3%	22.5%	5.8%	15.6
$\eta = 5.0$	11.7	58.5	70.2%	22.5%	2.5%	15.6
$= 15.0$	10.9	58.3	67.5%	22.5%	7.2%	15.6
$= 20.0$	10.6	58.2	66.1%	22.5%	9.4%	15.5
$Z = 2.0$	1.2	8.7	47.4%	22.5%	27.0%	2.3
$= 4.0$	4.5	26.0	64.0%	22.5%	12.2%	6.9
$= 10.0$	19.2	97.4	69.6%	22.5%	3.5%	26.0
$n = -0.01$	13.4	88.2	69.1%	20.0%	4.2%	17.6
$= 0.00$	12.1	70.7	68.8%	21.4%	5.0%	16.5
$= 0.03$	9.7	42.4	67.4%	24.0%	7.4%	14.1
$\rho = 0.00$	11.4	88.2	69.1%	30.0%	5.2%	17.6
$= 0.04$	10.5	37.0	67.0%	16.4%	6.5%	13.6
$= 0.11$	9.1	19.7	63.6%	10.6%	7.5%	11.2
$\beta = 0.30$	10.6	53.6	39.1%	22.5%	3.6%	14.3
$= 0.40$	10.4	53.6	53.3%	22.5%	4.9%	14.3
$= 0.55$	12.1	63.3	76.2%	22.5%	6.0%	16.9
$\alpha = 0.20$	5.5	18.3	55.9%	15.0%	10.1%	7.3
$= 0.25$	7.6	32.2	61.9%	18.7%	7.9%	10.3
$= 0.35$	18.0	112.5	75.2%	26.2%	3.9%	25.7

5.3 INTERNATIONAL MIGRATION AND ECONOMIC POLICY

If we now move on to migration patterns under conditions of
optimal capital accumulation, migration may become part of
economic policy. The theory of optimal migration is closely
linked to the theory of optimal population growth (see Arthur
and McNicoll [1977]). In the present setting I will only
consider the possibility of an immigration policy and I will
exclude the possibility of stimulating people to leave the
country. The question for a social planner is: given the ability
to control the number of immigrants, what should be the optimal
immigration flow? There are considerations to be made which may
make the optimal control of immigration a complex problem. The
first problem concerns the characteristics of individuals.
Individuals are born in a country and we usually assume that
their abilities and their preferences are given once and for
all. This assumption becomes quite untenable when we try to
discuss migration. Once the migrants (and their children) have
settled in the country of their choice, do they adapt their
characteristics to those of the domestic population or do they
remain the same? Empirical studies (e.g., Chiswick [1978]) show
that first-generation migrants still have origin-specific
characteristics, while later-generation migrants can hardly be
distinguished from the indigenous population.

The second problem is concerned with the analysis of a non-
stable population. An economic system that is inhabited by
population groups with different (positive) rates of
reproduction, implies an average population growth rate that
will always increase and in the limit will approach the rate of
the population group which has the highest birth rate.

Last but not least, the choice between trained and untrained
individuals leads to different effects on the human capital

stock. Trained individuals of a given level of education can simply be added to the existing stock; unskilled individuals will however have to be educated from scratch. Difficulties arise when these untrained migrants differ in their ability to learn. If they have more difficulty in learning than the indigenous population, extra costs will have to be incurred to transform them into skilled workers.

In the following section I will discuss the way in which the population growth rate is affected by migration. Section 5.3.2 will discuss the conditions for optimal immigration.

5.3.1 DEMOGRAPHICS

To demonstrate the complications which divergent growth rates imply, some demographic accounting is performed. The aggregate labour force and its growth rate are defined as:

$$(5.35) \quad L_i(t) = L_i^d(t) + L_i^m(t) - L_i^e(t) \quad \text{for } i = 1,2$$

$$(5.36) \quad \psi_i = \frac{\dot{L_i}}{L_i(t)} = n_i^d . \frac{L_i^d(t)}{L_i(t)} + n_i^m . \frac{L_i^m(t)}{L_i(t)} - n_i^e . \frac{L_i^e(t)}{L_i(t)}$$

where superscripts 'd', 'm' and 'e' denote the domestic population, immigrants and emigrants, respectively. There are two extreme options in dealing with population growth rates: (1) the birth and death rates depend on the country of origin or birth, or (2) the rates depend on the country of residence. We now illustrate the difference between these two definitions.

(1) *Constant characteristics*. Assume that migrants, wherever

they are, have a constant preference for children and their mortality rate is also constant. These rates differ from the growth rate in the country of destination. Once they have settled in this country the aggregate population growth rate is defined by:

$$(5.37) \qquad n = n_d . \frac{L_d}{L} + n_m . \frac{L_m}{L}$$

If the migrants (and their descendants) have a higher rate of increase than the indigenous population, the aggregate population growth rate will increase forever, approaching the migrant's rate of increase in the limit. In a two-country world, in which the growth rates diverge, the world population is inherently non-stable. Only when fertility and mortality rates converge, one can speak of a *stable* world population. A complication in the definition of the rate of migration is that it is composed of the flow of migrants as induced by economic forces *and* the reproduction and mortality rate of the migrants. Hence in a *steady state* the country of emigration is only affected in population size, but not in its growth rate. When time approaches infinity, the equality of growth rates is simply a consequence of high fertility individuals 'crowding out' low fertility individuals (see for this point, Keyfitz [1977]). High fertility individuals and their related characteristics (time preference, training costs, mortality) will under those assumptions, dominate the world population.

(2) *Changing characteristics*. Assume that once the migrants have settled in the country of their choice they adapt their behaviour, so that after a small interval in time they can hardly be distinguished from the indigenous population. This

implies for our definition of the aggregate growth rate (5.36) that a distinction between immigrants and domestic population is useless. The only way in which the immigrants affect the population growth in the country of destination is at the time of entrance:

$$(5.38) \qquad \psi_i = \frac{\dot{L_i}}{L_i(t)} = \frac{\dot{L_i^d}}{L_i(t)} + \frac{\dot{L_i^m}}{L_i(t)} = n_i^d + n_i^m$$

It is this latter definition of migration that we will use in our analysis of a selective immigration policy. Of course, the aggregate population growth rate in the country of emigration will now be affected due to the outflow of migrants. Note that the rate of immigration is rarely equal to the rate of emigration. A global steady state in this world is defined by equality of aggregate population growth rates: $\psi_1 = \psi_2$. If country 1 is the country of emigration and country 2 of immigration, this implies that $n_e L_1 = n_m L_2$. Given this simple identity it must be clear that if country 2 is small compared to country 1 ($L_2 \ll L_1$) and if the number of immigrants desired by the social planner of country 2 is positive, the emigration flow is going to be negligible for country 1.

5.3.2 OPTIMAL IMMIGRATION

Some of the differential equations which describe the asset development, change shape in an international setting. It should be stressed that the maximand (5.1) and the current-value Hamiltonian remain the same. Only the number of control variables change. The social planners each maximise consumption per capita of the local population, irrespective of the nationality of the inhabitants. Social planners can only control the immigration flow and not the emigration flow. Two additional assumptions are introduced: (i) in conducting an immigration policy, attracting immigrants is a costless activity, and (ii) the mortality rates in the two countries are identical[3], $\gamma_1 = \gamma_2 = \gamma$. The differential equations of physical and human capital now change to (for $i = 1,2$):

$$(5.39) \quad \dot{k}_i = s_i(t)y_i(t) - (\delta_K + \psi_i)k_i(t)$$

$$(5.40) \quad \dot{h}^s_i = v_i(t)y_i(t)/\eta_i - (\delta_H + \psi_i + \gamma_i)h^s_i(t) + n^s_m$$

$$(5.41) \quad \dot{h}^u_i = -\dot{h}^s_i$$

As one can easily see, the inflow of skilled and unskilled labour (n^m) affects the human capital stock as well as the physical capital stock in the country of immigration. One should make one qualification at this point. Skilled and unskilled labour are homogeneous across the two countries. There are no adjustment costs in transforming the skilled migrants of a technologically backward country to the requirements of a technologically advanced country[4].

We now move on to examine some cases where population growth

---

3. This assumption can also be interpreted as the possibility that migrants immediately adopt the mortality rate of the country of destination.

4. A more comprehensive model of migration would include costs of adjusting migrants educated abroad to production conditions at home. Drazen [1985] offers a nice framework for such resource allocation problems.

rates, training costs and production technologies differ. In order to concentrate on questions of economic policy, we will only consider interior solutions of capital investment. We can derive the immigration point of indifference for each of the two social planners, if we assume that the number of skilled and unskilled immigrants are controllable by the social planners. The first order conditions of the augmented Hamiltonian (5.10) become:

$$(5.42) \quad \frac{\partial H_i}{\partial n_s^m} = -\lambda_i k_i - \mu_i (h_i^s - 1) \quad \begin{cases} < 0: \ n_s^m = 0 \\ = 0 \neq n_s^m > 0 \end{cases}$$

$$(5.43) \quad \frac{\partial H_i}{\partial n_u^m} = -\lambda_i k_i - \mu_i h_i^s \quad < 0 : \ n_u^m = 0$$

It must be clear from the conditions mentioned above, that a social planner maximising welfare allows immigrants to enter the country as long as the level of welfare in the case of complete labour mobility is higher than the autarkic or restricted mobility level. Only for skilled labour benificial shifts of labour are imaginable. Unskilled labour merely increases the population density of the country of immigration and the subsequent demands on investment in physical and human capital to keep the migrants fully employed. Hence the welfare level of the receiving country in the situation, where an selective immigration policy is effectuated, is in general lower than the welfare level where a social planner abstains from such an effort (i.e. the autarky case). In the case of skilled immigrants the population density also increases, *but* a country saves on the investment in human capital. Hence there are possibilities of a positive welfare effect of free trade of skilled labour. The exact condition for allowing skilled migrants to enter a country has a straightforward interpretation. Immigration of skilled labour should be attracted to the point where the capital labour ratio equals the cost of training the unskilled labour force:

$$(5.44) \quad \eta + k = \eta h$$

Only if the autarkic situation in the country of immigration is such that the costs attached to training the unskilled part of the labour force exceed the capital/labour ratio ($k_i < \eta_i h_i^u$) an immigration policy is welfare improving. If the situation in the country of emigration is a mirror's image of its neighbour (i.e. $k_j > \eta_j h_j^u$, where $i,j = 1,2$ and $i \neq j$) the policy will be beneficial to both countries.

One should qualify this finding of a *selective* social planner, since unskilled migrants may differ in their ability to learn. If we modify the human capital equation to take account of the ability to learn of unskilled immigrants we obtain the following differential equation:

$$(5.45) \quad \dot{h}^s_{\,i} = v_i(t)y_i(t)/\eta_i^d - (\delta_H + \psi_i + \gamma_i)h^s_{\,i}(t) + n_j \Psi(\eta_j)$$

where $\Psi(.)$ describes the adjustment costs to transform an unskilled immigrant into a skilled worker and η^m and η^d, respectively, denote the training costs of an unskilled immigrant and an unskilled member of the indigenous population. Generally there are indeed additional costs attached to transforming migrants ($\Psi < 0$ if $\eta_j > \eta_i$). However, the presence of smarter immigrants may turn the 'costs' into gains ($\Psi > 0$ if $\eta_j < \eta_i$), and a selective immigration policy may not be restricted to merely skilled labour.

As a final point of qualification, in Ritzen and Van Dalen [1990] an additional effect is mentioned in evaluating the merits of the immigration of skilled individuals, viz. a foreign capital substitution effect. When international lending and borrowing is allowed for, the migration rate will affect the rate of return on foreign assets and, as a consequence, the amount of borrowing and lending.

5.4 A BRAIN DRAIN IN THE 'REAL' WORLD

This section discerns the various effects of migration by attaching numerical values to the parameters. Besides the practical interest in how this particular system works, the simulation is used to illustrate the pros and cons of the brain drain and try and trace the *size* of the welfare losses and gains.

The two case studies examined are perhaps at the forefront of economic policy. The first case examines two countries that decide to engage in an international labour market at a certain moment in time. Production technologies and population growth rates are identical, whereas the training costs differ.

The second case is concerned with the brain drain from developing countries to developed countries. This case is more complex since not only population growth rates and training costs differ, but the production technologies in the two regions of the world differ as well.

Any equilibrium in this world economy is assumed to be characterised by identical population growth rates, ψ^*, so that we can perform a steady state analysis. Under steady state conditions the optimal control variables concerning human capital are:

$$(5.46) \quad \dot{h}_1^s = 0 : \quad v_1^* = \frac{(\delta_H + \psi^* + \gamma)h_1^{s\,*}\eta_1}{y_1^*}$$

$$(5.47) \quad \dot{h}_2^s = 0 : \quad v_2^* = \frac{(\delta_H + \psi^* + \gamma)h_2^{s\,*}\eta_2}{y_2^*}$$

and consumption per capita in both countries amounts to:

$$(5.48) \quad c_1^* = y_1^* - (\delta_K + \psi^*)k_1^* - (\delta_H + \psi^* + \gamma)h_1^{s\,*}\eta_1 + n_s^m\eta_1$$

$$(5.49) \quad c_2^* = y_2^* - (\delta_K + \psi^*)k_2^* - (\delta_H + \psi^* + \gamma)h_2^{s\,*}\eta_2 - n_s^e\eta_2$$

where $n_s^e L_2 = n_s^m L_1$. As one can see from the right hand side of equations (5.48) and (5.49) the terms $n_s^m\eta_1$ represents the free rider effect of the brain drain for which the country of emigration has to pay $n_s^e\eta_2$. There are two effects, which have to be calculated before a country introduces a brain drain, viz.: (i) the capital dilution effect: $\Delta y_i - \Delta k_i - \Delta h_i^s\eta_i$ for $i = 1,2$ versus (ii) the free rider effect: $n_s^m\eta_1$ and $n_s^e\eta_2$. The condition for introducing a brain drain amounts to a positive sum of the capital dilution effect and the free rider effect, for at least one of the countries without affecting the welfare of the other country in a negative manner.

Table 5.5 shows some steady state simulations of the brain drain for constant population growth rates. Simulations of the two cases are performed so as to reflect the production per capita figures in different parts of the world. They must be seen as counterfactuals, since they show that a social planner conducts a policy which *lowers* welfare. As derived in the previous section 5.3.2, such an immigration policy will generally not be executed. Of course, one could calculate the optimal selective immigration rates by adding the condition (5.44), but this would yield either improbable rates of immigration not yet witnessed by world history, or no solution at all. Table 5.4 presents the parameter values for the two simulated case studies.

TABLE 5.4: PARAMETERS USED FOR THE BRAIN DRAIN SIMULATION[a]

Case: Country:	I		II	
	1	2	1	2
Technology Z	7.0	7.0	7.0	2.5
Physical capital share α	0.3	0.3	0.3	0.3
Human capital share β	0.5	0.5	0.5	0.2
Birth rate b	0.0	0.03	0.0	0.03
Mortality rate γ	0.01	0.01	0.01	0.01
Training costs η	12.0	9.0	12.0	20.0
Population size L	1.0	1.0	1.0	1.0
Depreciation rate physical capital δ_K	0.05	0.05	0.05	0.05
Depreciation rate human capital δ_H	0.09	0.09	0.09	0.09
Time preference ρ	0.05	0.05	0.05	0.05

a) For table 5.7 we have used other training costs parameters, viz. for case I: $\eta_1 = 150$; $\eta_2 = 9$ and for case II: $\eta_1 = 150$; $\eta_2 = 10$.

As one can deduce from table 5.5, the human capital intensity is not very much affected by the migration flow. The steady state welfare implications of the integration of labour markets (i.e. case I) confirm what we derived in section 5.2. The main

TABLE 5.5: A BRAIN DRAIN IN THE 'REAL' WORLD

Case:	I		II	
	$n_m^s = 0$	$n_m^s = 0.015$	$n_m^s = 0$	$n_m^s = 0.015$
k_1	49.3	39.5	49.3	39.5
k_2	32.7	39.6	6.7	8.3
h_1^s	67.9%	67.2%	67.9%	67.2%
h_2^s	67.8%	68.3%	10.9%	12.2%
y_1	14.8	13.8	14.8	13.8
y_2	13.1	13.9	2.7	2.9
s_1	13.3%	15.7%	13.3%	15.7%
s_2	17.5%	15.7%	17.5%	15.7%
v_1	4.4%	5.5%	4.4%	5.5%
v_2	5.1%	4.2%	9.0%	8.0%
c_1	12.2	11.1	12.2	11.1
c_2	10.1	11.0	2.0	1.9
free rider effect $i=1$	.	0.2	.	0.2
capital dilution effect $i=1$	.	−1.3	.	−1.3
free rider effect $i=2$	.	−0.1	.	−0.3
capital dilution effect $i=2$	.	1.0	.	0.2

conclusion from this simulation is that, for plausible parameters of tastes, technologies and endowments, the country of immigration loses, while the country of emigration gains from international integration. The investment rates in human capital for the two countries are in line with figures of public expenditures on education, as one can see in table 5.6. Table 5.6 gives an indication of the magnitude of public expenditures on education in 1975 and 1987. Although some spending on education is financed privately, the vast majority of education spending is financed by the government and Table 5.6 gives a fair impression of relevant magnitudes.

TABLE 5.6: PUBLIC EXPENDITURES ON EDUCATION, 1975-1987[a]

	Percent of GNP		Per Inhabitant (in US $)	
	1975	1987	1975	1987
Developed nations	6.0	5.9	270	704
Developing nations	3.5	4.1	14	29
Africa	4.5	6.6	18	37
Northern America	6.4	6.9	475	1257
Europe[b]	5.7	5.5	197	451
Latin America[c]	3.4	4.1	42	78
Asia	4.3	4.5	20	61
Oceania	6.5	5.8	329	524

a) Data on private expenditures are generally lacking for developing countries and for matters of comparability the table is compiled with public expenditures figures.
b) Including U.S.S.R.
c) Including the Caribbean

Source: Unesco [1989]

Finally, I want to show that a brain drain *can* be beneficial for both countries. Table 5.7 shows that when training costs are excessively high in the country of immigration, the free rider effect outweights the capital dilution effect. Table 5.7 shows clearly that the human capital structure of the country of immigration changes dramatically. The effects for the country of emigration are in line with the comparative statics results of section 5.2. It should be noted that there are no *potential* welfare improvements possible (i.e. the sum of welfare of the two countries, weighted by the relative population sizes) in the simulations presented. Thus the global objective function conforms to the global objective function of chapter 3:

$$(5.50) \quad V_0 = \int_0^\infty e^{-\rho t} \left\{ U_1[c_1] \frac{L_1(t)}{L(t)} + U_2[c_2] \frac{L_2(t)}{L(t)} \right\} dt$$

Only if a global planner uses an unweighted (i.e. the relative population shares are not taken into account) social welfare function, one can imagine that a case exists which offers potential welfare improvements, viz. the case of a very large country of immigration and a relatively small country of emigration. As the demographic accounting exercise of section 5.3.1 showed, one can arrive at a situation in which the immigrants hardly influence the aggregate population growth rate, whereas the migration flow could imply a substantial decrease in the population growth rate at the same time. Since the capital dilution effect dominates the free rider effect, this situation results in an increase in average world welfare. One would end up with the unlikely 'one nation, one vote' situation. The ethical justification of such a welfare function seems indefensible. The current welfare of millions of people

TABLE 5.7: A BENEFICIAL BRAIN DRAIN

Case:	I		II	
	$n_m^s = 0$	$n_m^s = 0.015$	$n_m^s = 0$	$n_m^s = 0.015$
k_1	21.5	12.9	21.5	12.9
k_2	32.7	39.6	7.2	8.8
h_1^s	14.3%	9.3%	14.3%	9.3%
h_2^s	67.8%	68.3%	16.8%	18.0%
y_1	6.4	4.5	6.4	4.5
y_2	13.1	13.9	2.9	3.1
s_1	13.3%	15.7%	13.3%	15.7%
s_2	17.5%	15.7%	17.5%	15.7%
v_1	26.7%	29.4%	26.7%	29.4%
v_2	5.1%	4.2%	6.4%	5.5%
c_1	3.9	4.7	3.9	4.7
c_2	10.1	11.0	2.2	2.3
free rider effect $i=1$	.	2.2	.	2.2
capital dilution effect $i=1$	.	−1.4	.	−1.4
free rider effect $i=2$	.	−0.1	.	−0.1
capital dilution effect $i=2$	.	1.0	.	0.2

would be set equal to the current welfare of one man. Of course, in an intertemporal context the discussion becomes quite different since one has to talk about real and potential (or 'to be born') persons.

5.5 SUMMARY

Should the U.S.A. welcome graduates from Mexico or India? Does the integration of domestic labour markets in one European labour market form an economic policy which is welfare improving for all countries concerned? These are questions at the forefront of economic policy debates (see e.g. Greenwood and McDowell [1986] and Simon [1990]) which have yielded different answers at different times. Part of the disagreement about effects of international migration can be explained by the social welfare function used. As noted by Quibria [1990] the Benthamite utility function would turn upside down the conclusions of the welfare analysis with a Millian utility function. With these warnings in mind, I have analysed in this chapter the welfare consequences of the 'brain drain' in a two-country general equilibrium model with Millian social welfare functions. Each country produces by means of physical capital and two types of labour (skilled and unskilled). If social planners strive for optimal (unweighted) per capita welfare, the brain drain will only be an optimal policy action under a limited number of economic states. Along optimal growth paths in a world with divergent population growth rates, there are essentially two effects to be taken into consideration, viz. (1) the capital dilution effect, and (2) the free rider effect if migrants *are* already *educated*. One could add a third effect, viz. if migrants are *not yet* trained, and the learning ability of migrants as represented by the training costs per unit of labour is lower than that of the indigenous population, a country might save on education expenditures. However, under quite general conditions the optimal immigration rate is zero. There are, however, possibilities for a positive aggregate world welfare effect of international migration, if the common objective function conforms to that of an unweighted social welfare function. Under those conditions, a positive welfare effect can arise. If the country of immigration is sufficiently large and the country of emigration sufficiently small, the sum of welfare effects of international migration is likely to be positive. This possibility implicitly assumes that the country that gains from migration will compensate the losing country. Explicit international transfers between governments is, however, a phenomenon that is not very likely to occur and quite difficult to design and execute (see Bhagwati [1985]).

The overall practical conclusion of this chapter must be that countries are well advised to educate their own labour force and not introduce a selective immigration policy. An extra reason for abstaining from a selective immigration policy is the consequent widening of the divergence in dynamic efficiency in capital accumulation. Developing countries invest far too little in education at present and instituting a brain drain would hardly affect the population growth rate and would harm the human capital stock significantly.

APPENDIX 5A: COMPARATIVE STATICS FOR THE MODEL OF HUMAN CAPITAL
ACCUMULATION

As a reference to the comparative statics analysis in section
5.2 the inverse matrix, A^{-1}, of reaction coefficients is given.
The comparative statics can be obtained by multiplication with
the matrix of parameter coefficients, B.

$$(5.A.1) \quad \begin{bmatrix} dk \\ dh^s \\ ds \\ dv \\ dc \end{bmatrix} = A^{-1}.B. \begin{bmatrix} d\delta_K \\ d\delta_H \\ d\gamma \\ dn \\ d\rho \\ dZ \\ d\eta \end{bmatrix}$$

where

$$A^{-1} = 1/\text{Det.} \begin{bmatrix} B_{11} & B_{21} & 0 & 0 & 0 \\ B_{12} & B_{22} & 0 & 0 & 0 \\ B_{13} & B_{23} & B_{33} & 0 & 0 \\ B_{14} & B_{24} & B_{34} & B_{44} & 0 \\ B_{15} & B_{25} & B_{35} & B_{45} & B_{55} \end{bmatrix}$$

and

$$B = \begin{bmatrix} 1 & 0 & 0 & 1 & 1 & -f'_k & 0 \\ 0 & \eta & \eta & \eta & \eta & -\Delta w & (\rho+\gamma+\delta_H+n) \\ k & 0 & 0 & k & 0 & -sf & 0 \\ 0 & \eta h^s & \eta h^s & \eta h^s & 0 & -vf & (\delta_H+\gamma+n)h^s \\ 0 & 0 & 0 & 0 & 0 & (1-s-v)f & 0 \end{bmatrix}$$

where:

$Det = (A_{11}A_{22} - A_{12}^2)y^2 > 0$

$B_{11} = A_{22}y^2 < 0$

$B_{12} = B_{21} = -A_{12}y^2 < 0$

$B_{13} = y(A_{21}sy_h - A_{22}A_{31}) > 0$

$B_{14} = y(A_{21}A_{42} - A_{22}A_{41})$

$B_{15} = y^2\{-A_{21}(sy_h + A_{42} - A_{52}) + A_{22}(A_{31} + A_{41} - A_{51})\}$

$B_{22} = A_{11}y^2 < 0$

$B_{23} = -y(A_{11}sy_h + A_{12}A_{31}) > 0$

$B_{24} = -y(A_{11}A_{42} + A_{12}A_{41})$

$B_{25} = -y^2\{A_{11}[sy_h + (A_{42} - A_{52})] + A_{12}[A_{31} + (vy_k - A_{51})]\} < 0$

$B_{33} = (A_{11}A_{22} - A_{12}^2)y > 0$

$B_{34} = y(A_{42}A_{11} - A_{12}vy_k)$

$B_{35} = -y^2\{A_{11}[A_{22} + (A_{42} - A_{52})] - A_{12}(A_{21} - vy_k + A_{51})\} < 0$

$B_{44} = (A_{11}A_{22} - A_{12}^2)y > 0$

$B_{45} = -(A_{11}A_{22} - A_{12}^2)y^2 < 0$

$B_{55} = (A_{11}A_{22} - A_{12}^2)y^2 > 0$

$A_{11} = Z\partial^2 f/\partial k^2 < 0$

$A_{12} = A_{21} = Z[\partial^2 f/\partial k\partial h^s - \partial^2 f/\partial k\partial h^u] > 0$

$A_{22} = Z[\partial^2 f/\partial h^{s2} + \partial^2 f/\partial h^{u2} - 2.\partial^2 f/\partial h^s \partial h^u] < 0$

$A_{31} = sy_k - (\delta_K + n) < 0$ if $\rho = 0$

$A_{41} = vy_k > 0$

$A_{42} = vy_h - (\delta_H + \gamma + n)\eta < 0$ if $\rho = 0$

$A_{51} = -y_k(1 - s - v) < 0$

$A_{52} = -y_h(1 - s - v) < 0$

CHAPTER 6: ON THE RELEVANCE OF THE RICARDIAN THEORY OF PUBLIC FINANCE TO CONDITIONS OF DEMOGRAPHIC CHANGE

The populations of industrialised countries are rapidly ageing. The economic consequences of this development are not as easily obtained as one might think. A non-stable age structure has dynamic consequences (see, e.g., Van Imhoff [1989a] and Cutler et al. [1990]) which are absent in many steady state analyses. The consequences for the public finance of age-related government expenditures during periods of demographic change are considered to be of a more complex order, since the tax base, factor prices and the demand for public goods change simultaneously. In order to see how demographic changes affect fiscal policy, I will confine my attention in this chapter to the fiscal policy of a government that has to finance an exogenous flow of public spending by the choice between lump-sum taxation and the use of public bonds. In other words, I will examine the conditions of debt neutrality, better known as the Ricardian equivalence theorem of public finance. Since the practice of economic theory can be characterised as a complete rat race[1] in generating Ricardian (non-) equivalence theorems, I am not going to join this race. Instead I will review, illustrate and bring together some of the demographically related contributions and point out that the realism of assumptions matters in the Ricardian theory of public finance.

---

1. There are numerous overviews on the subject of Ricardian equivalence and related issues, e.g., Tobin [1980], Buiter [1985], Aschauer [1988a], Leiderman and Blejer [1988], Barro [1989a,1989b], Bernheim [1989a] and some macroeconomics textbooks, such as Sargent [1987] and Blanchard and Fischer [1989].

To get acquainted with the issues at stake, this review starts in section 6.1 with a formal demonstration of Ricardian equivalence of public finance methods. The model chosen in this section is the basic macroeconomic model of an infinitely-lived representative consumer/producer, and it is used as a standard of argument for later sections. Section 6.2 then discusses some of the most crucial assumptions underlying the phenomenon of debt neutrality, especially with respect to the assumptions concerning an economy characterised by demographic change. Finally, sections 6.3 and 6.4 evaluate and sum up the use of the Ricardian theory of public finance and what the consequences of non-neutral debt are for economic policy in an ageing society.

6.1 THE IMMORTAL CONSUMER MODEL

The usual starting point for examining the economic effects of fiscal policy is the modelling of behavioural relationships of the private sector vis-à-vis the public sector. The most basic model is one in which an infinitely-lived consumer/producer decides on investing and consuming a composite commodity. The standard assumption is that finitely-lived individuals, interconnected through intergenerational transfers such as gifts and bequests, can be transformed into an infinitely-lived representative individual or family if utility functions are time-separable.

The government in this set-up is rather passive. It merely provides a stream of government expenditures which can be financed by either taxation or a combination of taxation and public debt. The first form leads to a *temporally* balanced budget and the second form of finance leads to an *intertemporally* balanced budget. The latter type of fiscal regime is characterised by Sargent [1982] as the polar Ricardian fiscal regime: public debt is fully backed by taxation. To gain an insight in these economies I will model both regimes.

6.1.1 THE IMMORTAL REPRESENTATIVE AGENT ECONOMY

One of the most puzzling theorems in macroeconomics is that overlapping generations of mortal consumers can be approximated by an infinitely-lived representative agent. In other words, they are observationally equivalent. To illustrate how one can arrive at such a conclusion, we can start with a rather simple model, similar in nature of the Barro [1974] model. It is assumed that the head of the family cares about his/her own consumption/ leisure path, in youth (c^y, x_t^y) and in old-age (c^o, x_t^o), and the utility of his/her children and through the children he/she cares about the children's children, etc., etc. The utility function for a member of the tth generation looks like:

$$(6.1) \qquad U_t = U[c_t^y, c_t^o, x_t^y, x_t^o, U_{t+1}^*]$$

In this utility function it is assumed that the parents' own consumption and leisure vector, c_t and x_t, are weakly separable from the utility of their heirs, U_{t+1}. The heirs are a non-separable entity for the initial decision maker. However, if one takes the representative household at face value, the correct strategy for modelling this family would be the Koopmans [1960,1964] formulation of 'time perspective' or its equivalent for the altruistically linked dynasty, the notion of 'intergenerational altruism':

(6.2) $U_0 = \sum\limits_{t=0}^{\infty} V[c_t, x_t, E_t U_{t+1}]$

The dynastic utility function contains the family head's own consumption and leisure stream, $\{c_t\}_{t=0}^{\infty}$ and $\{x_t\}_{t=0}^{\infty}$, and the expected utility of the heirs, $\{E_t U_{t+1}\}_{t=0}^{\infty}$, where E_t is the mathematical expectation conditional on information available at time t and V is called the aggregator function (Koopmans [1960]). By formulating the utility function in this way one essentially deals with the problem of *endogenous time preference*, as pointed out by Weil [1990]. Although this may look like a trivial extension to the standard Barrovian model, it cannot be considered so. The implications of the Koopmans-formulation are quite strong, since it narrows down the set of economies in which observational equivalence of models with infinitely-lived agents and overlapping generations prevails: only under conditions of stationarity of the utility function and period independence will the infinitely-lived representative agent model be observationally equivalent to the model of overlapping generations with intergenerational transfers. This condition boils down to the requirement that there is only one composite good in each time period (see Blackorby and Russell [1989] for a proof). This distinction is often overlooked by the assumption that the *family* acts *as if* it is an infinitely-lived *individual*. Since the purpose of this section is to show the conditions of debt neutrality, I will restrict my attention to this time separable utility function. To keep things simple, I will first start with the behaviour of the infinitely-lived dynasty in the absence of a government, and in sections 6.1.2 and 6.1.3 I will introduce the influence of government.

With these introductory remarks in the back of our mind,

consider the following utility maximisation problem for the family representative:

$$(6.3) \qquad \int_0^\infty e^{-\rho t} U[c(t), x(t)] \, dt$$

where ρ denotes the constant rate of time preference, $c(t)$ consumption per capita at time t and $x(t)$ denotes the leisure enjoyed. Leisure and its complement labour supply, $\ell(t)$, are constrained by the available amount of time per family. The utility function is assumed to be separable and increasing in its arguments, but at a decreasing rate (i.e. $U_i > 0$, $U_{ii} < 0$ and $U_{ij} = 0$ for $i,j = c,x$, $i \neq j$). Furthermore, the utility function is time-separable. If we normalize the available amount of time to 1 we can write the time constraint (holding with equality) as:

$$(6.4) \qquad x(t) + \ell(t) = 1$$

In his leisure time the agent performs his role as consumer. The consumer invests part of his income from labour and capital in assets and the remaining income is consumed. The dynamic (or flow) budget restriction amounts to:

$$(6.5) \qquad \dot{a} = w(t)\ell(t) + (r(t) - n_f)a(t) - c(t)$$

where the total amount of assets, $a(t) = k(t) - b_f(t)$. The variable $k(t)$ denotes physical capital and $b_f(t)$ the amount of borrowing or lending by the family. There is one representative family in this economy which grows at the rate, n_f:

$$(6.6) \qquad \dot{N_f} = n_f N_f(t)$$

The family increases its assets position (in per capita terms) by consuming less than the income received from work effort, $w(t)\ell(t)$, and interest income minus a correction for dilution of wealth per capita, $(r(t) - n_f)a(t)$. Note that the head of the family takes into account the growth rate of the family, n_f, which in the absence of mortality boils down to the family specific birth rate. Borrowing is however restricted by a condition imposed by the lenders on a capital market. The net asset position of the family should be a non-negative value as time approaches infinity:

$$(6.7) \qquad \lim_{t \to \infty} a(t)R(t) \geq 0$$

where the short term discount factor $R(t)$ is given by,

$$R(t) = \exp\left\{-\int_0^t [r(v) - n_f]\ dv\right\}.$$

The transversality condition (6.7), better known as the No-Ponzi-game condition, requires that the present value of wealth, arbitrarily far into the future, has to be a non-negative. In other words, the family's wealth per capita should not increase asymptotically faster than the interest rate corrected for the rate of population growth, $(r - n_f)$. Of course, an equilibrium path of asset accumulation will be such that the condition (6.7) holds with equality: ever increasing wealth at the rate $(r - n_f)$ is not desirable as long as the marginal utility of consumption is positive. In other words, this condition ensures that families will not leave over any resources that asymptotically have positive present value. This restriction is perhaps more illuminating if one replaces consumption per capita in the utility function by equation (6.5):

$$(6.8) \qquad U[w(t)\ell(t) + (r(t) - n_f)a(t) - \dot{a}; \; x(t)]$$

If there are no restrictions on borrowing, the individual will borrow (i.e. negative $a(t)$) sufficiently to maintain a level of consumption such that the marginal utility of consumption becomes zero. Net indebtedness will be growing at the rate $(r - n_f)$. It is, however, highly unlikely that a lending party will be willing to lend capital to a debtor who uses the capital to meet interest payments. Temporary fluctuations in the speed of accumulation are, of course permitted. What the No-Ponzi-game condition boils down to, is the requirement that no consumer should be a net creditor or debtor in present value terms.

During worktime the agent performs the role of producer by solving the static problem of profit (Π) maximisation in a competitive factor market:

$$(6.9) \qquad \text{Maximise } \Pi = \{f[k(t),\ell(t)] - r(t)k(t) - w(t)\ell(t)\}$$
$$k,l$$

This problem yields for the constant-returns-to-scale production function, the well-known factor price rewards:

$$(6.10) \qquad w(t) = \partial f/\partial \ell(t)$$

$$(6.11) \qquad r(t) = \partial f/\partial k(t)$$

In equilibrium, profits Π are zero and therefore need not be included in the budget constraint of the consumer.

The current-value Hamiltonian can now be formulated as:

(6.12) $H(c,x,a,\lambda) = U[c(t),x(t)] +$

$$+ \lambda(t)\{[r(t) - n_f]a(t) + w(t)\ell(t) - c(t)\}$$

The necessary and sufficient conditions for an interior solution amount to:

(6.13) $\dfrac{\partial H}{\partial c(t)} = 0 : \lambda(t) = \dfrac{\partial U}{\partial c(t)}$

(6.14) $\dfrac{\partial H}{\partial x(t)} = 0 : \lambda(t)w(t) = \dfrac{\partial U}{\partial x(t)}$

(6.15) $\dot{\lambda}(t) = \rho\lambda(t) - \dfrac{\partial H}{\partial a(t)} = \lambda(t)[\rho + n_f - r(t)]$

(6.16) $\lim\limits_{t\to\infty} a(t)\lambda(t)e^{-\rho t} = 0$

and budget and time constraints, (6.4) and (6.5) and the factor prices (6.10) and (6.11). Under certain circumstances, additional restrictions[2] on preferences are needed to ensure

---

2. When labour-augmenting technical progress takes place at a constant rate (as in King et al. [1988a, p. 201]), all quantities should be expressed in terms of per 'augmented capita'. When the rate of technical progress is positive, some restrictions are needed to ensure the compatibility with a steady state.

that the economic system exhibits steady state growth. In the
absence of a government or foreign sector the *aggregate* family
debt, b_f, is in equilibrium always zero, hence we can calculate
with the equilibrium condition $a(t) = k(t)$. In addition, the
interest rate is determined by the accumulated physical capital
stock, $k(t)$, and work effort, $\ell(t)$.

Given the previous relationships, we can rephrase the flow
budget constraint (6.5) in terms of an intertemporal budget
constraint. By integrating (6.5) forward in time and imposing
the No-Ponzi-game condition (only this time holding with
equality), we obtain the following budget restriction:

$$(6.17) \qquad \int_0^\infty c(t)R(t)\ dt = \int_0^\infty w(t)\ell(t)R(t)\ dt + a_0$$

The intertemporal budget restriction (6.17) boils down to the
condition that the present value of consumption must equal the
present value of labour earnings and initial assets.

6.1.2 FISCAL POLICY: TEMPORALLY BALANCED BUDGET

At this point, the government enters the scene and it follows
the extreme dictum of Adam Smith "the only good budget is a
balanced budget". At every moment in time, the government
finances its outlays $g(t)$ by taxing the representative agent a
lump sum of $\tau(t)$, so that the budget is balanced: $\tau(t) = g(t)$.
Government expenditures are assumed not to affect the consumer's
utility or the private sector's productivity. The intertemporal
budget constraint for the representative family can be written
as:

$$(6.18) \qquad \int_0^\infty c(t)R(t)dt = \int_0^\infty w(t)\ell(t)R(t)dt - \int_0^\infty \tau(t)R(t)dt + a_0$$

where $a_0 = k_0 - b_{f0}$, and the short term discount factor $R(t)$ is given by,

$$R(t) = \exp\left\{-\int_0^t [r(v) - n] \ dv\right\}.$$

The growth rate, n, in the short term discount factor $R(t)$ denotes the *aggregate* population growth rate, which in the presence of one representative family is equal to the family growth rate: $n_f = n$. By virtue of the balanced budget one could just as well replace the present value of taxes in (6.16) by the present value of government expenditures. Straightforward calculation of the utility maximisation shows that optimality conditions (6.13)-(6.16) are not affected by the introduction of a government. The only channel of influence is to be found in the private sector's budget constraint. Government consumption displaces through a lump-sum tax part of the private resource constraint, which could have been allocated to private consumption.

6.1.3 FISCAL POLICY: INTERTEMPORALLY BALANCED BUDGET

In another setting, the government may not always balance its budget. It has access to a capital market, which in this closed economy boils down to borrowing from (or lending to) the private sector. Public debt per capita, $b_g(t)$, must pay the *same* rate of return if the representative family wants to hold its assets. The competitive capital market assumption is sufficient to guarantee this equality. The flow budget constraint in per capita terms for the government comes down to,

$$(6.19) \quad \dot{b}_g(t) = g(t) - \tau(t) + (r(t) - n)b_g(t)$$

The intertemporal version can be obtained by integrating (6.19) forward and imposing the No-Ponzi-game condition, holding with equality:

$$(6.20) \quad \lim_{t \to \infty} b_g(t)R(t) = 0$$

Thus, the intertemporal government budget constraint amounts to:

$$(6.21) \quad \int_0^\infty g(t)R(t)dt = \int_0^\infty \tau(t)R(t)dt - b_{g0}$$

Given the initial value of public debt, the government need not balance its budget at every point in time, as long as the present value of spending equals the present value of taxes.

The possibility of running deficits and subsequent borrowing also modifies the private sector's budget constraint:

$$(6.22) \quad \dot{a} = w(t)\ell(t) + (r(t) - n)a(t) - c(t) - \tau(t)$$

where $a(t) = k(t) - b_f(t) + b_g(t)$.

The central question of public finance is: does the method of finance - balancing the budget temporally or intertemporally- influence the allocation of resources? The answer to this question is easily obtained if we substitute the government budget constraint (6.21) in the intertemporal budget constraint of the representative agent (again, integrate (6.22) forward and impose the No-Ponzi-game condition). We finally obtain the following intertemporal budget constraint:

$$(6.23) \qquad \int_0^\infty c(t)R(t)dt = \int_0^\infty w(t)\ell(t)R(t)dt - \int_0^\infty g(t)R(t)dt + a_0$$

One can see immediately that once we have substituted the temporal balanced budget constraint in equation (6.18), constraints (6.18) and (6.23) are identical. We can now state the Ricardian equivalence theorem:

> *For a given path of government expenditures $\{g(t)\}_{t=0}^\infty$ the method of public finance - a temporal or intertemporal balanced budget - is irrelevant for the time path of consumption and labour supply, $\{c(t),\ell(t)\}_{t=0}^\infty$, of the representative agent.*

This neutrality result is easily extended to the case of time-dependent population growth. The budget constraints are not affected in any fundamental way. If one's view coincides with the simple Ricardian model, public finance during a period of non-stationary population growth is going to be easy and the civil servant's life is indeed the quiet life. In the next section some of the strong assumptions of the Ricardian equivalence theorem are relaxed. It may not come as a surprise that Ricardian equivalence fails in models which do more justice to economic and demographic stylised facts.

6.2 THE BREAKDOWN OF THE IMMORTAL CONSUMER

In the present section I will discuss the reasons why government debt and taxation are generally not equivalent in a society that encounters changes in its population structure, and how budget deficits will affect the intertemporal resource allocation. To understand why public debt matters, one can proceed along the lines of discussing the strength of the underlying assumptions. Contrary to the 'F-twisted' methodology, as ascribed to Friedman [1953], there is a case to be made in questioning the realism of assumptions if one wants to *understand* the interaction between the public and private sector. Assumptions are never quite true, but despite this difficulty, which is inherent to the social sciences, the task of an economist is to make the complex transparent. Realistic explanations postulate entities on grounds additional to analytical convenience and involve a commitment to their further scrutiny. Any theory should therefore be examined by reflection on its assumptions vis-à-vis some relevant stylised facts[3]. This review is in no way different from such a procedure. As a quick refresher, the Ricardian equivalence theorem is based on the following set of assumptions:

1. Public debt is fully backed by *lump-sum* taxation[4].
2. The government and the representative agent have the *same planning horizon*.

---

3. It goes without saying that this approach should not turn a hair in the instrumentalist camp of enquiry.

4. Assumption 1 also rules out the case where public debt can be monetised. Any resulting inflation from monetary finance can be seen as an implicit distorting tax on nominally denominated assets.

3. Labour and capital markets are *perfectly competitive*. This implies that full-employment reigns the country and there are no borrowing constraints present: the public and private sector borrow at the same real interest rate and credit rationing is absent.

4. Individuals have *rational expectations* about the time path of future income and future taxes.

5. When the timing of tax payments is changed by the government, the distribution of taxes across agents in not changed in a present value sense.

It would be a trivial exercise to show that a violation of the first assumption will lead to real effects of public finance. It must be clear that distortionary taxes influence the relative prices of leisure, consumption and investment choices and on that account the debt neutrality proposition simply fails. The question for a benevolent government then is to choose a fiscal policy that minimises the deadweight loss (i.e. welfare loss due to the difference between allocations under conditions of lump-sum taxation and income taxation) brought about by such taxes necessary to finance public spending. It is beyond the scope of this chapter to analyse the welfare consequences of such taxes. This aspect of economic policy is postponed to chapter 7. At this point it suffices to mention a quite comprehensive overview of fiscal policies with real effects by Aschauer and Greenwood [1985] and a review by Barro [1989b].

In the remaining five sub-sections, I will take a closer look at the above stated assumptions of the Ricardian model and see how they are related to the demographic state of a country. The review will concentrate on: (1) the degree of altruism within the family; (2) international migration; (3) uncertain lifetime; (4) population growth uncertainty; and (5) capital market imperfections. The last aspect is added to the list of demographic factors since it turns out that some capital market imperfections are demographically related.

6.2.1 ARE WE A MEMBER OF ONE DYNASTY?

In the seminal contribution by Barro [1974] the public finance question of debt neutrality was set in the Samuelson [1958]-Diamond [1965] model of overlapping generations, augmented with an altruistic motive of parents to leave positive bequests behind for their children. Barro argued that voluntary transfers between parents and children cause the representative dynastic family to behave *as if* it is a *single, infinitely-lived individual*. There remains empirical ambiguity whether or not one can view the finitely-lived representative agent as a member of a dynasty. Despite this ambiguity, one can start from the assumption that agents are dynastically linked and examine if dynastic ties between overlapping generations are sufficient for generating the neutrality proposition. Weil[5] [1987,1989] puts the finger on the sore spot of Ricardian equivalence by developing such a model; a model in which infinitely-lived dynasties are the decision making units of an economy. The model stresses the disconnectedness of families as the root of non-neutrality of public debt. Each *new* dynasty is, by definition, not linked to pre-existing families through operative intergenerational transfers. In a way the model looks very much like the standard infinitely-lived representative agent model of

---

5. Weil's [1989] model of overlapping families of infinite lifetime is essentially an outcome of the uncertain lifetime model of Yaari [1965] and Blanchard [1985].

section 6.1. The point of departure is the presence of more than one dynasty. All dynasties are however identical and each decision maker of a dynasty is not connected in any way with the other families. Together with heads of other extended families he/she (or should I say 'it') decides on the optimal consumption/leisure path. At the beginning of time, one can still represent the private sector as inhabited by a representative dynasty. However, Weil argues that as soon as *new* dynasties are born (i.e. a positive birth rate), to be interpreted as unloved children, the discount rate of government and dynasties will diverge. If a government decides to postpone taxation by the issuance of public debt, it will make dynasties of today better off since the future tax base will include new agents to whom they are not related. The real interest rate must rise to maintain aggregate consumption at its equilibrium level. To answer the question posed by Barro in 1974 "Are government bonds net wealth?" Yes, as long as new dynasties are 'born'. A positive birth rate is tantamount to the existence of an infinity of traders and in the Weil-model, the infinity of dynasties allows the government to run a rational Ponzi-game or chain letter scheme (see O'Connell and Zeldes [1988]). The basic insight Weil's analysis offers, is that the length of the consumers' planning horizon bears no logical relation to the issues raised by the Ricardian equivalence theorem or the efficiency of competitive equilibria. Models in which agents have an infinite planning horizon and infinitely-lived representative agent models, are not interchangeable. Therefore, what seems crucial for the proposition of debt neutrality to go through, is the validity of the use of the dynastic family. Bernheim and Bagwell [1988] have most vehemently criticized the dynastic family as a modelling tool for questions of public finance. The crux of their critique is that family linkages form complex, interlocking networks in which each individual may belong to *many* dynastic groupings. If one carries the assumptions of the dynastic family to extremes, a host of neutrality results arises, such as the irrelevance of distortionary taxation and public redistribution. These neutrality results are incomparably stronger than the standard representative agent results, since they apply under weaker conditions than those imposed by Barro *et al*. No wonder, Bernheim and Bagwell exclaim "Is everything neutral?" The implicit suggestion by Bernheim and Bagwell [1988] is that economic theory should pay more attention to household formation and dissolution, and at least depart *a priori* from the dynastic family notion for the study of questions concerning public finance.

The assumption that individuals act as if they have an infinite lifetime can therefore only be legitimised if the family ties between generations are indeed tight. The central assumption of debt-neutrality is then the strength of altruism: do parents love their children enough for transfers to come about? The suggestion offered by research on the role of intergenerational transfers in the U.S. economy (see Kotlikoff and Summers [1981]) seems to support the altruistic model. However, the data Kotlikoff and Summers present seem quite innocuous, since they cannot distinguish between intentional and accidental transfers. One is still left wondering whether parents love their children or not. The strength of altruism has also been studied quasi-empirically by means of simulation. For instance, Weil [1987] examined the operativeness of an altruistic transfer motive in an overlapping generations model. Simulations by Weil indicate that parents must 'love their children' very much for the transfer motive to be operative. For a class of plausible parameter configurations, he finds that it is impossible for parents to love their children enough for transfer motives to operate. However, Altig and Davis [1989] have reached a strikingly different conclusion for a model closely related to that of Weil [1987]: for reasonable lifetime productivity profiles and a modest desire to smooth consumption intertemporally, parents need to love their children only a little bit for the transfer motive to be operative. The reason why Weil's result is reversed, finds its cause in the life-time productivity profile: Altig and Davis [1989] use an upward sloping profile over the first two periods of life (life amounts to three periods in their model), whereas Weil [1987] uses a two-period model in which the profile is simply downward sloping. With a *downward*-sloping profile, steady state transfers serve only to pass the economy's capital stock from one generation to the next, and if the economy operates inefficiently, i.e. in overaccumulating savings, transfers are not useful and hence, the altruism motive fails to operate. However, when lifetime productivity profiles contain an *upward* sloping segment, life-cycle considerations are less likely to generate competitive inefficiency in capital accumulation, and the motive for intergenerational transfers is more likely to be operative. Parents are not going to transfer resources to their children when the economy operates inefficiently. This would be like throwing good money after bad money.

The bequest motive of parents has mainly been treated as independent of the labour efficiency of their heirs. Buiter [1986,1988] has shown that technical progress by itself does not destroy Ricardian equivalence. However, if one assumes that the bequest motive depends on the rate of technical progress, fiscal policy may have real effects (see Drazen [1978]). If, e.g., altruistic parents take into account the wealth of their children and productivity growth is very high, the parents may want to leave a negative bequest since their children will be much wealthier than they are. In general, the imposed non-negativity constraint on bequests will be effective, thus impeding the optimal intergenerational transfer. A tax cut will therefore increase current consumption, since it enables parents to consume in accordance with their optimal plans. A related source of non-neutrality is presented by Laitner [1979] in a dynastic family model. The reason why bond financed and tax-financed fiscal policies are not identical, is to be found in the uncertainty concerning the bequest motives of children: no family can be certain that all of its descendants will have operative bequest transfers. In other words, there is uncertainty whether intergenerational linkages are strong enough. An extra factor destroying altruism within the family may well be the size of the family. As pointed out by Andreoni [1988], the degree of altruism decreases as the size of the economy grows. In case of a dynastic family, this property boils down to the size of the family. Also the Bernheim and Bagwell-critique hinges strongly on the degree of altruism within the family. As mentioned earlier, they forcefully state their point by pushing the dynastic family to its limits, thereby effectively neutralising any public policy effort. However, Andreoni [1989] has shown that public debt in the presence of *impure altruism* within the dynastic family still can have non-neutral effects. Egoism and altruism within the family play a major role in individual behaviour. For instance, imagine a two-period world in which parents care about their own consumption, c^p, and consumption of their heirs, c^h. In addition, the utility of the parents also depends on the size of the bequest, b: $U_p(c^p, c^h, b)$. The utility of the heirs is simply $U_h(c^h)$. Since the parents and heirs care about the same good, c^h, the dynastic family has a public good. When a person experiences a "warm glow" in giving resources to another person, the donor is said to be 'impurely altruistic' with respect to the gift. The recipients' behaviour is said to be 'purely altruistic' (and egoistic at the same time) with respect to their own consumption. The terminology is quite confusing but what it boils down to is that heirs are willing to step down to receive a gift and by this 'altruistic' act he/she can make another person feel better. As an illustration, consider the example of social security. In traditional societies the old are taken care of by their children. The young are in effect making gifts to the old, whereby the consumption of the old was a public good. If the young get a 'warm glow' from supporting the old in their needs, then the old are more altruistic with respect to their own consumption. Now, in a modern society, the old are taken care of by the social security system, which redistributes resources among the young and the old. The difference between the two systems is that in the traditional society transfers were voluntary, whereas under the current social security regime transfers have become involuntary and impersonal. A redistribution from the young (less altruistic) to the old (more altruistic) will increase the supply of the public good, i.e. the consumption of the old. Children will reduce their gifts, but not by the full amount of the transfer. Private gifts are imperfect substitutes for public 'gifts'. Regardless of the direction of the intergenerational transfers, consumption will increase in the period the debt is incurred.

In conclusion, if a government is endowed with eternal life and our own lives are of a finite nature, the homogeneity assumption (no. 2) boils down to the question "Are we all a member of *one* big family or dynasty?" The reason why we all have to be a member is that the Ricardian theory of public finance is a *macro*economic theory. Therefore, if one wants to maintain the Ricardian theory as an approximation of the entire economy, one can either assume that the economy consists of identical families[6] or one can assume that individuals are different, but still are members of one family. If this assumption is untenable, lump-sum taxes will induce economic actions and can no longer be considered non-distortionary. Empirical estimates of the measure of altruism within the family, plausible models of intergenerational transfers and the stylised facts of demography point out that this assumption is indeed highly questionable.

6.2.2 INTERNATIONAL MIGRATION

Closely related to the issue of the number of new dynasties, is the issue of immigration. The immigration of new members in a society makes it attractive for a government to shift resources forward and pay later. The reason for that can again be found in Weil's [1989] model of overlapping families. Immigrants are essentially new dynasties that cannot avoid in any way the extra levies (as a consequence of earlier tax cuts). Pre-existing families have profited from the earlier tax cuts. There are a number of weak spots in the interpretation of new dynasties as immigrants. Immigrants are supposed to have no rational expectations about the future path of taxes and income in the country of their destination. Furthermore, one cannot analyse the consequences of emigration in Weil's model, since he makes the assumption that dynasties can never disappear. This is unfortunate, since emigration of certain family members may affect the family growth rate, which would again destroy

---

6. A fact which seems highly unlikely to be a real-to-life description. See, e.g., Pestieau [1984].

Ricardian equivalence but this time the result hinges on divergence in family and dynastic growth rates.

It is ironic that in the early nineteenth century David Ricardo himself mentioned some exceptions to his proposition that under certain circumstances taxation and public debt are equivalent means for financing public expenditures. Ricardo [1817, p. 244] suggested two reasons why this theoretical proposition could not be applied in practice. One of these reasons was that bond finance would be advantageous if the owner of the bonds, i.e. the private sector, emigrated before taxes were levied to pay off the bond issue[7]. Ricardo gives in fact an example which amounts to a violation of the assumption of lump-sum taxation. If taxes would be truly lump-sum, they would not have induced a reaction on the side of the private sector. Emigration (or more generally, tax evasion) is an economic activity and the only way the distortion caused by lump-sum taxation can be cancelled out is by levying a tax independent of the place of residence[8].

Another reason for using public debt as a method of finance is found in the free rider behaviour of immigrants when the country possesses a durable public good (see Leeds [1989]). Public debt may promote a more efficient immigration flow by the reduction of the ability to free-ride on the capital provided by the indigenous population. Public debt allows parents to

---

7. The second reason amounted to the argument that bond owners would act as if bond finance were genuinely advantageous. In other words, he thought it likely that they did not understand that it implied higher future taxes.

8. In a multi-region or multi-country setting with mobile labour, governments are sure to encounter public finance effects similar to those found in the literature on fiscal competition (Wildasin [1988]) and the Tiebout model (see for an overview Stiglitz [1983]).

(Pareto) improve their resource allocation by transferring funds from immigrants to their heirs. Therefore public debt is preferable to paying current taxes because it transfers some of the burden of paying for the durable good to the free-riders c.q. immigrants. Public debt works like a deterrent and immigrants are no longer attracted by the potential for free-riding.

Again, if one concludes that emigration and immigration are widespread, unpredictable and non-negligible phenomena, the proposition of debt neutrality fails.

6.2.3 UNCERTAIN LIFETIME

The cliché goes that there are two things in life which are certain: death and taxes. The *timing* of your death is, however, an aspect of life that is far from certain. The uncertainty concerning the length of lifetime was first introduced in models of intertemporal consumption by Yaari [1965]. Twenty years later Blanchard [1985] and subsequently Buiter [1986,1988,1989] exploited a simple fact of life: mortal individual consumers are likely to adjust their propensity to consume out of lifetime wealth if the length of lifetime is itself uncertain[9]. The mortality rate is assumed to be constant at every point in time. In addition to this simplified assumption, Blanchard assumed that the birth rate and death rate are exactly equal. Buiter

---

9. An interesting extension to the Blanchard-Buiter analysis is a two-country model of international lending and borrowing by Masson [1989]. One can study different population age structures by simply assuming identical population growth rates, but different birth and mortality rates. Countries with a relatively old (young) age structure will be net creditors (debtors) in equilibrium.

corrected for this unrealistic assumption by incorporating divergent birth and death rates into the Blanchard model. Although the assumption of age-independent probability of death still defies demographic reality, it does capture one aspect of mortality, viz. that the chance that you will be alive in, say, twenty years from now is smaller than the chance of being alive tomorrow. The issue of uncertain lifetime raises the problem of unintended (positive) bequests if the consumer's wealth is positive, or unintended negative bequests if the consumer dies in debt. If we exclude the possibility to die in debt, the consumer has to choose the best consumption path that excludes the possibility of negative bequests at death. A government differs from the consumer in that it does not suffer from mortality. In its endeavour to choose the optimal consumption path, the consumer can rely on the services of an insurance company. In the Yaari-Blanchard model there is room for such an insurance company since the uncertainty of lifetime is tied to the individual; in the aggregate there is no uncertainty. The insurance company makes premium payments to the living in exchange for receipt of the consumer's remaining wealth in the event he or she dies. In a competitive insurance industry, the insurance premium will be equal to the probability of death. Now there are two channels present through which uncertainty of lifetime works. First, an efficient insurance industry enables consumers to increase the marginal propensity to consume out of lifetime wealth by exactly the probability of death. Second, future utilities are discounted at a higher rate than would have been the case in the absence of uncertainty. The public and private sector have fundamentally different discount factors and only by sheer coincidence they will be identical. The main point of the Blanchard-Buiter analysis is that public debt can have real effects since the persons who enjoy the tax cut today are not certain whether they will have to face an increase in taxes tomorrow, simply because as the chances are, they may not be around anymore. One can also deduce that the further the increase in taxes is postponed into the future, the larger the initial wealth effect will be, since the probability that the agent will still be subject to a tax increase will be smaller.

6.2.4 POPULATION GROWTH UNCERTAINTY

Uncertainty in demographic developments, as summed up in the population growth rate $n(t)$, is likely to affect the individual resource allocation in two different ways. First, if the *future income* of the individual is uncertain and this type of uncertainty is non-insurable, uncertainty will lead to reactions that will depend on the public finance method at hand. Since population growth is one of the underlying determinants of the long-run real interest rate, it is a short step to deduce that future income is uncertain when population growth is uncertain. A study that stresses the uncertainty of income is the one of Barsky, Mankiw and Zeldes [1986]. Two-period lived agents have a future income given by

$$(6.24) \qquad y_h(t) = \alpha_h + \epsilon_h(t)$$

where α_h is constant over time and $\epsilon_h(t)$ is a random term with mean zero such that $\Sigma_h^H \epsilon_h(t) = 0$ and $E[\epsilon_h, \epsilon_j] = 0$ for $h \neq j$. In addition to these assumptions we assume that (1) preferences are time separable, (2) consumption is a normal good and (3) there is non-increasing absolute risk aversion. If non-lump sum taxes are levied on uncertain future income at the uniform rate τ, such that the total amount raised is equal to an amount of debt

created in the first period, consumption *rises* in the event of a
current period tax cut. The reason why this happens is that the
tax cut replaces an uncertain claim to future income by a
certain claim, in other words it reduces the uncertainty
attached to future disposable income. Feldstein [1988] also
analyses the consequences of uncertain income, but without
relying on the assumption of non-lump sum taxes or imperfections
in annuity markets. His conclusion is that when income is
uncertain, bequests are also uncertain. Consumption therefore
rises more in response to an increase in current disposable
income than to an equal present value increase in the disposable
income of the next generation.

The second source of uncertainty arises from the *uncertain
future taxes*; a feature which is likely to apply to countries in
demographic transition. Government spending is demographically
related and so is the subsequent burden. However, public choices
are bound to change in democracies where interest groups change
size. In an uncertain world, a current tax cut will signal
future increases in tax rates, but the exact timing, the type of
tax to be increased and the incidence of taxation across
individuals are all uncertain. In section 6.2.4, on uncertain
lifetime, we already saw how the timing of taxation affects
consumption. The type of taxation is perhaps a question wich
should be allocated to the theory of dynamic optimal taxation.
The risk attached to future tax claims, yields a reaction quite
different from the reaction to uncertain future income. Chan
[1983] examined the uncertainty of taxation in a two-period
world where future gross income is known in advance. Assume that
tax liabilities of agent h are given by,

(6.25) $\tau_h(t) = \theta_h(t) + \gamma \epsilon_h(t)$

where $\theta_h(t)$ denotes a time and state invariant share of aggregate taxes levied on agent h and $\epsilon_h(t)$ is a mean zero stochastic term with property $\Sigma_h^H \epsilon_h(t) = 0$. The term γ represents an increase in the risk of income redistribution across households. Under the same restrictive assumptions on preferences as mentioned above, Chan shows that consumption *falls* in the presence of a tax cut. Risk-averse consumers will increase their savings in the presence of increased uncertainty about future net income, thereby aiming at a smooth consumption path over time.

6.2.5 CAPITAL MARKET IMPERFECTIONS

Agents are usually not as homogenous and well-behaved as an economic theorist might wish them to be. Preferences and endowments play a major role in the modelling of capital market imperfections. For instance, a standard assumption in the Ricardian model is that private and public bonds are perfect substitutes in the agent's portfolio of securities. However, if government policy appears as incredible, government bonds are not very likely to be a perfect substitute for private bonds. Agents may also differ in their ability to borrow capital (e.g., due to a lack of collateral), in order to finance a smooth lifetime consumption/leisure path. The borrowing constraints usually refer to capital market phenomena, such as credit rationing or differential interest rates on borrowing and lending. The raison d'être of these types of borrowing constraints can, to a large extent, be found in the information sets of market participants. Unobservable risk characteristics of borrowers can, for example, give rise to the problem of adverse selection and, in many cases, to credit rationing.

Whether informationally imperfect capital markets provide a theoretical basis for the failure of debt neutrality, is a question, that has been examined by Yotsuzuka [1987]. He assumes from the start an asymmetry of information on the capital market, viz. that borrowers have exclusive information regarding their probability of default. Lenders can only infer the hidden information by the use of some signal. Yotsuzuka uses the case where the contracts purchased by the consumer serve as a signal of his/her risk characteristics. The crucial element in answering this question turns out to be the extent to which information is shared among lenders. In Yotsuzuka's model with full communication amongst lenders (resulting in equilibria better known as 'signaling equilibria'), there are only two types of contracts: separating and pooling contracts. If (separating) contracts can be designed to make high risk borrowers reveal themselves then a separating equilibrium obtains. A pooling contract makes all types of borrowers borrow at the same interest rate. The reason why public debt has non-neutral effects is then to be found in the *existence* of the pooling contract. In the case where lenders do not communicate with each other, the private sector cannot offer the pooling contract, while the government can. The point is that liquidity constraints change endogenously in response to public policy and the possibility might arise that the resulting change neutralises policy actions. It should be stressed, however, that this neutrality result is a knife-edge case. Yotsuzuka comes to the conclusion that adverse selection in capital markets does not necessarily mean a failure of Ricardian equivalence. Debt neutrality only fails in models where lenders (1) do not communicate with each other about their customer's indebtedness, or (2) have full and shared information (i.e. contract purchases can be perfectly monitored). These capital market imperfections rest, however, on arbitrary restrictions on the extent of communication. When one considers the incentives for communication explicitly one arrives at the conclusion that debt neutrality prevails. In case of endogenous communication debt neutrality can survive, because the private loan market supports the pooling contract regardless of the intertemporal reallocation of taxes. Separating contracts are not possible in case of endogenous communication, since there is always an incentive for a bank to enter the market and offer a customer a loan with a profitable interest rate and choose not to divulge the names of the customers to other banks. Banks will, however, suffer losses since each of them will attract a higher share of high-risk customers than the share that would make the banks break even. Hence, banks offering pooling contracts have an incentive to share information. An equilibrium is supported by one group of lenders that chooses to disclose information on their customers while the other group does not. A government in such a setting has lost its ability to force the pooling contract on all customers. The size of the pooling contract offered by banks will adjust so that the total size of the two pooling contracts, public and private, remain constant.

The models in which Ricardian equivalence fails, such as Yotsuzuka's [1987], carry the implication that in many cases it is *possible* to achieve a Pareto-improvement by a debt-financed tax cut. Under conditions of liquidity-constrained individuals it is as if the government is borrowing on behalf of the liquidity-constrained individuals.

Abel [1989] introduces another kind of market imperfection.

234

He examines the case where insurance is not actuarially fair[10], by assuming that there are administrative costs of servicing life insurance and that these costs are proportional to the size of the insurance contract. His model is an extension of the Yaari-Blanchard analysis. For a two-period world inhabited by selfish consumers (i.e. consumers with no bequest motive) Abel shows that under Blanchard's demographic assumptions (i.e. when death rate equals birth rate) and sufficiently high administrative costs, consumers will not buy life insurance and one obtains the remarkable result that debt neutrality holds. In other words, the Ricardian equivalence theorem holds only in the presence of selfish consumers and the absence of an insurance industry. It fails to hold in the presence of a perfect insurance market, in which case we are back in the Yaari-Blanchard-Buiter world (see section 6.2.3).

Still another case examined by Abel [1989], is one in which consumers have altruistic bequest motives towards some, but perhaps not all of their children. The setting is again a two-period world. Each parent has to choose a portfolio of riskless bonds and annuities, which offer a rate of return at least as high as the return on bonds. In case the parents do not survive, some children inherit the wealth of their parents while the unloved children have only their own endowments to fall back on. The children are only alive in the second period of this (two-period) world and they simply consume their entire resources minus the lump-sum tax. If the rate at which 'disinherited' (or perhaps unwanted) children are born equals zero, and insurance is actuarially fair, debt neutrality will hold. This is exactly

---

10. Another source of imperfection in the annuity market is adverse selection. The fiscal policy consequences of adverse selection are discussed in Abel [1986].

the point made by Weil [1989], who refers to those children as 'unloved' children. All children must be a member of one 'loving' family, otherwise new families will be born and consumer heterogeneity slips into the model. If the insurance market is *missing*, debt neutrality will only hold if and only if the birth rate of disinherited consumers is equal to the death rate. The intuition behind this knife-edge theorem is that in the case of a tax cut in period 1, the additional wealth that the parents will leave behind, will be just sufficient for each heir to pay for the higher tax in period 2, and so parents and children can maintain the initially planned consumption paths. In the case that the parents disinherit some of their children, the heirs will receive a greater inheritance. In such a case of selective altruism, the heirs pay in effect for the disinherited children, who did not receive any bequests.

In conclusion, the conduct of fiscal policy in economies with capital market imperfections is such that generally public debt matters, but before one condemns the public debt neutrality proposition, one should make the rules of the game explicit (e.g., the degree of communication amongst lenders, whether annuities are actuarily (un)fair, and the presence of collateral-conditions on borrowing).

6.3 LESSONS IN RICARDIAN PUBLIC FINANCE

What are the lessons that we can draw from a theory of public finance that seems to defy reality? The lesson one can draw from this review is that the Ricardian model of the immortal consumer serves a useful purpose in debates about fiscal policy because it takes on the role of a standard of argument, albeit a Utopian standard of argument. But, as in court any man is considered innocent until proven guilty, so is the Ricardian equivalence theorem (although one may suspect that it is guilty). It is generally felt that the interaction between private and public sector in the Ricardian model does not approximate real world decision making; it merely functions as the yardstick of more sophisticated models of economic behaviour. In this review several reasons have been presented in explaining why public debt could matter in actual economies. These reasons are to be found in the description of the decision making units, the form of public spending and taxation and the prevailing rules of the game. The economies described by the pure Ricardian theory are restricted to such a small set that one can easily dismiss it as 'not relevant for present day economies', and this final statement is beyond a reasonable doubt. The 'good' of the Ricardian theory of public finance is that it has stimulated or provoked many bright minds to 'prove' the guilt of this model. The 'bad' of this theory is that it has led people to believe in this model, perhaps on account of its simplicity.

The *pure* Ricardian theory of fiscal policy is ill-suited as a normative theory. It cannot provide any guidelines whatsoever: the method of public finance is irrelevant. In addition, the theory does not tell us whether the consumption paths chosen are optimal; it merely states that fiscal policies do not affect private choices, whether efficient or inefficient. One notable exception to this rule is the case where capital market imperfections exist (see Yotsuzuka [1987]). The Ricardian theory of public finance *seems* to be more suited as a positive theory of fiscal policy. Ricardian economies function as the yardstick of economic and econometric models of government, because it provides a clear-cut hypothesis: whatever method of public finance the government chooses, it will leave the intertemporal allocation of resources unaffected. Econometric analysis of the

Ricardian proposition has, however, yielded ambiguous results. I could present an endless list of econometric studies which support and others which reject the Ricardian equivalence theorem, but as De Haan [1989, chapter 4] has already presented it, I will not. As made clear in the previous sections, the restricted set of economies that display debt-neutrality is so small that any macroeconomic test of Ricardian equivalence is bound to yield a rejection. A lot of empirical work muddles through by showing ambiguous tests without giving attention to what the source of this ambiguity really is. An anecdote told by Jan Tinbergen on a friendly clash between a theorist, who relied strongly on *a priori* reasoning - John Maynard Keynes - and an econometrician - Tinbergen himself - is perhaps telling in this respect:

> *"In a survey on the maximum amount of compensation of war damages Germany could pay, Keynes assumed a price elasticity of the demand for export goods of -2. A figure, by the way, which he assumed not to be applicable to the German situation in particular, but to all economies in general. I told Keynes that I and some of my colleagues at the CBS (the Netherlands Central Bureau of Statistics) had done some regression analyses and we found indeed the figure -2. I thought this result would be good news for Keynes. On the contrary, Keynes thought that we at the CBS should be the ones to be happy, since we had found the right number. Keynes undoubtedly found his economic intuition far more reliable than econometric estimates. Perhaps rightly so", Tinbergen [1987, p. 1092] adds.*

Like Keynes we know the right number; however, one glance at the scribblings of academic economists shows that we have not acted upon this intuition lately. The ambiguity will remain in the econometric testing of the debt neutrality hypothesis, as long as the determination of structural (or 'deep') parameters of the Ricardian model is left aside. If one does not pay attention to intergenerational links and intertemporal preference formation, any conclusions extracted from empirical work are likely to be wishful thinking.

There are three roads to improve the state of the art. One line of research is to conduct experimental (or laboratory) tests of Ricardian equivalence (see, e.g., Cadsby and Frank [1989]). By practising 'economics by lobotomy' one may gather information on the question "How Ricardian is the representative consumer really?" Another, more common, route is to examine the altruistic linkages within the family (as done by Altonji et al. [1989]). In that case, microeconometric research should dominate macroeconometric research, in order to give meaningful answers to questions of deficit finance. Last but not least, econometricians and economic theorists should pay attention to the aggregation of individual behaviour. The microeconomic foundation of macroeconomic general equilibrium theories involves temporal[11] and intertemporal aggregation problems. The observational equivalence of models of overlapping generations and the model with an infinitely-lived representative agent requires that certain consistency conditions are satisfied before one can speak of a macroeconomic theory of public finance (see Aiyagari [1985] and Blackorby and Russell [1989] on this point). The majority of non-neutral effects of public debt are based on violations of the conditions for observational equivalence. In the case of the Ricardian theory of public finance, there are two conditions which need to be satisfied: (1) Observational equivalence: a model of overlapping generations with bequest motives can mimic the behaviour of an

---

11. For instance, in a static model a representative agent exists if and only if the utility functions of all agents are quasi-homothetic (i.e. characterised by linear Engel-curves) and the Engel-curves of the agents are parallel (see Gorman [1961]).

infinitely-lived representative agent; and (2) Perfect
representation: the government should have the same preferences
as the representative agent. As shown by Bernheim [1989b], the
occurrence of the latter property is a rare occasion.
Intergenerational altruism renders objectives of social planners
time inconsistent. The planner can only solve this problem by
placing weight on the welfare of deceased generations. It does
not require a great fantasy to imagine that the economist who
favours a Ricardian view of the world is skating on thin ice.

6.4 SUMMARY

Barro [1974] rekindled a vintage question of public finance,
viz. is public debt issued by a government today a burden to
future generations? In retrospect, Barro's provocative statement
that "public debt does not matter" must be seen as a reaction to
the Keynesian stance in public finance, as it reigned in the
sixties. Ensuing Barro's seminal 1974-paper, public finance
theories in the seventies and eighties were at their intellec-
tual height and numerous econometricians estimated the relevance
of the neutrality proposition by using naive reduced form
equations. In the closing of the 1980s Bernheim and Bagwell
[1988] produced perhaps the final blow to Ricardian equivalence
theories by taking the underlying assumptions at face value and
showing that the use of the dynastic family as a central
decision making unit leads to untenable conclusions, unless
one's view of the world is distorted. The question of Ricardian
equivalence therefore evolves essentially around one big issue:
how realistic are the underlying assumptions? One of the most
important keys to understanding the question why public debt
matters is to be found in the heterogeneity of agents. Two types

of heterogeneity must be distinguished: temporal and intertemporal. Intertemporal heterogeneity of agents is present in
assumptions on the identical planning horizons of the private
and public sector and the form of the utility function. Temporal
heterogeneity is, of course, to be found in agents with
different temporal preferences, endowments and abilities.

For the first type of heterogeneity, various assumptions need
to be made to ensure that the representative individual and the
government have the same planning horizon. Usually it is thought
that successive generations of finite-lived agents are linked to
each other through operative transfer motives. Although one
would expect that infinity of lifetime is one of the most
unrealistic assumptions of the Barro-model, it is not crucial
for the Ricardian equivalence theorem to hold. Weil [1989] shows
that the disconnectedness of dynasties, or the love for
children, is a far more important aspect of the model. Besides
the theoretical argument, Poterba and Summers [1987] have shown
that the length of the planning horizon is unlikely to matter,
as far as short-run policy effects are concerned. Even if
consumers have no motive for intergenerational transfers, the
average lifespan seems long enough, relative to the typical time
horizon of public deficit policies, to make infinite horizon
models a good approximation. Elements which do break the chain
of intergenerational transfers are (1) unloved or unwanted
children, (2) uncertain lifetime, and (3) migrants.

The second type of heterogeneity is far more straightforward
than the first type. Different agents at one point in time can
give rise to redistribution effects of fiscal policy. The
assumption of different agents or disconnected families is
however untenable if one assumes that intergenerational links
exist. Dynastic families are in the long run interrelated in one
big family and as a consequence, the effects of redistribution

can be neutralised. Capital market imperfections give rise to another type of temporal heterogeneity. In case agents differ in terms of initial and life time endowments and in terms of honesty, lenders will fall back on borrowing restrictions, such as interest differentials and credit rationing, to circumvent enforcement problems caused by the need of satisfying the intertemporal budget constraint. A different type of market imperfection is the case of uninsurable risk. The reactions to uncertain future income and taxation are both of some relevance in an ageing society. The reactions do, however, differ per type of uncertainty.

The overall conclusion of this review is that, under quite general circumstances, public debt matters in a world characterised by demographic change. One could of course still take on the role of the devil's advocate and claim that the realism of assumptions does not matter. No assumption is quite true or 'real'. But as Robert Lucas [1980] once put it: "The more dimensions on which the model mimics the answers actual economies give to simple questions, the more we trust its answers to harder questions". In that respect, the *pure* Ricardian economy lacks credibility in answering the hard questions of public finance.

CHAPTER 7: DYNAMIC OPTIMAL TAXATION AND ENDOGENOUS PUBLIC SPENDING

Should a government accumulate a trust fund for the covering of future increases in public spending, or should tax rates establish a balanced budget in each and every period? Are current income tax rates too high? These and related questions are at the center of the theory of dynamic optimal taxation. The theory is of particular relevance to the question of public finance of an ageing society. The prospects of large flucuations in public spending as a consequence of ageing are indeed real and in this chapter I try to disentangle the various factors at work: a change in the demand for public goods and a changing tax base.

This chapter applies the theory of optimal taxation to conditions of demographic change and it examines the optimal use of consumption taxation and public spending. Conventional wisdom tells us to use public debt in smoothing out irregularities in financing government spending. This wisdom is often applied to a distortionary tax and an exogenous supply of public goods. As soon as the public goods supply is endogenous, the question of optimal taxation becomes quite complex, because one has to determine the entire time path of taxation and public consumption.

The dynamic fiscal policy solutions will be discussed, as well as their applicability for a country with a non-stationary population growth rate. First, in section 7.1 the issue of tax smoothing is discussed for a better understanding of the issues at stake. Sections 7.2 and 7.3 examine the optimal tax policy that is relevant for the goverment of a small open economy in the presence of international differences in demographic change.

To get a feel for the channels through which a tax affects the private sector, an *ad valorem* consumption tax will be discussed under various assumptions. Throughout the analysis, public spending is assumed to be a variable of choice of a government. Demographic shocks are discussed as an illustration of the principles derived. Section 7.4 discusses some elements of fiscal policy in an interdependent world economy, such as time consistency and cooperation. Finally, section 7.5 summarises the general conclusions on the principles of dynamic optimal taxation.

7.1 SHOULD A GOVERNMENT SMOOTH TAX RATES?

This section provides an introduction to questions of optimal taxation for a thorough understanding of the principles of taxation. The design of dynamic fiscal policies is concerned with the choice of the optimal sequence of distortionary tax rates and public spending over time. The reason why a government has to *choose* a fiscal policy is to be found in the distortionary nature of taxation and the existence of public goods. The discussion departs from conditions of debt neutrality. This Ricardian theory of public finance amounts to the proposition that the manner in which a government finances a given path of expenditures does not matter. The distortionary nature of taxes influences the choices of consumers and producers for the worse. A benevolent government tries to minimise this welfare loss, better known as *excess burden* or *deadweight loss*. The static theory of optimal taxation, as initiated by Ramsey [1927] and later extended by Samuelson [1951] and Diamond/Mirrlees [1971], has made clear that the excess burden of taxation is minimised when a government follows the (Ramsey) tax rule: concentrate taxation on goods in relatively inelastic demand or supply, or goods that are close complements to the untaxed goods. The power of the optimal taxation theory lies not so much in this particular inverse elasticity rule, but in the provision of a standard of argument in the discussion of the positive and normative questions of fiscal policy. The notion of excess burden of distortionary taxation enables one to rank fiscal policies in terms of efficiency. Critics of the practical use of the theory of optimal taxation, such as Harberger [1990], often aim their grudge at the flawed knowledge (or measurement) of elasticities. The applicability of (static) optimal taxation rules is indeed questionable if one tries to project it in a one-to-one relationship on reality, but so is any high brow theory which tends to lay down *principles* of policy design.

The dynamic counterpart of the static optimal taxation problem has been an enrichment of the theory of public finance, since the theory enables one to base a macroeconomic theory of taxation on the microeconomics of individual decisions on consumption and labour supply. The theory owes its intellectuel debt to the permanent income theory of consumption, as pioneered by Friedman [1957]. In a nutshell, this theory amounts to the hypothesis that decisions made by consumers are based on the present value of their lifetime income rather than their current income. The theory implies that if consumers experience an unexpected one-time windfall gain in income (say, a stroke of perfect foresight in the pools), then they will not consume their entire good fortune. Instead, they will raise their consumption by the amount to which their permanent income rises. Barro [1979], who recognised the similarities between public and private intertemporal decision making, formulated the hypothesis that tax rates are smoothed over time. The model he used was rather *ad hoc* in that it did not provide an explicit solution of the excess burden or the sequence of decision making steps in setting taxes. Barro simply based his idea of tax smoothing on a tax collection function with increasing marginal costs. As it turns out, this rather crude approximation *does* seem to reflect the dynamic choices government faces. Tests do not seem to reject the tax smoothing hypothesis for postwar U.S. data (Barro [1979] and Sahasakul [1986]) and data for the U.K. for the period 1701-1918 (Barro [1987]). There are, however, indications that other factors (including political ones) influence the path of tax rates significantly, as Roubini and Sachs [1989a,1989b] show for a selected number of industrial economies. They find that tax rates do not follow a random walk. Kremers [1989] examined the question whether the tax rate setting since the 1920s in the U.S. was set within bounds of long-run sustainability. During most of the inter- and post-war period, fiscal policy in effect stabilised the federal debt relative to gross national product. However, after 1981 the tax rate smoothing hypothesis has to be rejected, since the build-up of public debt has gone well beyond the capacity of a smooth tax rate.

The general idea behind the 'tax smoothing' hypothesis is that the excess burden of taxation typically rises more than proportionately with the tax rate. A benevolent government faces in fact a Laffer curve[1] in determining its optimal fiscal policy. Later extensions paid explicit attention to the intertemporal distortions brought about by taxation. A central point of discussion in the dynamic theory of taxation is *which taxes* should be used to counter real shocks and, in the case of only one tax, whether this tax rate should be *smoothed*, remain *constant* or move in line with public spending and hence *balance*

---

1. See Fullerton [1982] for a discussion of the Laffer curve.

the budget at every point in time. The question is analogous to the optimal taxation question in a static setting to a certain extent. Under such conditions, the optimal tax problem boils down to the question whether one should use uniform taxation for all goods consumed. In a dynamic setting, a constant tax rate is a simple result which is generally based on equally simple models: the utility function is separable across time as well as across the arguments of leisure and consumption (see Deaton [1981]), policy is time consistent and factor prices are exogenous. The tax rate constancy result stems from a general theorem of uniform taxation by Atkinson and Stiglitz [1972], which rests on the separability and iso-elasticity properties of the welfare function. The separability is introduced to rule out cross effects of distortionary taxation on labour supply, and the iso-elasticity is required to ensure that there is no time dependence in government plans: the intertemporal elasticities of substitution are constant. Aiyagari [1989] has shown for a restricted set of preferences[2], viz. preferences implying that the income effect of a change in the net wage on work effort is zero, that tax rates should move in line with unexpected permanent changes in government expenditures. Constant or smooth tax rates are only applicable if government spending shows no unexpected changes. For a more general preference structure, but with an exogenously determined interest rate, Kremers [1986b] has shown for a two-period economy without capital that the property of tax rate constancy applies if *discounted* after tax (nominal) wages are equal in the two periods *and*, above all, if

─────────────────

2. The utility function introduced by Aiyagari [1989] is: $U(c(t))$, where $c(t)$ is net consumption, i.e. net of the opportunity cost of work in units of foregone consumption, $c(t) = C(t) - H[\ell(t)]$, where $H(.)$ is an opportunity cost function of work with properties, $H' > 0$, $H'' > 0$, $H(0) = 0$.

the preferences for leisure are symmetric across the two periods[3]. This might indeed be of some relevance to fiscal policies in ageing economies, since it stresses the fact that for economic policy design, it matters *when* one prefers to enjoy leisure. A symmetric preference for leisure amounts to the assertion that there exists indifference between the timing of leisure, in youth or in old age. In other words, this restriction requires that the representative agent does not subjectively discount future leisure. Aschauer [1988b] extends the analysis and goes on to show that tax rate constancy applies if undiscounted real wages are equal and the form of momentary utility is stationary.

The dynamic theory has generally concentrated on labour income taxation and has generally ruled out the taxation of capital income. The problem tied to capital income taxation is that, in general, it is seen as a time-inconsistent policy option, i.e. it always pays for a benevolent government to surprise the private sector with a capital income levy, since capital is a fixed factor in the short run and its supply is elastic in the long-run (a feature that is pointed out by Fischer [1980] and Kydland and Prescott [1980]). This result is restricted to the conditions of a closed economy. If, for instance, firms in a small open economy have tax arbitrage opportunities by moving profits abroad, time consistency may still go through. The general result of time inconsistency arising from capital taxation does not imply that the choice of other taxes is automatically time consistent. E.g., a tax on

---

3. The Kremers result is a generalisation of the Corlett-Hague [1953-54] result to a dynamic setting. The Corlett-Hague rule boils down to the condition that uniform taxation of goods is an optimal policy if the cross elasticities between the taxed and the untaxed goods are equal.

labour income may also be time inconsistent (see Persson and Tabellini [1990]). It is outside the scope of this section to consider solutions that overcome problems of time consistency (see section 7.4 for a more extensive discussion). It is assumed that the fiscal policy which the government announces at time zero is adhered to forever. In other words, a commitment technology (law, contracts) is available. Despite this shortcoming, principles of optimality without the property of time consistency are interesting as they stand. For a closed economy Chamley [1986] examined the combination of wage and capital taxation. A first-best policy would be for the government to raise an initial capital levy by an amount equal to the present discounted value of future public consumption. The existence of an initial capital stock in a growth model corresponds to the existence of pure profits in the static case. A general result in questions of optimal taxation is that it is always efficient to first tax pure profits (Munk [1978]). In the absence of a lump-sum tax solution, a government has to consider taxing production factors and consumption. The capital tax has two effects: it raises revenues on fixed capital, $k_0 > 0$, but it also introduces intertemporal distortions in saving. Chamley [1986, p. 616] found that there are two regimes for capital income taxation in an infinitely-lived representative agent model: in the short run, capital income is taxed as high as possible, viz. at a 100% capital income tax rate. In this short period the lump-sum effect exceeds the distortionary effect. Of course, a one-time capital levy would not bring about any distortions. The time interval of capital taxation becomes smaller (greater) when the capital stock is relatively small (large) with respect to its steady state value. After some time (and certainly in the steady state) capital income is not taxed at all[4]. Without going through the complete proof, the result is quite intuitive. Physical capital is irreversible, and taxing this production factor initially as high as possible and abstaining from labour income taxation as much as possible, would bring about the smallest possible welfare loss. After the period of capital taxation, wage taxation is the only tax rate left and with the accumulated fund, the wage income tax rate can be smoothed whenever irregularities appear in government spending.

However, as soon as heterogeneity of agents (e.g., over-lapping generations of individuals) is introduced into the model the Chamley result disappears. For instance, Stiglitz [1987] shows that interest income is taxed in the steady state if there are two (or more) types of individuals, and if a government cannot offset the changes in relative wages induced by the tax policy. Under those circumstances the government will wish to take these changes into consideration and an interest income tax will be desirable. Sandmo [1985] goes on to show that in an overlapping generations model, where the demand for future consumption is inelastic, the interest income is the ideal tax base from an efficiency point of view. In general, the relative tax rates depend on the relative magnitudes of the elasticities of labour supply and demand for future consumption. However, capital taxation involves a question where *ex ante* and *ex post* elasticities differ[5] and thereby the incentive for government to act time-inconsistent.

---

4. Auerbach [1979] has shown that the steady state tax rate on capital income is equal to zero in the infinite horizon model, with a discount rate equal to the growth rate. Chamley [1986] performs in that respect a more general analysis.

5. See Persson and Tabellini [1990, ch. 6] for an exposition of this point.

In the following sections I will examine how a distortionary tax should be set during periods of non-stationary population growth. I will discuss the behaviour of a representative family and the fiscal policy rules of a benevolent government. I will treat the case of an *ad valorem* consumption tax cum public debt. The analysis aims at obtaining some general *principles* of taxation. The theory of optimal taxation is a branch of welfare economics and as Hahn [1973] has argued: "Welfare economics is the grammar of arguments about policy, not the policy". At this point the calibration of fiscal policies to actual conditions and measuring welfare losses is going to be an arbitrary excercise. The question "How high should the tax rate be?" depends, among other factors, on the planning horizon, the initial public debt, the future path of government expenditures and population growth. These issues are beyond the scope of this chapter.

7.2 A SIMPLE MODEL OF THE REPRESENTATIVE FAMILY

As the basis for the theory of dynamic optimal taxation I will consider the infinitely-lived agent or dynasty. The head of the representive dynasty faces the following utility maximisation problem:

$$(7.1) \qquad \text{Maximise } W_0^P = \int_0^\infty e^{-\rho t} U[c(t), x(t), g(t)] \; dt$$
$$c, x$$

where ρ denotes the constant rate of time preference, $c(t)$ consumption per capita at time t, $x(t)$ the leisure enjoyed and $g(t)$ denotes the amount of government spending which gives rise to consumption externalities. It depends on the character of the public spending how much the consumer enjoys[6]. The usual distinction of public good characteristics is the following:

$$g(t) \equiv \frac{G(t)}{N(t)^{\kappa}} \quad \text{where } \kappa \in [0,1]$$

The parameter κ denotes the degree of *rivalry* in public consumption. A value of $\kappa = 0$ denotes the pure public good as analysed by Samuelson [1954]. A value of κ larger than 0, indicates that the use of the public good by a member of the population will limit the use by other members of the population. In case $\kappa = 1$, the degree of rivalry is complete and the public good has got private good characteristics. To keep things simple, I will restrict my attention to non-excludable public goods and services and the perfectly divisible public good (i.e. $\kappa = 1$) in the remainder of this chapter. The government maximises with respect to per capita public consumption, g ($\equiv G.N^{-\kappa}$, with $\kappa = 1$). In a growing economy, i.e. $n(t) > 0$, one should restrict κ to 1 if the government uses a social welfare function defined in per capita terms. Other values for this rivalry parameter will lead, under those circumstances, to time-dependent public spending rules and a steady state cannot exist.

The head of the representative dynasty has perfect foresight and behaves competitively: the family faces an international capital market at which it can borrow or lend capital at the world interest rate, $r(t)$. The utility function satifies the following assumptions:

---

6. See Djajić [1987,1989] for an analysis of (exogenous) public spending in the presence of lump-sum taxes and various assumptions concerning the interaction between public and private consumption.

A.1: $U: R_+ \rightarrow R$ with $\partial U/\partial i > 0$, $\partial^2 U/\partial i^2 < 0$, $\partial^2 U/\partial i \partial j = 0$ for

$i,j = c,x,g$ and $i \neq j$

$\lim_{i \to 0} \partial U/\partial i = \infty$ and $\lim_{i \to \infty} \partial U/\partial i = 0$

Leisure, public consumption and private consumption are separate arguments in the utility function which rules out any direct interaction between the three. This separability assumption is introduced to provide an analytically tractable model. The fiscal policy question for more general utility functions can only be examined in a tractable manner if one makes use of a model without capital (such as in Lucas and Stokey [1983], Kremers [1986b] and Aschauer [1988b]).

The representative family or dynasty consists initially of N_0 family members. As time passes by, the family size grows at the rate $n(t)$:

$$(7.2) \qquad N(t) = N_0 \exp \int_0^t n(s) \, ds$$

Leisure, $x(t)$, and its complement labour supply, $\ell(t)$, are constrained by the available amount of time per family. The utility function is additively separable in the arguments c, x and g. If we normalize the available amount of time to 1 we can write the time constraint as:

$$(7.3) \qquad x(t) + \ell(t) = 1$$

The consumer invests part of his income from labour and assets in and the remaining income is consumed. The consumer can borrow or lend at the world capital market at the rate r. The size of the economy is too small to be of any influence on the factor price formation. The dynamic (or flow) budget restriction amounts to the following differential equation:

$$(7.4) \qquad \dot{a} = w\ell(t) + [r - n(t)]a(t) - c(t)[1 + \varsigma(t)]$$

where the net foreign assets of the family are denoted by a (= m + k + b), and consist of foreign assets, $m(t)$, physical capital, $k(t)$, and one-period government bonds, $b(t)$, respectively. Furthermore, $\varsigma(t)$ denotes the tax rate on consumption, r the interest rate and w the wage rate.

Factor prices are exogenous and therefore the development of saving and investment develop independently. During worktime the head of the family performs the role of representative producer by solving the static problem of profit (Π) maximisation in a small open economy:

$$(7.5) \qquad \underset{k,\ell}{\text{Maximise }} \Pi = \{f[k,\ell] - rk - w\ell\}$$

The production function $f(.)$ is written in the intensive form. It represents the well-known neoclassical production function and it suffices to state that it produces the composite commodity under conditions of constant returns to scale and that it is well behaved ($\partial f/\partial k, \partial f/\partial \ell > 0$ and $\partial^2 f/\partial k^2, \partial^2 f/\partial \ell^2 < 0$, $\partial^2 f/\partial k \partial \ell > 0$). Througout the analysis it is assumed that capital does not depreciate. The profit maximisation problem of the representative producer yields under conditions of a small open economy the production factor relationships:

$$(7.6) \qquad w = \partial f/\partial \ell(t)$$

(7.7) $r = \partial f/\partial k(t)$

In equilibrium, profits Π are zero and therefore need not be included in the budget constraint of the consumer. With given factor prices, one can deduce from equation (7.7) that the amount of capital to be accumulated should be kept in line with the growth rate of the labour force (differentiate condition 7.7 with respect to time):

(7.8) $\dot{k} = (\dot{l}/l)k$

Borrowing by the consumer is restricted by a condition imposed by the lenders on a capital market. The net asset position of the family should be a non-negative value as time approaches infinity:

(7.9) $\lim_{t \to \infty} a(t)R(t) \geq 0$

where the short term discount factor $R(t)$ is given by,

$$R(t) = \exp\left\{-\int_0^t [r - n(s)]\ ds\right\}$$

The No-Ponzi-game condition (7.9) requires that the present value of debt, arbitrarily far into the future, has to be non-negative. In other words, the family's debt should not increase asymptotically faster than the interest rate. Of course, an equilibrium path of asset accumulation will be such that the condition (7.9) holds with equality: forever increasing wealth at the rate $(r - n(t))$ is not desirable as long as the marginal utility of consumption is positive. This condition ensures that families will not leave over any resources that asymptotically have positive present value. The intertemporal budget constraint for the representative family can therefore be written as

$$(7.10) \qquad \int_0^\infty c(t)(1 + \varsigma(t))R(t)dt = \int_0^\infty w\ell(t)R(t)dt + a_0$$

The current-value Hamiltonian for the representative consumer can now be formulated as:

$$(7.11) \qquad H(c,x,a,\lambda) = U[c(t),x(t),g(t)] +$$

$$+ \lambda(t)\{[r - n(t)]a(t) + w\ell(t) +$$

$$- c(t)[1 + \varsigma(t)]\}$$

The necessary and sufficient conditions for an interior solution amount to:

$$(7.12) \qquad \frac{\partial H}{\partial c(t)} = 0 : \lambda(t)[1 + \varsigma(t)] = \frac{\partial U}{\partial c(t)}$$

$$(7.13) \qquad \frac{\partial H}{\partial x(t)} = 0 : \lambda(t)w = \frac{\partial U}{\partial x(t)}$$

$$(7.14) \qquad \dot{\lambda}(t) = \rho\lambda(t) - \frac{\partial H}{\partial a(t)} = \lambda(t)[\rho + n(t) - r]$$

$$(7.15) \qquad \lim_{t \to \infty} a(t)\lambda(t)e^{-\rho t} = 0$$

Assuming separability of the arguments of the utility function, each of the marginal utility conditions (7.12) and (7.13) is shown as functionally dependent on a shortened list of arguments of $U(.)$. This assumption becomes extremely helpful later on, when we consider dynamic optimal taxation rules. Combining equations (7.12)-(7.14) one obtains the following dynamic relations:

$$(7.16) \quad \frac{U_x(.t)}{U_c(.t)} = \frac{w}{(1 + \varsigma(t))}$$

$$(7.17) \quad \frac{U_{cc}(.t)}{U_c(.t)} \dot{c} = \rho + n(t) - r + \frac{\dot{\varsigma}}{1 + \varsigma(t)}$$

The fiscal policy instruments are treated parametrically by the individual consumer. One can easily see how proportionate taxation affects the individual resource allocation. The marginal rate of substitution between leisure and consumption should equal the marginal rate of transformation in equilibrium, i.e. the real wage rate corrected for the consumption tax: $1/(1 + \varsigma)$. The exclusion of capital income taxation in the present set-up of a one-sector growth model is not that great a loss of reality: a *change* in the *consumption* tax rate has consequences which can be equivalent to a proportionate tax on *capital* income (see RHS of equation 7.17).

The government of this small open economy is constrained by the following flow budget constraint:

$$(7.18) \quad \dot{b} = (r - n)b(t) + g(t) - \varsigma(t)c(t)$$

which can be transformed into the intertemporal budget
constraint by imposing the No-Ponzi-game condition:

$$(7.19) \qquad \int_0^\infty g(t)R(t)dt = \int_0^\infty \varsigma(t)c(t)R(t)dt - b_0$$

where b_0 denotes the initial public debt position.

Given the exogenous factor prices, a steady state is defined
by the following rules of allocation of consumption, capital and
leisure:

$$(7.20) \qquad \frac{U_x}{U_c} = \frac{w}{(1 + \varsigma)}$$

$$(7.21) \qquad r = n + \rho$$

$$(7.22) \qquad (r - n)h + w\ell - c - g = 0$$

where the level of national assets (consisting of foreign assets
and domestic capital) is denoted as $h = a - b$. Equation (7.20)
is the standard consumption/leisure trade-off equation. Equation
(7.21) is the steady state condition for a small open economy:
the parameters population growth and time preference should
equal the (exogenous) world interest rate. And finally, each
allocation of consumption, investment and labour supply should
satisfy the aggregate resource constraint (7.22).

7.3 DYNAMIC FISCAL POLICY

To disentangle the consequences of fiscal policies for countries
with a non-stationary population growth, I will present the
question of optimal consumption taxation. I could also have

examined the case of wage taxation, but in this deterministic model the distortionary nature of a consumption tax is the same as the distortionary effect of a wage tax. The neglect of this type of taxation is therefore not very serious. An *ad valorem* consumption tax rate performs two roles in dynamic general equilibrium models, viz. that of a tax on (i) saving, if the consumption tax is varied over time, and (ii) labour effort through the consumption/leisure trade-off. The first effect is equivalent to a capital income levy or subsidy. Thus, because a consumption tax indirectly taxes the fixed capital whereas a wage tax does not, the former is always more efficient than a wage tax in raising an equal amount of revenues. However, a commitment technology rules out this role of a consumption tax.

7.3.1 SECOND-BEST FISCAL POLICY PROBLEM

The benevolent government takes into account the behaviour of the family in its choice of second-best fiscal policy $\pi(t) = \{g(t), \varsigma(t)\}_{t=0}^{\infty}$. The problem we are dealing with in this section is second-best because the government cannot control the levels of c and x directly, but it chooses a fiscal policy that satisfies the optimisation restrictions of the private sector. Because the government is situated in a small open economy, it cannot affect the factor prices in this economy[7]. The government first solves the optimal values of the consumption tax rate and the amount of public spending, g, in such a way that consumer welfare is maximised.

---

7. Bovenberg [1988] brings forward empirical results for the period 1961-1985 that support the view that fiscal deficits in the U.S. have raised the real long-term interest rates. The assumption of exogenous factor prices is therefore only a good approximation of a small open economy.

The constraints faced by the government are the family's optimising behaviour and the government budget constraint. After the solution has been computed, the government announces the values of consumption tax rate and the amount of public spending. As soon as one has determined the optimal sequence of tax rates and public spending, one can also determine the flow of public bonds. Then the private sector computes its optimal solution. Under conditions of perfect foresight, the *individual* solution is *identical* to the *social* solution, because private optimal behaviour is taken into account in designing the social solution. I will start by considering a *general* utility function in which consumption and leisure choices are interdependent. The optimal consumption/leisure choice can be substituted in $U(.)$ as functions of $\zeta(t)$, w and $\lambda(t)$ and summarised in the function $U[c(\zeta,w,\lambda),x(\zeta,w,\lambda)] + V(g)$. The amount of public consumption enters the social welfare function separably. The utility function over the private consumption/leisure combination is the same function as the one of the private sector. The optimal fiscal policy problem can be stated as follows[8]:

$$(7.23) \quad \text{Max}_{\zeta,g} \ W_0^G = \int_0^\infty e^{-\rho t} U[c(\zeta,w,\lambda),x(\zeta,w,\lambda)] + V(g) \ dt$$

subject to the national resource constraint, the government budget constraint, non-negativity constraints on public and private consumption:

$$(7.24) \quad \dot{h} = w\ell + (r - n(t))h - c - g$$

---

8. For notational convenience I will drop time indicators where no confusion can arise.

(7.25) $\dot{b} = [r - n(t)]b - \varsigma c + g$

(7.26) $c(t), g(t) \geq 0$

where, for notational reasons, the level of national assets (consisting of foreign assets and domestic capital) is denoted as $h = m + k$ (or $h = a - b$)[9]. The goverment may have positive as well as negative wealth. The current-value Hamiltonian of the second-best fiscal policy choice is given by:

(7.27) $H(\pi,h,b,w,\lambda,\mu_i) = U[c(\varsigma,w,\lambda),x(\varsigma,w,\lambda)] + V(g) +$

$$+ \mu_1 \{w\ell + [r - n(t)]h - c - g\} +$$

$$+ \mu_2 \{[r - n(t)]b - \varsigma c + g\}$$

The shadow price μ_2 represents the marginal social value of public debt. It can also be interpreted as the marginal value of replacing lump-sum taxation by distortionary taxation. In other words, μ_2 denotes the value of the marginal excess burden of taxation and is always non-positive (see Atkinson and Stern [1974]).

The necessary and sufficient conditions for an optimal tax/debt policy are given by the following first order conditions for an interior solution (where variables with subscript letters denote partial derivatives):

---

9. One can check that the government problem is consistent with the private sector problem by summing the assets: $da/dt \equiv dm/dt + dk/dt + db/dt$.

$$(7.28) \quad \frac{\partial H}{\partial g(t)} = V_g - (\mu_1 - \mu_2) = 0$$

$$(7.29) \quad \frac{\partial H}{\partial \varsigma(t)} = U_c . c_\varsigma + U_x . x_\varsigma - \mu_1 [c_\varsigma + w.x_\varsigma] +$$

$$- \mu_2 [\varsigma c_\varsigma + c] = 0$$

$$(7.30) \quad \dot{\mu}_1 = \rho\mu_1 - \frac{\partial H}{\partial h(t)} = \mu_1 [\rho + n(t) - r]$$

$$(7.31) \quad \dot{\mu}_2 = \rho\mu_2 - \frac{\partial H}{\partial b(t)} = \mu_2 [\rho + n(t) - r]$$

$$(7.32) \quad \lim_{t \to \infty} h(t)\mu_1(t)e^{-\rho t} = 0$$

$$(7.33) \quad \lim_{t \to \infty} b(t)\mu_2(t)e^{-\rho t} = 0$$

The shadow prices of private assets, $\lambda(t)$, public debt, $\mu_2(t)$, and national resources, $\mu_1(t)$, all grow at the same rate[10]. The development of the marginal excess burden over time is described by equation (7.31). The government should take into account how the individual consumer values fluctuations in consumption. The rate of change and the level of the shadow price of private consumption is given by equation (7.14) and λ, respectively. The

---

10. This makes once again clear the importance of the assumption concerning atomistic government behaviour on the capital market. If, e.g., government could affect the real interest rate it would be able to influence the interest payable on its outstanding debt.

optimal fiscal policy is more concerned with the *relative* price of the excess burden, μ_2/λ, rather than with its absolute value, μ_2. Equation (7.28) indicates that the government should supply public goods up to the point where the marginal utility of public goods is equal to the marginal social value of national resources used, μ_1, and the marginal excess burden of distortionary taxation, μ_2. By definition, the excess burden amounts to a welfare loss (and negative), hence the marginal utility of public consumption, V_g, is always positive. If the marginal excess burden of taxation rises, government spending will fall (and vice versa). One cannot derive the optimal tax formula directly, but one can write out the marginal efficiency cost of taxation. Given the parameters of tastes, population growth and time preference, we know that tax rates should be smoothed over time (see Chamley [1985a,1986], since there exists a constant ψ such that:

$$(7.34) \quad \frac{\mu_2(t)}{\lambda(t)} = \psi \quad \text{or} \quad \frac{\mu_1(t) - V_g(t)}{\lambda(t)} = \psi$$

The value of ψ depends on the initial levels of public debt and physical capital. Under quite general conditions the initial level of public wealth is smaller than the present value of future public expenditures. Distortionary taxation is therefore necessary and the value of ψ is negative. Only in the case where a government finds some wealth in the garden of Eden (say, a renewable resource in case of an infinitely-lived government) which is equal to the present value of expenditures, a government can abstain from using distortionary taxation. One can also see that the non-stationarity of population growth does not matter for the tax rate constancy result, as long as the variations in population growth are expected. This infinite horizon model gives rise to a result of indeterminacy: in the steady state, the level of public debt cannot be ascribed a unique value, i.e. it is not independent of the initial state. In general, one can expect that a relatively high level of public debt at the start of the planning process also generates a relatively high level of public debt in the steady state. The marginal value of the excess burden depends on the amount of revenues which are raised through distortionary taxation. As mentioned above, this amount of tax revenue also depends on the level of public debt at the beginning of time. The optimal steady state level of public debt, b_∞, is therefore not independent of the initial level of public debt, b_0. This is the 'indeterminacy of public debt' result as first described by Barro [1979] and later derived in a general equilibrium model by Chamley [1985a].

If we return to condition (7.34) and substitute the optimal public goods condition (7.28) in the optimal tax rate condition (7.29) and divide both sides by $\lambda(t)$, we obtain the following expression for the marginal value of excess burden:

$$(7.35) \quad \psi = \frac{(1 + \varsigma)c_\varsigma(1 - V_g/U_c) + wx_\varsigma[1 - V_g/U_c(1 + \varsigma)]}{c + c_\varsigma(1 + \varsigma) + wx_\varsigma}$$

or rewritten in terms of tax elasticities:

$$(7.36) \quad \psi = \frac{(1 + \varsigma)[1 - (V_g/U_c)(1 + Q)] + Q}{\varsigma(1 + 1/\epsilon_c) + 1 + Q}$$

where we define $Q = \dfrac{w.x}{c} \dfrac{\epsilon_x}{\epsilon_c}$, $\epsilon_x = \dfrac{\varsigma}{x} \dfrac{\partial x}{\partial \varsigma}\bigg|_{d\lambda=0}$ and $\epsilon_c = \dfrac{\varsigma}{c} \dfrac{\partial c}{\partial \varsigma}\bigg|_{d\lambda=0}$

Since condition (7.35) is time dependent, the tax rate constancy result does not apply under the conditions of a general utility function. There is only one case where tax rate constancty applies, viz. if one assumes that the consumption tax has no effect on labour supply and falls entirely on consumption, i.e. the separability assumption that the *partial* derivative $x_\varsigma = 0$. Under those conditions (7.36) boils down to:

$$(7.37) \qquad \psi = \frac{(1 + \varsigma)[1 - (V_g/U_c)]}{\varsigma(1 + 1/\epsilon_c) + 1}$$

This information can be derived from the private sector's first order condition for the leisure choice, if and only if the welfare function is additively separable. For the remaining analysis we can consider the additively separable and iso-elastic utility function with $\sigma, \epsilon, \gamma > 0$ and $\sigma, \epsilon, \gamma \neq 1$:

$$(7.38) \qquad W_0^G = \int_0^\infty e^{-\rho t}\left\{ \beta_1 \frac{c^{(1-\sigma)}}{(1-\sigma)} + \beta_2 \frac{x^{(1-\epsilon)}}{(1-\epsilon)} + \beta_3 \frac{g^{(1-\gamma)}}{(1-\gamma)} \right\} dt$$

with $\Sigma_i^3 \beta_i = 1$, and for $\sigma = \epsilon = \gamma = 1$ we use the logarithmic utility function $U(c,x,g) = \beta_1 \log c + \beta_2 \log x + \beta_2 \log g$, where $1/\sigma$, $1/\epsilon$ and $1/\gamma$ represent the elasticities of intertemporal substitution in private consumption, leisure and public consumption (and as one can check they are independent of time). Under those circumstances, the implicit consumption and leisure functions amount to $c(\varsigma,\lambda)$ and $x(w,\lambda)$, respectively (see also Flemming [1987] and Kingston [1989] for this approach). This assumption does not imply that labour supply is inelastic: through the shadow price, λ, the distortionary consumption tax has an indirect influence on the labour supply.

As one can see in condition (7.36), the ratio between the marginal utility of public and private consumption will not change as long as one uses a constant tax rate. This property can be seen by differentiating the ratio V_g/U_c with respect to time:

$$(7.39) \quad d(V_g/U_c)/dt = (V_g/U_c)[\sigma\hat{c} - \gamma\hat{g}] = 0 \text{ if } d\varsigma/dt = 0$$

where a variable with a circumflex denotes a percentage change of that variable. From the differential equation for private consumption, equation (7.14), and the differential equation for public consumption is derived by differentiating condition (7.25) with respect to time:

$$(7.40) \quad \hat{g} \equiv \frac{\dot{g}}{g(t)} = \frac{1}{\gamma}(r - \rho - n(t))$$

$$(7.41) \quad \hat{c} \equiv \frac{\dot{c}}{c(t)} = \frac{1}{\sigma}(r - \rho - n(t) - \frac{\dot{\varsigma}}{1 + \varsigma(t)})$$

hence if $\varsigma(t) = \varsigma$, $\dot{g}$, $\dot{c} \gtreqless 0$ if $r \gtreqless \rho + n(t)$.

Failing the above mentioned conditions of tax rate constancy, a government's objective should therefore be to smooth out fluctuations between periods in the marginal value of the excess burden of taxation, μ_2, in terms of the private value of a unit of consumption, λ. The LHS of (7.36) is a constant, ψ, hence the government should decide on setting the consumption tax rate with this restriction in mind. Given the additive separability of the utility function, one can show that the marginal efficiency cost of taxation goes to zero as the elasticity ϵ_c goes to zero, and the marginal cost of taxation can become quite large if the marginal utility of public consumption by far exceeds the marginal utility of private consumption. Summarising,

$$(7.42a) \qquad \lim_{\epsilon_c \uparrow 0} \psi = 0$$

$$(7.42b) \qquad \lim_{\epsilon_c \to -\infty} \psi = 1 - V_g / U_c < 0$$

In conclusion, the tax rate constancy result hinges strongly on the assumptions of (i) an additively separable utility function; and (ii) the constancy of the (compensated) tax elasticity of consumption, ϵ_c. Failing this last condition, tax rates should be set at a low rate in times of relatively elastic reactions and at a high rate in times of relatively inelastic reactions.

7.3.2 FIRST-BEST FISCAL POLICY PROBLEM

It is of some interest to see according to what rules a government proceeds in a first-best world and contrast this benchmark case with the second-best fiscal policy. A first-best optimality rule can be derived by solving the reaction of consumption to an unexpected permanent change in consumption taxation, c_ς, giving rise to a permanent change in consumption explicitly, from the consumer's budget constraint, assuming meanwhile labour supply to be inelastic (hence in the model of section 7.3.1: $x_\varsigma, x_\lambda, x_w = 0$):

$$(7.43) \qquad c_\varsigma = - \frac{c}{(1 + \varsigma)}$$

Equation (7.43) expresses the manner in which a lump-sum tax displaces private consumption in the private budget constraint.

The consumption tax displaces private consumption, divided by the price of consumption, $(1 + \varsigma)$. If we substitute this relation in the optimal tax rate condition (7.36), we can see that the optimal consumption tax should establish the equality between the marginal utility of private consumption and the marginal utility of public consumption for each and every period:

$$(7.44) \quad V_g = U_c$$

Equation (7.44) is an elegant way of showing that a first-best allocation is possible in a potentially second-best world. One should notice that this rule distinctly differs from the second-best rule of the previous section, even with the restriction x_ς = 0. One can check that with an explicit lump-sum tax the same allocation rule (7.44) would apply and hence the marginal value of the excess burden of taxation is zero: μ_2 = 0. It is potentially a second-best world because without the public debt instrument, a government has to balance its budget and resort to varying the consumption tax rate. To see why the equality, $V_g = U_c$, naturally prevails, suppose that the marginal utility of private consumption exceeds that of public consumption, then utility could be increased by increasing the amount of private consumption by one unit and reducing the amount of public consumption by one unit via *lump-sum* taxation[11]. In this model the welfare obtained in the first-best world, i.e. with lump-sum taxes, is equal to the welfare obtained in the potentially second-best world: government can use a constant consumption tax

---

11. See for an application of this rule the fiscal policy model as developed by Foley and Sidrauski [1971].

rate, so that the present discounted value of tax collections equals the present discounted value of government consumption[12]. This is exactly what equation (7.44) amounts to, and second-best is no longer second but first best. There are two reasons why the problem of the second best collapses to conditions of the first best. First of all, a *constant* consumption tax rate does not distort capital accumulation. The development of the shadow price of capital is the same in a second-best world as in a first-best world. Secondly, by fixing the consumption tax, one taxes in effect all available goods. A general result in (static) optimal taxation is that one can set tax rates in a lump-sum fashion if there are no untaxed goods (see Auerbach [1985]). As a disclaimer, one must notice the restrictive conditions under which this result applies: *separability* in public and private consumption and *inelastic* labour supply. Despite its simplicity, it does offer us a simple optimal taxation formula in terms of consumer preferences. If we use the iso-elastic utility function with $\sigma, \gamma > 0$ and $\sigma, \gamma \neq 1$ throughout the remaining part of this analysis:

$$(7.45) \quad W_0^G = \int_0^\infty e^{-\rho t} \left\{ \beta_1 \frac{c^{(1-\sigma)}}{(1-\sigma)} + \beta_2 \frac{g^{(1-\gamma)}}{(1-\gamma)} \right\} dt$$

with $\Sigma_i^2 \, \beta_i = 1$, and for $\sigma = \gamma = 1$, we use the logarithmic utility function $U(c,g) = \beta_1 \log c + \beta_2 \log g$, where $1/\sigma$ and $1/\gamma$ represent the elasticities of intertemporal substitution in private consumption and public consumption. An alternative interpretation of this elasticity is one which applies to stochastic environments: σ is the coefficient of relative risk

12. This possibility was alluded to by Kenneth Arrow in discussing J.S. Flemming [1988, pp. 224-225]), but not proven.

aversion. A high value of this coefficient indicates that the representative consumer/producer would prefer a smoother path of consumption than the agent whose preferences are reflected in lower coefficients of risk aversion. Estimates for $1/\sigma$ are found to be low[13]. Mankiw [1981] reported a value of about 0.25, Hansen and Singleton [1982] found parameter values in the range between 1.0 and 1.5, while Mankiw *et al.* [1985] found extremely high values in the range between 1 and 10. Hall [1988] concludes, however, that there is no strong evidence for the elasticity of intertemporal substitution to be positive, and might be zero indeed. One of the reasons why a positive $1/\sigma$ may not be found is the presence of liquidity constraints (see Hayashi [1987]). There are no empirical findings of the intertemporal elasticity in public consumption, $1/\gamma$, whatsoever, but it would be reasonable to assume that public consumption is more inelastic than private consumption: $1/\gamma < 1/\sigma$, because public consumption is more likely to be tied to current conditions. The desire to shift public consumption across time is assumed to be less than the desire to shift private consumption and leisure.

The optimal tax rate can be given in quite general terms by rewriting the intertemporal budget constraint, given that the tax rate is a constant:

$$(7.46) \qquad \zeta = \frac{g^* + b_0}{c^*}$$

where $g^* = \displaystyle\int_0^\infty g(t)R(t)\ dt$, and $c^* = \displaystyle\int_0^\infty c(t)R(t)\ dt$.

---

13. See Mao [1989] for a discussion of the biases one may encounter in estimating the elasticity of intertemporal substitution.

If we term the variables g^* and c^* as 'permanent' (as short for the present discounted value) public and private consumption, we can say that the optimal tax rate should equal the permanent public consumption plus initial public debt, divided by the permanent tax base, which in this case boils down to private consumption.

At this point we can illustrate how a government should act in case it encounters shocks in one of the parameters of the economy. One movement, which is quite standard in case of an expected shock, is the co-movement of public and private consumption. Optimality condition (7.42) implies for the utility function (7.43) that public and private consumption should move together according to:

$$(7.47) \qquad \beta_1 \, \frac{\dot{c}.\sigma}{c^{1+\sigma}} = \beta_2 \, \frac{\dot{g}.\gamma}{g^{1+\gamma}}$$

Whether a government should accumulate or decumulate public debt depends on the intertemporal elasticities and the type of shock. For a thorough understanding of debt dynamics one should keep in mind the two types of public budget constraints: the inter-temporal and the flow budget constraint. If we rewrite the flow budget constraint we can see how debt should evolve:

$$(7.48) \qquad \zeta = \frac{[r - n(t)]b(t) - \dot{b}}{c(t)} + \frac{g(t)}{c(t)}$$

We established earlier that the optimal tax rate should be constant hence the RHS of equation (7.48) should be constant. With the allocation rule $U_c = V_g$, we can write (7.48) as:

$$(7.49) \quad \zeta = \frac{[r - n(t)]b(t) - \dot{b}}{c(t)} + A.[g(t)]^{(\sigma-\gamma)/\sigma}$$

where $A = (\beta_2/\beta_1)^{1/\sigma}$. Now if public and private consumption are equally elastic, i.e. $\sigma = \gamma$, the second term on the RHS of (7.49) becomes a constant and public debt should not be used. The reason is rather simple: the tax base - consumption- changes just enough to support the change in public spending. Things become quite different when the elasticities differ. To facilitate insight into the basic analytics, we can combine the intertemporal and the flow budget constraint to see whether a shock induces a government to finance public spending with a deficit ($db/dt > 0$) or a surplus ($db/dt < 0$). The change in public debt is given by the following equation (combine eq. 7.46 and 7.48):

$$(7.50) \quad \dot{b} = (r - n)b(t) + g^* \left\{ \frac{g(t)}{g^*} - \frac{c(t)}{c^*} \right\} - \frac{c(t)}{c^*} b_0$$

or, by reshuffling some terms, one can also write (7.50) as:

$$(7.50') \quad \dot{b} = (r - n)b(t) + c(t) \left\{ \frac{g(t)}{c(t)} - \frac{g^*}{c^*} \right\} - \frac{c(t)}{c^*} b_0$$

From equation (7.50) we can discern three public debt implications of tax rate smoothing:

1. The deficit rises in a one-to-one relationship with $b(t)$ if the economy is dynamically efficient (which seems like a reasonable approximation of industrialised economies, see Abel et al. [1989] for the U.S. economy).

2. The central part of equation (7.50) concerns the endogenous

variables c and g. A shock has two effects per definition: an immediate or temporal effect ($c(t)$ and $g(t)$) and a permanent or lifetime effect (c^* and g^*). When public spending reacts immediately more heavily to a shock than private consumption ($g/g^* > c/c^*$), the government will finance this shock by initially running budget deficits, to be compensated later on by budget surpluses. The size of the financial response is multiplied by the permanent government expenditure, g^* (see eq. 7.50)

3. The deficit rises if a government initially has public wealth, $b_0 < 0$ (and vice versa for initial public debt). This is quite logical: if one has positive wealth, one can start depleting it by running a sequence of deficits.

We can also discern a relationship between the steady state public debt, b_∞, and the initial public debt by solving equation (7.50) for $db/dt = 0$:

$$(7.51) \quad b_\infty = \left\{ g^* \left[\frac{c(\infty)}{c^*} - \frac{g(\infty)}{g^*} \right] + \frac{c(\infty)}{c^*} b_0 \right\} . \rho^{-1}$$

One can immediately see that a smaller rate of time preference enables a government to sustain a larger steady state public debt.

The crucial aspect about whether government should run a deficit or a surplus depends on the endogenous reactions of public and private consumption. With the help of optimality condition (7.44) we can say that the level of public and private consumption varies according to the following condition[14] (for $\beta_1 = \beta_2$):

$$(7.52) \quad c(t) \gtreqless g(t) \text{ if } \sigma \lesseqgtr \gamma$$

and given (7.47),

$$(7.53) \quad \hat{c} \gtreqless \hat{g} \text{ if } \sigma \lesseqgtr \gamma$$

For cases where $\beta_1 \neq \beta_2$, one can get mixed settings. For example, if $\beta_2 > \beta_1$ but $\gamma > \sigma$ the level of private consumption can be either larger or smaller than public consumption. However, for a plausible set of utility shares ($\beta_1 > \beta_2$) and intertemporal elasticities, such as in the case where $\gamma > \sigma$ (i.e. public consumption is intertemporally less elastic than private consumption), one can still say that the level of private consumption is larger than the level of public consumption. Now let us consider, for simplicity's sake, the case where $\gamma > \sigma$ and $\beta_1 = \beta_2 = \frac{1}{2}$ and $b_0 = 0$. Whether the government finances public spending with budget deficits or with surpluses is, in a way, straightforward. Take for instance the case of a shock in population growth. For some time interval, $t \in [0,T)$, the domestic population growth rate, n^*, lies above the world population growth rate, n (assuming that the world interest rate equals the world population growth rate and the rate of time preference, i.e. $r = n + \rho$, with $\rho^* = \rho$, $n^* < n$).

---

14. The optimality condition $U_c = V_g$ can be written down explicitly as: $c(t) = (\beta_2/\beta_1)^{-1/\sigma} \cdot g(t)^{\gamma/\sigma}$, with the following extreme properties,

$$\lim_{\sigma \to \infty} c(t) = 1 \qquad \lim_{\beta_2 \uparrow 1} c(t) = 0 \qquad \lim_{\gamma \to 0} c(t) = (\beta_2/\beta_1)^{-1/\sigma}$$

At time T the domestic growth rate converges towards the world rate. This scenario of population growth decline essentially amounts to a permanent positive shock in lifetime wealth, as it affects the short-run discount factor, $R(t)$, over the planning horizon. It gives rise to an increase in lifetime private and public consumption, levels of consumption which initially exceed their temporal counterparts. Both private and public sector wealth rise according to the divergence in r and $\rho^* + n^*$. The initial reaction of a government is to finance the consequences of this shock by dissaving, in other words by running a deficit $(g/c > g^*/c^*)$. At some point in time the public consumption levels fall below the permanent consumption levels and government starts running budget surpluses. Of course, if the parameters are reversed, e.g. the domestic population growth rate lies for the time interval $[0,T)$ below the world population growth rate (or the same scenario but this time public consumption reacts more to shocks than private consumption), one would end up with the mirror image of the previous scenario. A government starts to build a trust fund and depletes this fund at some point in the future.

7.4 FISCAL POLICY IN AN INTERDEPENDENT WORLD ECONOMY

The previous section was set in a small open economy in which policymakers are assumed to commit themselves to their original plans. The strategic interaction with other countries and the endogeneity of factor prices has however been neglected. This extension is of some importance for the issue of economic policy under conditions of demographic change. The populations of industrialised countries are ageing and it is highly likely that this change will induce public spending increases. The problem of ageing will be apparent in all industrialised countries with some differences in the timing of the transition. However, one country may have a sharper increase in public spending than another country because of different preferences or production technologies. If we add to this observation the finding that the degree of capital mobility has increased in recent years (see Obstfeld [1986]), and is likely to increase even further in years to come, one can see the relevance of paying attention to international aspect of economic policy. Data on international interest rates and data on national saving and investment patterns (Feldstein and Horioka [1980]) are consistent with a world in which capital mobility is substantial, at least among OECD countries.

In considering the effects of fiscal policy in an inter-dependent world economy two issues are apparent:

1. Design: How should taxes be set with and without commitment?
2. Cooperation: Does cooperation of fiscal policies offer an improvement in welfare compared to a noncooperative solution?

To start with the first question, in the standard deterministic one-sector growth model, the optimal fiscal policy rules with commitment would not change very much in a two-country setting with international lending and borrowing. Institutions, as represented in a stylised manner by the No-Ponzi-game condition, require that the countries should not be net creditors or debtors in a present value sense. What has changed is the scope for smoothing tax rates. For a small open economy, the government can perfectly absorb shocks in public spending by borrowing and lending abroad. In an interdependent world economy one would obtain effects of public spending that are a mixture of the closed and small open economy. Complications arise if there is no commitment technology, and when there are

externalities to decision making that are not realised in a
noncooperative setting. In this section I therefore want to
discuss the issues of time consistency and cooperation.

7.4.1 TIME CONSISTENCY

Ever since the seminal paper by Kydland and Prescott [1977] the
economics profession has become aware of the dimension of time
in economic policy formulation[15]. Conventional analysis of
taxation proceeded along the lines of imposing the restriction
that governments or social planners should be committed to their
original plans for a considerable time. Economic policy
formulation in the western world, and I dare say in any possible
human world, is characterised by a succession of governments of
different colours. I stress the word colour and not so much the
usual distinction left wing/right wing. It is the place in time
which determines the colour of a government in office. It might
not come as a surprise to an inhabitant of such economies, that
an inconsistency arises due to unforeseen disturbances,
preference changes[16], miscalculated policy effects or simply a
difference between social and private objectives. A recent
strand in the literature of economics has, however, detected a
surprising fact of economic policy formulation, namely that time
inconsistency arises even when there is no uncertainty,
preferences are fixed, all agents have perfect foresight and the
government is completely benevolent. The reason why plans can be

---

15. It must be considered a serious caveat that the authors in
volumes I and II of the authorative *Handbook of Public Economics*
[1985,1987], edited by Alan Auerbach and Martin Feldstein, do
not even mention the issue of time consistency once.

16. The case of time inconsistency of plans as a consequence of
preference changes was examined by Strotz [1955-56].

time inconsistent can be explained in rather simple terms. *Ex ante*, before some choices have been made by the private sector, an optimal policy induces some reaction on the side of the private sector. But *ex post*, after the choices have been made, the response to the policy measures taken, may be very different from the ex ante response, which makes the ex post constraints of a government quite different from its ex ante constraints. Whenever there is an imperfection (such as externalities or distortions) which makes the ex ante policy second best rather than first best, there is ex post an incentive to deviate from the ex ante policy. Any dynamic economic policy suffers from this problem of time inconsistency unless, of course, a commitment technology is available or unless all players have the same objective (see Chari *et al.* [1989]). Public policy without commitment must therefore be sequentially rational, i.e. policy rules must maximise the social welfare function at each date given that private agents behave optimally. Likewise, optimality on the part of the private agents designing allocation rules, requires that they forecast future policies as being sequentially rational for society. A sequence of policy rules, allocations and prices that satisfy these conditions, is called a *time consistent* or *sustainable equilibrium* (cf. Chari [1988]).

Lucas and Stokey [1983] and Persson and Svensson [1984,1986] showed how an optimal tax policy will be rendered time consistent by the choice of the maturity structure of public debt. Time-consistency is only guaranteed when a government can manipulate intertemporal prices, a condition which is likely to be fulfilled in a closed economy. In a small open economy this possibility is lost and optimal fiscal policy cannot be rendered time-consistent. Since the domestic restructuring of the debt has been addressed in full by Lucas and Stokey [1983] and

Persson and Svensson [1984,1986], I will merely repeat some of the intuitive reasoning behind their solutions here. A source of time inconsistency is the non-stationarity of the shadow price of distortionary taxation or the *cost of public funds*. The ability of the government to influence the intertemporal prices can resolve the time-inconsistency problem. Persson and Svensson [1986] interpret it as follows. Think, for example, of a planning horizon T (where T approaches infinity). Each goverment has a set of T first-order conditions corresponding to the path of T tax rates that are the direct choice variable of each government. The reason why time $t > 0$-governments will choose tax rates in accordance with the plans of time $t = 0$-government, is found in the ability of each government to manipulate the debt structure, thereby influencing the T cash flows inherited by its successors. In effect, each government has T instruments to affect the T choice variables of its successors.

The optimal taxation problem becomes more complex in an interdependent world economy, since *ex ante* fiscal policies suffer from *double credibility* problems: one from the interaction between the dominant player/government and the follower/consumer, and one from the interaction between the two (or more) governments. In a world where private capital mobility is allowed and intertemporal prices are equalised, fiscal policy can still be made time consistent if each of the governments thinks itself large enough to affect the world interest rate. When governments treat the world interest rate parametrically, time-inconsistency will be the result, since each of the goverments will have lost the debt instrument to affect the constraints of its successors. Under those circumstances, only international policy coordination can be of help where the world government solves the 'closed' economy problem. Asymmetry in government behaviour can also lead to time inconsistency, even though one of the economies is large enough to influence its terms of trade and intertemporal prices. Persson and Svensson [1986] state that if a country is large enough to affect the $2T$ choice variables of its successors (i.e., T tax rates and T implicit interest taxes given by the difference between home and foreign interest rates), fiscal policy can be made time consistent by the use of the $2T$ debt instruments to influence the constraints of their successors, viz. the debt structure of both the domestic and foreign debt. When one of the countries is a Stackelberg-leader and the other player is a follower, the follower cannot make his fiscal policy time consistent and subsequently, the foreign debt demanded c.q. supplied by the follower will not coincide with the optimal foreign debt as would have been materialised under conditions of commitment.

Persson *et al.* [1987] and Kotlikoff *et al.* [1988] have enriched the standard model of Lucas and Stokey [1983] with extra assets, thereby finding a way around the problem of time-inconsistent discretionary behaviour. Persson *et al.* [1987] extend the analysis to an economy with money, so that a government chooses distortionary inflation taxes (i.e. money growth rates) in addition to wage tax rates. A restructuring scheme still exists which makes the second-best policy credible: the benefit of raising revenue by the issue of seigniorage is counteracted by a loss of revenue if the government holds claims on the private sector in the form of nominal bonds. If each government inherits a zero nominal position against the private sector, the incentive for an ex post surprise inflation will disappear.

The majority of these models of optimal taxation are however restricted to economies without capital, thereby reducing the applicability of the time-consistency result to actual economies. To circumvent credibility problems with a capital levy, Kotlikoff *et al.* [1988] introduce social contracts. In a model with overlapping generations, the old in each period have an incentive to tax already accumulated capital in order to avoid distortionary wage taxation. A social contract, which prescribes the second-best policy, may effectively be sold from each generation to the next by an intergenerational transfer from young to old. If the social contract is violated it becomes valueless, and the prospective capital loss introduces a cost for ex post deviations that may help enforcing an equilibrium with no capital levy.

The critical assumption in models of time inconsistency concerns the expectations of individuals with respect to the future government policies. In the absence of a commitment technology, governments can achieve the equilibrium path that approaches or coincides with the equilibrium path of a government with commitment. However, a government has to use trigger strategies to support such sustainable equilibria (Chari [1988]). The difficulty with policy design in such environments is that whenever government deviates from its original plans, people's beliefs can change quite dramatically. In the case of trigger strategies: small changes in one player's decision - the government - trigger large changes by other players. Sometimes, when a policy change is seen as a desirable move, the public might expect a change in policy regime, leading to large and undesirable outcomes. The theoretical implication of modelling the interaction between government and individuals in this fashion, is that sustainable equilibria can only be supported by discontinuous changes in people's beliefs. The practical implication of this result is that a government can forestall the problem of undesirable (large) reactions to a change in government policy by undertaking those changes only after extensive public debate, so that a government can bring about the change in beliefs.

7.4.2 COOPERATION VERSUS NONCOOPERATION

International trade and finance theories of interdependent economies are dominated by the question whether cooperation provides extra benefits compared to the case of noncooperation. In each case one has to formulate explicitly how policymakers interact. The idea that social welfare can differ under these two regimes presupposes that policymakers have some monopoly power in affecting relative prices. As noted by some authors (Frenkel and Razin [1985], Chari and Kehoe [1990a]), some results on fiscal policy cooperation are similar to those obtained in the optimal tariff literature. Substantial distortions and a reduction in world welfare can be the result if governments cannot commit to cooperation. These distortions arise from monopoly power. As one would expect from results obtained in the optimal tariff literature, these distortions vanish if countries become small compared to the rest of the world. Countries are thus back in surroundings of perfect competition, where they are led by Smith's invisible hand to promote social well-being. Chari and Kehoe [1990a] show in a *static* international trade model with two commodities, that the optimal tariff result holds for fiscal policies if a government has access to lump-sum taxes. In case the government is relatively large, public spending can affect world relative prices and the noncooperative equilibrium yields a lower level of welfare than the cooperative equilibrium. If countries become small this particular distortion vanishes and the two regimes of cooperation converge. However, the analogy with the tariff result ceases if public goods are financed with distortionary taxes: even though countries may become small in the limit, the cooperative and noncooperative policies are generally different. Domestic distortions seem to be unremovable, and international cooperation can offer welfare gains that surpass the economic policy choice made in markets where governments have no monopoly power. The basic insight behind the Chari and Kehoe [1990a] result is that governments in a static setting may not be aware of the fact that there is an externality to the coordination of fiscal policies. In a cooperative framework, i.e. an equilibrium in which governments choose policy jointly to maximise a world objective function, the marginal rates of substitution (MRS) between private and public consumption are equated to the marginal rates of transformation. In a noncooperative equilibrium, allocations will generally differ because each government chooses its fiscal policy taking the world price as given. Governments try to equate the MRS between private goods to the world price, and at the same time they try to establish the equality of the marginal utility of private and public consumption. These two goals are in conflict. On the one hand, the distortionary consumption tax drives a wedge between the MRS between private goods and the world price. The first goal can be achieved by setting the tax rate equal to zero. On the other hand, one needs to set a non-negative tax if governments want to achieve the second goal. The optimal fiscal policy in a noncooperative regime involves a certain trade-off between these two goals of which neither is achieved completely. In the cooperative equilibrium case, governments recognise that the world price does not reflect the MRS between private goods of other countries' consumers because of tax distortions. Thus, with a global objective function, governments seek to equate MRS across countries.

The Chari and Kehoe [1990a] model of cooperation was, however, set in a static model of international trade, in order to avoid the problems associated with the time inconsistency of optimal policy. Examining the desirability of cooperation in a dynamic setting has given rise to a host of counterintuitive results. Rogoff [1985a] was perhaps one of the first to challenge the standard view that cooperation among countries is desirable. He shows for a simple monetary two-country model that cooperation leads to a lower level of welfare than noncooperation does. Criticism of Rogoff's startling result was aimed at one of his key assumptions, viz. the objective function of each country's policy maker does not coincide with the objective function of the indigenous population (see Canzoneri and Henderson [1988]). The Rogoff result could indeed be overturned under conditions of microeconomically founded public policy and it may lead one to interpret the Rogoff result as follows: if policy makers form a coalition against the private sector, the policy makers may be worse off than if they do not cooperate. The crux of the Rogoff result does not entirely rest on the difference of individual and government preferences. For example, Kehoe [1989] has shown that cooperative equilibria may be Pareto-dominated by noncooperative equilibria, in the case of representative governments with the use of capital taxation interacting in a (dynamic) two-country world economy. This nonoptimality result follows directly from the fact that the cooperative equilibrium is time inconsistent, whereas in a non-cooperative two-country setting competition among governments produces a different set of incentive constraints, viz. that the tax on capital should always be zero. The intuition behind this result is that competition[17] may perform the role of a

---

17. In a two-country inflation tax model with a somewhat different notion of equilibrium, Van der Ploeg [1988, pp. 12-15] comes to more or less the same conclusion: competitive decision-

commitment technology. It forces governments to act in
accordance with the rules of competition instead of the rules of
monopoly.

In a somewhat different setting, Buiter and Kletzer [1991]
have shown that in a standard overlapping generations model,
where conditions that deliver Ricardian equivalence are absent
and fiscal policy is time consistent[18], government can use lump-
sum transfers to affect both the static and intertemporal terms
of trade. It can alter the pattern of saving and consumption and
it allows in effect the government to exploit the country's size
in world trade and international lending and borrowing. The
strategic use of lump-sum taxes does not result in overall loss
in world surplus. It does, however, imply that a redistribution
of total surplus will take place between foreign residents and
the domestic population. The difficulty with evaluating
cooperation is the construction of a yardstick that measures
welfare. In an interdependent world economy one should make a
distinction between Pareto-optimality with respect to individual
preferences and the preferences of policy makers, separately and
jointly. Lump-sum redistributions chosen by the planners under
free trade and complete capital mobility, assure that the
equilibrium is Pareto optimal with respect to the individuals'
preferences. While policies necessary for a Pareto-optimal
equilibrium growth path for a two-country world economy under
free capital mobility need not be coordinated, a Pareto optimum
with respect to the two national planners' preferences and a

---

making has a built-in *disincentive* to renege plans.

18. Buiter and Kletzer [1991] adopt a utilitarian social welfare
function as constructed by Calvo and Obstfeld [1988]; a function
that requires no constraints on government behaviour to assure
time consistency of the command optima.

global social optimum are attained only through coordinated policy selection. The reason why cooperation is necessary, is similar to the static case: with noncooperative behaviour (say Nash behaviour) the social planners will not face the same shadow prices of capital.

If one goes one step further, the optimisation of global social welfare in a world with perfect capital mobility requires, besides coordination, the use of intergenerational transfers within each country, and international lump-sum transfers between countries. The basic insight Buiter and Kletzer [1991] offer with this result is that to ascertain competitive equilibrium allocations to be global social optima, there must be scope for lump-sum redistributions between *all* agents alive at the same time. If these international transfers are infeasible, one can still achieve the global second best by either: (i) the use of intergenerational lump-sum redistribution to affect the world interest rate and thus the international distribution between debtors and creditors; or (ii) policies that affect the payments to the immobile factor, labour. Governments can create wage differentials by subsidising investment in one country and taxing it in the other. An example of the first solution would be a redistribution towards the old; such a policy would raise the interest rate and this increase will redistribute resources from borrowers to lenders.

Needless to say, the elements of cooperation discussed here in short are but one aspect of the plethora of issues concerning cooperation and coordination (see for a broader discussion Horne and Masson [1988]).

7.5 SUMMARY

Dynamic fiscal policy design in a world characterised by changes in parameters is difficult to characterise precisely. Non-stationary population growth is such a real world phenomenon and a case in point when it comes to considering the fiscal policy consequences of such a development. This chapter aimed at bringing together some literature on the question of dynamic optimal taxation and examined principles of taxation.

Tax rate smoothing and its extreme version, tax rate constancy, is a simple policy guideline which applies to the case of a government that encounters shocks in public spending. It borrows a leaf from the static theory of optimal taxation where uniform taxation applies, given suitable symmetry, homogeneity and separability assumptions. The dynamic conditions under which tax rate constancy applies narrow the proposition down to conditions of (i) additive separable utility function; (ii) constant (compensated) consumption elasticity with respect to the consumption tax; and (iii) time-consistent fiscal policy. The case of non-stationary population growth is merely an application of this constant tax rule. In the absence of the possibility of running a Ponzi-game, a distortionary consumption tax should depend on the discounted present value of government spending divided by the discounted present value of consumption (or more generally the tax base). This principle of dynamic optimal taxation implies that, at times of relatively low public spending, a government should accumulate a trust fund (or a 'war chest') to smooth the tax rate across periods of relatively high public spending. One should however never forget that posing a question in (time-)symmetric terms implies already a symmetric answer. In addition, it should be noticed that the countercyclical use of budget deficits that characterises the economy if a government adheres to the 'tax smoothing' principle, has no connection with the Keynesian notion of countercyclical fiscal policy or stabilisation policy, although the constant tax does work as a stabiliser. The neoclassical argument is based on an equilibrium approach of the business cycle, while the Keynesian theory refers to markets in disequilibrium.

In case of inelastic labour supply and utility separability in public and private consumption, the fiscal policy choice between consumption taxation and the use of public debt can give rise to a first-best allocation, only if a government keeps the consumption tax rate *constant*. Although it is a knife-edge case, it proves that public debt has an important role to play in a world characterised by change and that a flat rate tax need not be distortionary at all times. Furthermore, if public and private consumption are equally intertemporally elastic, one need not use public debt, since any shock is absorbed by the change in the tax base, viz. consumption.

In an interdependent world economy, the standard questions of optimal taxation should be extended to cover questions of time consistency and cooperation. Optimal cooperative policy internalises the externalities by maximising a weighted sum of the objectives of the fiscal authorities concerned. Questions of time consistency reveal that optimal fiscal policy is extremely vulnerable to hierarchies in economic decision making in an interdependent world economy. The state of the art is quite sophisticated in terms of game theoretic constructs, and time and again one wonders how sophisticated policy design should be to find a solution. A serious caveat in the development of the field of dynamic economic policy is the absence of measurement of the welfare loss of time inconsistency.

The practical message for ageing societies is that in the long-run governments should base their fiscal policies, c.q tax rates, on the ratio of the present discounted value of public spending (plus the initial public debt) and the present discounted value of the tax base. In this model this amounts to per capita consumption. This latter variable is likely to be higher in a steady state that is characterised by a lower population growth rate. An economy moving over time to a lower population growth rate can initially run budget deficits, in the case where public consumption is intertemporally less elastic than private consumption. The running of budget deficits with a declining population is contrary to conventional wisdom. One of the open questions of economic theory is, however, how technical change, tastes and demography interact. For example, if a relatively old population structure results in a lower rate of technical progress or a change in the composition of public and private consumption, the public financial consequences of ageing or population decline may well be overturned. If ageing implies higher public spending and a *smaller* tax base, it would be in accordance with principles of optimality to form a trust fund now, by fixing the tax rate(s) at levels which can cover the future level of public spending. A government accumulates assets (i.e. buys public bonds), since the constant tax rates are in excess of the level of public spending of today.

The transition in the next 30-40 years can in effect be smoothed *if* the population growth settles down to a stationary rate. The crux of policy design for an ageing society is whether the change in (total) fertility is permanent or temporary and how parameters of taste develop over time. Although the first element of uncertainty in economic policy design could be incorporated it would not modify the basic insights offered by the principle of tax rate smoothing[19].

---

19. See Kingston [1989] for an extension to stochastic environments. Tax rate constancy applies if, in addition to the conditions of section 7.3.1, there is constant relative risk aversion.

CHAPTER 8: ECONOMIC POLICY IN A DEMOGRAPHICALLY DIVIDED WORLD

*"At this festive season of the year, Mr. Scrooge," said the
gentleman, taking up a pen, "it is more than usually desirable
that we should make some slight provision for the poor and
destitute, who suffer greatly at the present time. Many
thousands are in want of common necessaries; hundreds of
thousands are in want of common comforts, sir."
"Are there no prisons?" asked Scrooge.
"Plenty of prisons," said the gentleman, laying down the pen
again.
"And the Union workhouses?" demanded Scrooge.
"Are they still in operation?"
"They are. Still," returned the gentleman, "I wish I could say
they were not."
"The Treadmill and the Poor Law are in full vigour, then?" said
Scrooge.
"Both very busy, sir."
"Oh! I was afraid, from what you said at first, that something
had occurred to stop them in their useful course," said Scrooge
"I am very glad to hear it."*

A Christmas Carol, Charles Dickens [1843]

Practical questions of economic policy are sometimes solved by
methods of Uncle Scrooge, in other words, by defining the
problem away. The economic policy consequences of ageing are a
case in point when it comes to solving problems by definition.
The problem of financing expenditures on social security during
periods of demographic change has until now been approached in a
rather pragmatic way by governments and their advisers. The
lowering of benefit levels, an increase of the retirement age,
an increase of the social security premiums c.q. tax rates or
simply the promotion of fertility, are all policy options which
have far-reaching consequences for the intergenerational
distribution of resources and economic growth. Of course, such

solutions do not conform to economic principles but to principles of accounting. Foresight should be the essence of government. The principle of dynamic economic policy is that one has to make a choice between scarce means to achieve given ends over a certain planning horizon. Decisions about the choice of particular ends is not an economic subject, it belongs to the field of ethics in the case of normative questions and political science in the case of positive questions. As Lionel Robbins has argued persuasively, economics can only illustrate how one can satisfy given ends "in so far as the achievement of *any* end is dependent on scarce means" [1935, p. 24]. This classical viewpoint and the modesty that goes with it is still shared by many economists today. E.g., Lucas [1990b, p. 667] asserts that:

> "Theory does not provide us a blanket vindication of any
> single universally applicable policy conclusion, but it
> does provide a coherent framework for examining specific
> policy interventions on their merits, case by case. I
> think it is a mistake to ask more than this from
> economic analysis."

The analysis of the policy implications of demographic developments is perhaps one of the most debatable questions around. Populations perform a dual role in economies. On the one hand, they are the decision makers who determine fluctuations in economic activity through various allocation mechanisms; and on the other hand, they are one of the endowments of an economy. In designing intertemporal economic policy rules, one must decide whether one should take account of future generations in contemporary decisions. The difficulty with this aspect of economic policy is that an asymmetry arises in the treatment of future generations: the initial decisionmaker can take account of future generations by leaving a bequest, but who guarantees that future generations will take account of past (or deceased) generations? Traditional welfare economics largely addressed policy options that have no effect on the number of persons nor their personal identities. New extensions deal with the issue of endogenous fertility, i.e. when members of the present generation decide on how many individuals will exist in the next generation and the possibilities they face (see Parfit [1984] and Dasgupta [1988]). Although I could have started from scratch with models of endogenous fertility, I have remained within the bounds of traditional welfare economics since the problem of a demographically divided world still has not been dealt with in a satisfactory way.

In this closing chapter I first want to sum up the main findings concerning economic policy in a demographically divided world (section 8.1), and then point out some caveats and qualifications of the models used in this thesis (section 8.2). The dual role of the latter section is to guide thoughts on future research on the interaction between demography and economics.

8.1 ECONOMIC POLICY IN A DEMOGRAPHICALLY DIVIDED WORLD

In this thesis I have tried to disentangle the most important issues at stake in a demographically divided world. The economic consequences of demographic division are challenging, in a practical as well as a theoretical sense. There is, however, also the danger that the demographic division of countries with different population growth rates will remain as it is today. If the joint objective of economic policy is concerned with the average world welfare, one will encounter a situation of an ever decreasing level of welfare that eventually ends up in a world that 'enjoys' the welfare of the developing world. In case each region is concerned with its own welfare, the prospects are equally repugnant, viz. a world in which widespread poverty reigns amidst negligible plenty. If the developing world *does* complete the transition to the status of 'developed', the world capital market will become increasingly dependent on the developments in large economies, such as in India and China. In the past and at present, the role of developing countries in international capital markets is of a secondary nature, since the amount of saving established in these countries was and is small compared to the amount of consumption foregone in technologically superior countries, such as Japan and Germany. Up to 1950 the developed world made up roughly 30% of the world population (see Table 8.1). Anno 1989, the developed world makes up approximately 23% of the world population. One should,

TABLE 8.1: DEMOGRAPHICALLY DIVIDED WORLD 1900-1989 (in millions)

	1900	1950	1989
Developing regions	1,070	1,681	3,954
Africa	133	224	626
Asia[a]	867	1,292	2,886
Latin America	70	165	442
Developed regions	560	835	1,209
Europe, USSR, Japan, Oceania	478	669	936
Canada, USA	82	166	273
World	1,630	2,516	5,162

a) Excluding Japan

Source: World Resources Institute [1988]

however, change these figures for the age-group that makes decisions on saving and dissaving. By excluding children below the age of 15 years, the developed world covers 27% of the 'adult' world population.

The *practical* challenge is to make the transition through policy actions to a world economy in which the world population is stable and stationary, and in which the environment is left intact. The reason why it would be reasonable to strive for a zero population growth rate is that the world is a finite renewable resource if one treats it well, and it is likely to become an exhaustible resource if it is treated badly. The relatively high consumption levels of the developed world makes one wonder whether the transition of developing countries, such as India and China, to the status of 'developed' is a viable option if these countries adopt the current living standard of industrialised countries. Table 8.2 gives an impression of the per capita use of commercial energy in the world. Problems of acidic deposition, climate change and stratospheric ozone depletion are already exacerbated by wasteful energy use. Therefore, a positive population growth rate for the world as a whole is bound to lead to repugnant conclusions in a world economy with a finite carrying capacity. Practical measures of "decreasing the surplus population" seem to be family planning programmes and the education of people. Especially the last option is recognised as a measure that may yield lasting effects on population developments in developing countries (see Schultz [1990]), while this option still guarantees the 'freedom to choose'. The wealth of nations is to a large extent embodied in the knowledge and abilities of the people. The externality that knowledge may have on population growth is a point neglected in this thesis but it may be worthwile pursuing this point further.

The *theoretical* challenge of a demographically divided world economy is to discover behavioural rules that can lead to a better world than the situation in which two entities remain autarkic. Dixit [1981, p. 283] once drew attention to the theoretical difficulties involved in the treatment of different growth rates in countries engaging in international trade: "...during the course of the supposed steady state, trading prices must change from the autarky prices of one country to

TABLE 8.2: PER CAPITA CONSUMPTION OF COMMERCIAL ENERGY

	1986 (gigajoules)	Perc. change over the period 1970-1986
Africa	12	44
North and Central America	195	n.a.
U.S.A.	278	-12
Canada	284	10
Mexico	47	54
South America	30	n.a.
Asia	20	n.a.
China	21	106
Japan	106	13
India	8	97
Europe	130	18
France	114	1
Germany	166	10
Netherlands	211	57
U.K.	157	n.a.
U.S.S.R.	187	54
Oceania	145	35
World	56	9

Source: World Resources Institute [1988]

those of the other". These consequences of different growth rates are "inconsistent with the logic of a steady state". The Global Golden Rules (of Chapter 3), which apply to the centralised case of a planner that governs investment in a two-region world, constitute a simple way of modelling influences of countries with different sizes and growth rates in an interdependent world economy. If one decentralises decision making in this two-country world, and imposes the property that the rich country cares about the (unweighted) per capita welfare in the poor country, there is a limit to the help the rich country can offer to the poor country when population growth rates differ. If the planner of the rich country uses the Benthamite objective of total utility, the rich country will generally keep on transferring resources to the poor country. The weighted objective function gives an ever increasing (relative) weight to the welfare of the poorer country. The attitude of the rich country would, however, be quite naive: the help it offers hardly affects per capita welfare, whereas the Millian planner is more realistic (but harsh) in that it cares about the entire nation's standard of living.

In a more 'decentralised' planning problem with constant rates of time preference (Chapter 4), the only condition which has to be fulfilled is the convergence of population growth rates at some point in time. In case this 'transversality' condition does not materialise, and we encounter a permanent difference between population growth rates, the country with the high population growth rate will act in the long run as if it is a closed economy borrowing a negligible amount (in per capita terms) from the country with the low population growth rate. The country with the low population growth rate will eventually act as a small open economy with the world interest rate permanently higher than the autarkic interest rate. The change in consumption in the high growth country will approach zero as the world population growth rate coincides with the high population growth rate eventually, while the consumption in the low growth country will accelerate as time goes by, since the population growth divergence increases with time. One must, however, consider the normative significance of the resulting outcome. A state of ever increasing indebtedness and a non-stationary world wealth distribution with a steadily increasing number of people living on a subsistence level are undesirable outcomes and it is subsequently ruled out by authors as Ramsey [1928] and Lucas and Stokey [1984]. A possible avenue for analysing a demographically divided world is to make the rate of time preference depend on present consumption levels and the utility thereof. In such a setting the social planner of the relatively low population growth rate will not postpone consumption forever and he will start consuming today what otherwise would never have been consumed. In case population growth rates diverge, the ultimate steady state is characterised by a small open economy with a relatively high rate of time preference and a large, almost closed, economy with a relatively low rate of time preference.

Another policy option in a demographically divided world is closing the population growth gap by migration flows. To simply move people permanently from one country to the other, turns out to be a misguided policy measure (Chapter 5). First of all, in a one-sector world economy this may not be so surprising if one thinks of the world as an integrated closed economy. Moving people from one region to the other does not change the world population growth rate and its economic consequences. Secondly, in a more decentralised fashion the reason for being cautious with the instrument of immigration is that under quite general conditions, selective immigration will give rise to a (negative) capital dilution effect that dominates the (positive) free rider effect of not paying for the training costs of the attracted skilled labour. Only under exceptional circumstances, e.g., if the developing world is inhabited by people who are ten times smarter (i.e. less costly to train) than the people in the developed world, a brain drain would be a beneficial arrangement. A selective immigration policy is, by and large, an inferior policy to the policy of training indigenous labour. The practical implication is that countries are well advised to educate their own labour force and not introduce a selective immigration policy.

The second part of this thesis has been devoted to the discussion of the fiscal policy implications of demographic change. First of all, the possibility of debt neutrality in a world characterised by demographic change was discussed in Chapter 6. A government that chooses any combination of lump-sum taxes and public debt to finance a given flow of public expenditures, will not influence the intertemporal resource allocation of the private sector. The premises that deliver this result, better known as debt neutrality, or the Ricardian equivalence of taxation and deficit finance, are, however, farfetched if one pays attention to demographic stylised facts: lifetime is uncertain, migration is widespread, families are not all that altruistic, the population may differ in terms of borrowing-risk characteristics and finally, future population and the fiscal consequences thereof are uncertain. The overall conclusion is that public debt matters in a world characterised by demographic change, or stated in a more straightforward manner: (1) in a closed economy the decision to substitute budget deficits for current taxation affects real factor prices, interest rates and wages, and tax cuts will generally make present generations better off at the expense of future generations; (2) in a small open economy, budget deficits would have a negligible effect on factor prices. Persistent budget deficits do, however, affect the amount of borrowing and lending, thereby giving rise to the possibility of twin deficits (i.e. a current account and a public budget deficit) in case the government is the only party engaged in international lending. In an interdependent world economy, one would obtain a mixture of the economic consequences of fiscal policies in a small open and closed economy.

To frame the dynamic fiscal policy question of demographic change in a slightly more realistic environment, I have discussed in Chapter 7 the use of a distortionary tax - an *ad valorem* consumption tax - in combination with public debt and endogenous public spending for a small open economy. The interaction of these elements is pivotal for understanding public finance questions in an economy characterised by demographic change. A changing tax base and a change in the demand for public goods are likely to occur simultaneously. Given these probable developments one must try and discern robust policy guidelines. The policy rule that can be extracted from the analysis of Chapter 7, is that tax rates should be constant across time and should be set in such a manner that it equals the present discounted value of public spending (plus initial public debt) divided by the present discounted value of the tax base, which amounts to consumption in the case of chapter 7. Perfect foresight of government enables one to save resources in the good times and deplete this fund in the bad times. The property of tax rate constancy is however derived under quite limiting assumptions regarding preferences and market conditions: (i) the utility of leisure, private and public consumption are additively separable; (ii) the compensated elasticity of consumption with respect to a tax change is constant; and (iii) economic policy is time consistent. In a way, the guideline of tax smoothing is not essentially different from the proposal made by Keynes in 1939 on *How to Pay for the War*[1]. The finance of war and peace is still a policy issue and if one expects a war, the theory of public finance suggests that one should not go to war on a 'pay-as-you-go' basis. Accumulating a 'war chest' or trust fund is more likely to be sound economic policy. However, if war strikes a country as a 'Blitzkrieg', the accumulation of a war chest which preceeds the event of war, is an option impossible. One can only resort to spreading the burden of taxation by partly financing the war by the issuance of public debt. Demographic changes may not be entirely different from the economic consequences of war and peace. The economic consequences of ageing can be foreseen to a large extent, since the births of today are the work force of tomorrow and the work force of today is the group of old-aged of tomorrow. The practical policy implication of this tax smoothing principle is to accumulate a trust fund now to smooth the increase in public spending in the near future.

Among the different settings there is indeed one case where a consumption tax does *not* lead to second-best allocations. If the levels of private and public consumption are independent, and labour supply is inelastic, a flat rate consumption tax will not induce any distortions. The theorem of tax rate smoothing confirms the common sense intuition towards dynamic economic policy. Indeed, if one wants to act the historian one must concede that neither Barro nor Friedman were the originators of

---

1. It should be remembered that Keynes actually wrote *How to Pay for the War* before the start of the second world war. The book, published in February 1940, developed from two long articles that Keynes wrote for *The Times*, which appeared 14 and 15 November 1939.

the idea of 'smoothing' but the idea can be traced back to the biblical records of Genesis (41:1-45), where Joseph interprets the Pharaoh's dreams and gives the advice to smooth the (expected) yields of seven abundant and seven lean years. One must, however, realise that by posing a question set in a time-symmetric environment, one is bound to receive a time-symmetric answer. Given the ambiguous empirical results, one should perhaps either pay attention to the conditions that violate tax rate constancy, or develop the theory of dynamic optimal taxation by focussing on possible channels of preference drift.

In an interdependent world economy, tax rate smoothing is still a property which guides economic policy actions, but the extent to which tax rates can be smoothed depends on the economic developments abroad. The inherent difficulty of models of an interdependent world economy is that, under certain plausible conditions, the property of time consistency is lost. In a closed economy, the government could render fiscal policy time consistent by manipulating the maturity structure of public debt in such a fashion that subsequent governments will not depart from the original plan. In an open economy this opportunity is only left open for a (Stackelberg) leader in the world economy. Small open economies, Stackelberg followers and Nash equilibria are settings in which the fiscal authority cannot influence the intertemporal terms of trade. Under those circumstances, cooperation should be the intermediate objective in order to internalise the externalities of joint decision making. In a different setting (capital taxation, inflation tax), the desirability of cooperation may not be as evident as public discussions suggest. The absence of competition among fiscal authorities may create an environment in which incentives exist that give rise to a time-inconsistent equilibrium.

8.2 QUALIFICATIONS AND POSSIBLE EXTENSIONS

Economic policy seems simple enough if one frames questions in
equally simple models. The optimal control solution to the
optimal growth problem in a closed economy is usually referred
to as playing a game 'against nature'. There is only one
immortal decision maker who has complete control, whereas its
trading partner, Mother Nature, will always give way to this
decision maker. As soon as more agents are introduced into the
model, such as explicit trading partners or successive
governments, the resource allocation problem becomes more
complex since one has to spell out who gains and who loses from
trade. A heterogenous population can give rise to (static)
strategic interactions whereas the succession of governments or
generations can give rise to a problem known as the
inconsistency of optimal plans (see Kydland and Prescott
[1977]), or dynamic strategic interactions. At this point it may
therefore seem like a good opportunity to point out the
qualifications and pitfalls one may encounter when discussing
economic policy.

Dynamic inconsistency occurs when a future policy decision
that forms part of an optimal plan formulated at an initial date
is no longer optimal from the viewpoint of a later date, even
though no new information has appeared in the meantime. This
simple though path breaking result has led to a host of
intertemporal planning insights which were kept in the dark by
the assumption that policy rules are set out and adhered to
forever. The phenomenon of time inconsistency puts government
behaviour in an entirely new daylight. Previously, one would
only have discussed the possible mechanisms, such as reputation,
in policy conduct in a 'cocktail hour' fashion (although the
discussion will continue to be larded with platitudes if

measurement does not keep up with theory). Dynamic inconsistency
is a major argument for the use of policy *rules* rather than
discretion. Further developments have analysed the trade-off
between the gains from flexibility produced by discretion and
the losses due to dynamic inconsistency (see Rogoff [1985b]).
The game-theoretic approach of economic policy puts a stress on
the credibility of policy makers. E.g., it is possible that a
rational concern for reputation by policy makers will produce
time consistent behaviour (see Barro and Gordon [1983]). It may
also help to understand why governments of different persuasions
pursue a certain fiscal policy not consistent with their
behaviour had they been in power in the future. Persson and
Svensson [1989] show why a conservative government will collect
less revenue in taxes and leave more public debt than its
liberal successor would prefer. And conversely, a 'stubborn' or
'pragmatic' liberal government would choose to borrow less if it
knew it would be succeeded by a more conservative government. Up
and till today the theory of time inconsistency has been strong
on game-theoretic expositions but rather poor on empirical
testing. In a field so rich in different settings, measurement
is certainly no luxury. Economic policy is in dire need of
quantitative answers as to the desirability and feasibility of
certain actions of interference. Simulation of certain policy
actions offers a help in answering questions of an "How big?"
nature. The welfare costs of monopoly and the stabilisation of
business cycles, as calculated by Harberger [1954] and his
former graduate student Lucas [1987], respectively, have
provoked many policy-minded economists by the assertion that
scope for welfare improvements by means of public action is
negligible. Although one may be overwhelmed by the highly
technical analysis, one should always bear in mind that certain
calculations are not as 'model free' as their authors argue.

This thesis has not pursued such empirical goals and they may be interesting in their own right. For example, how big are the welfare costs of balancing the public budget against the alternative of tax rate smoothing? When these costs are considered small[2], a balanced budget may not be so bad after all, since the fiscal discipline, necessary for a successful 'tax rate smoothing' policy, does not seem to be one of the most distinguishing marks of politicians. An equally important issue is the question "How big are the welfare improvements of cooperation of fiscal and monetary policies?" The answers to this question are particularly vulnerable to the formulation of common objective functions and the type of market in which public authorities interact.

Another shortcoming of the models presented in this thesis is the abstraction from aspects of technical progress, market imperfections, different goods and adjustment costs in investment. Incorporation of each element would, of course, tone down some of the conclusions. Despite these more realistic elements, I still think the principles of economic policy derived in this thesis are relevant. Adding realism starts to count when one tries to calibrate the models to actual economies and when one tries to *quantify* welfare gains and losses.

The principles derived in this thesis are straightforward calculations of a non-stable world population. Future research of questions of the economic consequences of a demographically divided world should perhaps concentrate on threshold levels in

---

2. This is what the calculations by Cutler *et al.* [1990] suggest. However, the level of aggregation makes their analysis quite intractable and the outcome suspect. E.g., the small efficiency losses of a variable tax rate could have been the result of (unintentional) interest rate smoothing; this would indeed be the case where optimality is the result of innocence rather than design.

economies. Thresholds refer to the regions of control in the
presence of multiple equilibria, where below a certain level of
the state variables, the economy unwinds until it reaches an
inferior equilibrium. Above the critical cut-off point the
economy approaches the stable, more desirable, stable
equilibrium. In general, there are four threshold levels which
are important for the understanding of the interaction between
population and economic activity, viz. (1) production
technology; (2) carrying capacity of natural resources; (3) the
function of children; and (4) debt accumulation. These threshold
levels are basic for the understanding of the myriad of
development problems.

The thresholds in production imply that multiple equilibria
are possible, of which some could be unstable. It may not be
optimal to accumulate capital because the marginal product of
capital is so low, it will take too long to get to the point
where capital accumulation pays off. Recent studies indicate
that technology thresholds exist in the accumulation of human
capital. Standard one-sector neoclassical growth models exhibit
the property that economies with basically similar technologies
will converge to a common balanced growth path. The stylised
facts point (see Azariadis and Drazen [1990]), however, in the
direction of the existence of similar countries with a wide and
persistent divergence in growth rates.

The threshold called 'carrying capacity' is perhaps the most
vital one. The point where the use of a renewable resource turns
it into an exhaustible resource[3] is crucial for understanding
development problems and some unstable trajectories in the
demographic transition. The fall in mortality preceeds the fall
in birth rates, which leads to quite high population growth

---

3. Koopmans [1980] discusses the reverse side of this problem.

increases. Once populations expand to the point where their demands exceed the sustainable yield of natural resources, they begin to consume directly or indirectly the resource base itself. Forest and grasslands disappear, water tables fall and soils erode with the ultimate danger that countries will never complete the demographic transition. This negative externality of births is not easily recognised by individuals. Table 8.3 gives an impression of the sustainability of populations in Africa.

TABLE 8.3: MEASURES OF SUSTAINABILITY IN SEVEN AFRICAN COUNTRIES[a] BY ECOLOGICAL ZONES, 1980

	Food			Fuelwood		
Zone	Agriculturally Sustainable Population	Actual Rural Population	Food Dis- parity	Fuelwood Sustainable Population	Actual Total Population	Fuel Dis- parity
			(million)			
Sahelo-Saharan	1.0	1.8	−0.8	0.1	1.8	−1.7
Sahelian	3.9	3.9	0.0	0.3	4.0	−3.7
Sahelo-Sadunian	8.7	11.1	−2.4	6.0	13.1	−7.1
Sadunian	8.9	6.6	2.3	7.4	8.1	−0.7
Sahelo-Guinean	13.8	3.6	10.2	7.1	4.0	3.1
Total	36.3	27.0	9.3	20.9	31.0	−10.1

a) Burkina Faso, Chad, Gambia, Mali, Mauritania, Niger, and Senegal. The five ecological zones are delineated by amounts of rainfall.

Source: Worldbank [1985]

In the two most northern zones, where the rainfall is lowest, sustainable agricultural and fuelwood yields are already being matched or exceeded. In all countries and all zones, forests have less capacity than croplands and grazing lands to support people sustainably. Although one can, of course, increase the carrying capacity of certain resources, such as cropland, by investment in capital and technology, other resources are inherently fixed without some fundamental technological breakthrough. The Worldbank [1985] concludes in a down-to-earth manner that the "available intensive production techniques that would increase the carrying capacity have not proven sufficiently remunerative for wide adoption, despite the pressure on land". A viable policy alternative can therefore be sought in decreasing the population to a more sustainable level. Although I discuss the sustainability of populations for the case of developing countries here, it could equally apply to the developed world, where the situation is more acute. Taking into consideration the quite drastic environmental pollution in the developed world, the population decline, which some industralised countries already experience, may indeed be a blessing in disguise.

This brings me to the third threshold level, viz. the function of children. In primitive societies the (extended) family performs a dominant role as a resource allocation mechanism. Within the family children function, for instance, as social security, production factor and status symbol. With the introduction of a social security system provided by the State children loose their function as old-age support within the family. However, within a country, children are still necessary to provide old-age support. The difference between the two societies is that children have become a public good in the advanced society, whereas in the primitive society they are still a private good. The point where children change their role from production to that of a consumption good or from private to public good is quite important for understanding positive and normative questions of demographic transition[4]. The ethical questions that are tied to endogenous fertility are, because of the dual nature of the commodity 'children', extremely difficult to sort out (see Nerlove *et al.* [1987]).

The last threshold level concerns the amount of debt that a country and a fiscal authority can credibly sustain. As pointed out in chapters 4 and 7, in the standard neoclassical model of the infinitely-lived agent, the long-run private and public debt are indeterminate (see on this point Becker [1980] and Chamley [1985a], respectively). The steady state public debt depends on the initial public debt and the entire future path of government spending and tax revenue. However, models of debt accumulation usually impose the condition that Ponzi games or chain letter schemes are not allowed. By imposing this condition one takes a short cut in determining sustainable debt positions. On the empirical side of the question of sustainable debt, Kremers [1990] and Horne *et al.* [1989] found that in long-run equilibrium net foreign assets depend on international differences in public debt and demographic factors. It is however of some importance to discover whether the foreign asset position serves other purposes than merely a claim on agents abroad to shift resources intertemporally. The traditional function of debt is threefold: consumption smoothing, consumption tilting and consumption augmenting (see Frenkel and Razin [1987]). Theoretical extensions as of late have considered

---

4. Hansson and Stuart [1990] move along the same line in trying to discover why certain countries develop and others not.

the strategic role of debt[5]. Private and public debt can be used strategically by the option of (partial) default. And, as we saw in chapter 4 (section 4.3), the amount of debt accumulated can also give rise to a change in time preference. Although the last extension needs further scrutiny the strategic debt theory has opened up avenues for understanding developments in world capital markets that may have previously been swept aside by assumptions of convenience.

8.3 CAVEAT EMPTOR

In this thesis I have tried to come to grips with some of the basic policy issues that are relevant to a world characterised by demographic change. Elegance in modelling this world economy has not been the prime objective. I have merely tried to lay bare the bones of economic reasoning. The policy solutions presented are, of course, tied to the personal views of the consumer of economic theory. One is free to argue that the way in which I present stylised facts, my choice of the social welfare function and the manner in which I model economies are not very plausible. Unambiguous policy advice is as a consequence of such disagreement a scarce commodity in economic theory. The price one has to pay for practicing the profession of an applied economist is that one tends to fall back on tractable but simple models; models that may neglect important mechanisms or policy issues. This thesis is no exception to this. The policy maker who hopes to extract some instant guidelines will therefore be looking in vain. Economic policy

---

5. See, e.g., the analyses by Chari and Kehoe [1989,1990b], Aghion and Bolton [1990] and Tabellini [1991].

design is directed at constructing robust guidelines, given a particular view of the world. Economists can only hope to convince men of practical affairs of their view by practicing the art of persuasion, which comes down to combining the rhetorical tetrad of logic, fact, metaphor and story telling in a balanced manner (cf. McCloskey [1990]). Economic policy *decisions* are eventually tied to the intuition of Keynes' "madmen in authority" in choosing the right model, while they should be aware that a 'caveat emptor' clause is part and parcel of every economic theory. The inability to make the distinction between design and decision has led on many occasions to exclamations similar in vigour of the outburst made by U.S. President Warren G. Harding (1920-1924) when he talked to his secretary after a hearing on matters of public finance:

> *"John, I can't make a damn thing out of this tax problem. I listen to one side and they seem right, and then - God! - I talk to the other side, and they seem just as right. I know somewhere there is a book, that will give me the truth, but hell, I couldn't read the book. I know somewhere there is an economist who knows the truth, but I don't know where to find him and haven't the sense to know and trust him when I find him. God! what a job!"* (from S.E. Morison [1965, p. 920])

Policy making still is, and will always be, a 'hell of a job' and it is no use shouting like the Mad Queen at the messenger-economist "Off with his head!" as soon as a policy advice turns out to be disastrous. Policymakers might be under the impression that policy making is like the art of painting-by-numbers, where the theorists provide the numbers. It is eventually the responsibility of the policy maker to apply economic theory and not of the theorist. One can only hope that policy makers improve their intuition in using the right models for the right issue.

The models of economic policy design presented in this thesis are intended to provide insight in the economic and ethical consequences of demographic change. The most pressing ethical questions are yet to be faced, for instance that technical progress in medical science lengthens lives and decreases child mortality. But it turns out that such progress has been a mixed blessing: population growth in the developing world has shown a steep increase and this increase has had a disastrous effect on the standard of living. Our judgement concerning such developments falls into two extremes in a world with finite resources. Policymakers with a Benthamite outlook on life will not judge the present development as very harmful, thereby leaving us with the Repugnant Conclusion of Classical Utilitarianism (Parfit [1984]): a very low standard of living for a very large population. The other extreme, the Millian planner, will act as a prophet of doom and judge the rapid increase of the world population as extremely harmful. One should, of course, look behind the façade of the Millian planner whose ultimate goal would be a one-person population (see Sumner [1978]). The screening of arguments on their ethical content might indeed be the greatest contribution economic theory can make to a policy debate. By pushing the consequences of a certain criterium to its limits one can start making a judgement about a desirability and feasibility of public action. Given the tacit extreme views of the dominant criteria used in mainstream economic theory, it should be considered a desirable trait of future welfare analysis to construct social welfare functions that explicitly value population size and growth rate.

Finally, a lasting impression of the analysis of the consequences of demographic change is the manysidedness of the problem: simple policy questions turn out to be complex ethical questions. I cannot but conclude that *any* economic policy in a demographically divided world is debatable, and it will remain so, since a conflict of *values* is inherently human. In coming to a close, one should therefore keep in mind the reprimand Ebenezer Scrooge received from the Ghost of Christmas Present when they together observed the dwindling prospects of Tiny Tim; a reprimand which is perhaps the best approximation to the complexity of the ethics of life and death:

> "If these shadows remain unaltered by the Future, none other of my race", returned the Ghost, "will find him here. What then?
> If he be like to die, he had better do it, and decrease the surplus population".
> Scrooge hung his head to hear his own words quoted by the Spirit and was overcome with penitence and grief.
> "Man", said the Ghost, "if man you be in heart, not adamant, forbear that wicked cant until you have discovered What the surplus is, and Where it is. Will you decide what men shall live, what men shall die? It may be, that in the sight of Heaven, you are more worthless and less fit to live than millions like this poor man's child. Oh God! to hear the Insect on the leaf, pronouncing on the too much life among his hungry brothers in the dust!"

REFERENCES

Abel, A.B. (1986), Capital Accumulation and Uncertain Lifetimes with Adverse Selection, *Econometrica*, 54, 1079-1097.

Abel, A.B. (1989), Birth, Death and Taxes, *Journal of Public Economics*, 39, 1-15.

Abel, A.B., N.G. Mankiw, L.H. Summers, and R.J. Zeckhauser (1989), Assessing Dynamic Efficiency: Theory and Evidence, *Review of Economic Studies*, 56, 1-20.

Aghion, Ph., and P. Bolton (1990), Government Domestic Debt and the Risk of Default, in: R. Dornbusch and M. Draghi (eds.), *Capital Markets and Debt Management*, Cambridge University Press, Cambridge, forthcoming.

Aiyagari, S.R. (1985), Observational Equivalence of the Overlapping Generations and the Discounted Dynamic Programming Frameworks for One-Sector Growth, *Journal of Economic Theory*, 35, 201-221.

Aiyagari, S.R. (1989), How Should Taxes Be Set?, *Quarterly Review*, Federal Reserve Bank of Minneapolis, Winter 1989, 22-32.

Altig, D., and S.J. Davis (1989), Government Debt, Redistributive Fiscal Policies, and the Interaction between Borrowing Constraints and Intergenerational Altruism, *Journal of Monetary Economics*, 24, 3-29.

Altonji, J.G., F. Hayashi, and L.J. Kotlikoff (1989), Is the Extended Family Altruistically Linked? Direct Tests Using Micro Data, mimeographed, National Bureau of Economic Research, May 1989, Cambridge, Mass.

Andreoni, J. (1988), Privately Provided Public Goods in a Large Economy: The Limits of Altruism, *Journal of Public Econo-*

mics, 35, 57-73.

Andreoni, J. (1989), Giving with Impure Altruism: Applications to Charity and Ricardian Equivalence, *Journal of Political Economy*, 97, 1447-1458.

Arrow, K.J. (1950), A Difficulty in the Concept of Social Welfare, *Journal of Political Economy*, 58, 328-346.

Arrow, K.J. (1951), An Extension of the Basic Theorems of Classical Welfare Economics, in: J. Neyman (ed.), *Proceedings of the Second Berkeley Symposium on Mathematical Statistics and Probability*, University of California Press, Berkeley.

Arrow, K.J. (1964), *Social Choice and Individual Values*, John Wiley, New York.

Arrow, K.J., and C. Fischer (1974), Environmental Preservation, Uncertainty, and Irreversibility, *Quarterly Journal of Economics*, 88, 312-319.

Arrow, K.J., and F.H. Hahn (1971), *General Competitive Analysis*, North-Holland, Amsterdam.

Arrow, K.J., and M. Kurz (1969), Optimal Allocation over an Infinite Horizon, *Journal of Economic Theory*, 1, 68-91.

Arthur, W.B., and G. McNicoll (1977), Optimal Time Paths with Age-Dependence: A Theory of Population Policy, *Review of Economic Studies*, 44, 111-123.

Aschauer, D.A. (1988a), The Equilibrium Approach to Fiscal Policy, *Journal of Money, Credit and Banking*, 20, 41-62.

Aschauer, D.A. (1988b), Tax Rates, Deficits and Intertemporal Efficiency, *Public Finance Quarterly*, 16, 374-384.

Aschauer, D.A. (1989), Is Public Expenditure Productive?, *Journal of Monetary Economics*, 23, 177-200.

Aschauer, D.A., and J. Greenwood (1985), Macroeconomic Effects of Fiscal Policy, *Carnegie-Rochester Conference Series on Public Policy*, 23, 91-138.

Atkinson, A.B., and N.H. Stern (1974), Pigou, Taxation and

Public Goods, *Review of Economic Studies*, 41, 119-128.

Atkinson, A.B., and J.E. Stiglitz (1972), The Structure of Indirect Taxation and Economic Efficiency, *Journal of Public Economics*, 1, 97-119.

Auerbach, A.J. (1979), The Optimal Taxation of Heterogenous Capital, *Quarterly Journal of Economics*, 94, 589-612.

Auerbach, A.J. (1985), The Theory of Excess Burden and Optimal Taxation, in: A.J. Auerbach and M.S. Feldstein, *Handbook of Public Economics*, Volume I, North-Holland, Amsterdam.

Auerbach, A.J., and M. Feldstein (1985/1987), *Handbook of Public Economics*, Volume I, 1985, and Volume II, 1987, North-Holland, Amsterdam.

Auerbach, A.J., and L.J. Kotlikoff (1987), *Dynamic Fiscal Policy*, Cambridge University Press, Cambridge.

Azariadis, C., and A. Drazen (1990), Threshold Externalities in Economic Development, *Quarterly Journal of Economics*, 105, 501-526.

Bardhan, P.K. (1965), Optimum Accumulation and International Trade, *Review of Economic Studies*, 32, 241-244.

Bardhan, P.K. (1967), Optimum Foreign Borrowing, in: K. Shell (ed.), *Essays on the Theory of Optimal Economic Growth*, MIT Press, Cambridge, Mass.

Barro, R.J. (1974), Are Government Bonds Net Wealth?, *Journal of Political Economy*, 82, 1095-1117.

Barro, R.J. (1979), On the Determination of the Public Debt, *Journal of Political Economy*, 87, 940-971.

Barro, R.J. (1987), Government Spending, Interest Rates, Prices and Budget Deficits in the United Kingdom, 1701-1918, *Journal of Monetary Economics*, 20, 221-247.

Barro, R.J. (1989a), The Neoclassical Approach to Fiscal Policy, in: R.J. Barro (ed.), *Modern Business Cycle Theory*, Basil Blackwell, Oxford.

Barro, R.J. (1989b), The Ricardian Approach to Budget Deficits, *Journal of Economic Perspectives*, 3, 37-54.

Barro, R.J., and G.S. Becker (1989), Fertility Choice in a Model of Economic Growth, *Econometrica*, 57, 481-501.

Barro, R.J., and D. Gordon (1983), Rules, Discretion and Reputation, *Journal of Monetary Economics*, 12, 101-121.

Barsky, R.B., N.G. Mankiw, and S.P. Zeldes (1986), Ricardian Consumers with Keynesian Propensities, *American Economic Review*, 76, 676-691.

Becker, G.S., and R.J. Barro (1988), A Reformulation of the Economic Theory of Fertility, *Quarterly Journal of Economics*, 103, 1-25.

Becker, R.A. (1980), On the Long-Run Steady State in a Simple Dynamic Model of Equilibrium with Heterogenous Households, *Quarterly Journal of Economics*, 95, 375-382.

Becker, R.A., and C. Foias (1987), A Characterization of Ramsey Equilibrium, *Journal of Economic Theory*, 41, 173-184.

Becker, R.A., and M. Majumdar (1989), Optimality and Decentralization in Infinite Horizon Economies, in: G.R. Feiwel (ed.), *Joan Robinson and Modern Economic Theory*, MacMillan, London.

Benhabib, J., and K. Nishimura (1981), Stability of Equilibrium in Dynamic Models of Capital Theory, *International Economic Review*, 22, 275-293.

Benhabib, J., and R.H. Day (1982), A Characterization of Erratic Dynamics in the Overlapping Generations Model, *Journal of Economic Dynamics and Control*, 4, 37-55.

Bernheim, B.D. (1989a), A Neoclassical Perspective on Budget Deficits, *Journal of Economic Perspectives*, 3, 55-72.

Bernheim, B.D. (1989b), Intergenerational Altruism, Dynastic Equilibria and Social Welfare, *Review of Economic Studies*, 56, 119-128.

Bernheim, B.D., and K. Bagwell (1988), Is Everything Neutral?, *Journal of Political Economy*, 96, 308-338.

Bhagwati, J.N. (1985), The Brain Drain: International Resource Flow Accounting, Compensation, Taxation and Related Policy Proposals, in: J.N. Bhagwati, *Dependence and Interdependence, Essays in Development Economics*, Vol. II, Oxford University Press, Oxford.

Bhagwati, J.N., and C.A. Rodriguez (1976), Welfare-Theoretical Analyses of the Brain Drain, in J.N. Bhagwati (ed.), *The Brain Drain and Taxation, Theory and Empirical Analysis*, Vol. II, North-Holland, Amsterdam.

Biddle, J.E., and D.S. Hamermesh (1990), Sleep and the Allocation of Time, *Journal of Political Economy*, 98, 922-943.

Blackorby, C., and R.B. Russell (1989), On the Observational Equivalence of Models with Infinitely Lived Agents and Models with Overlapping Generations, mimeographed, University of California.

Blanchard, O.J. (1985), Debt, Deficits and Finite Horizons, *Journal of Political Economy*, 93, 223-247.

Blanchard, O.J., and S. Fischer (1989), *Lectures on Macroeconomics*, MIT Press, Cambridge, Mass.

von Böhm-Bawerk, E. (1959), *Capital and Interest*, Vol. 2, *Positive Theory of Capital*, Libertarian Press, South Holland, Ill.

Börsch-Supan, A., and K. Stahl (1991), Life Cycle Savings and Consumption Constraints: Theory and Empirical Evidence and Fiscal Implications, *Journal of Population Economics*, 4, forthcoming.

Bovenberg, A.L. (1988), Long-Term Interest Rates in the United States, *IMF Staff Papers*, 35, 382-390.

Bovenberg, A.L. (1989), The Effects of Capital Income Taxation on International Competitiveness and Trade Flows, *American Economic Review*, 79, 1045-1064.

Boyer, G.R. (1989), Malthus Was Right after All: Poor Relief and Birth Rates in Southeastern England, *Journal of Political Economy*, 97, 93-114.

Boyer, M. (1978), A Habit Forming Optimal Growth Model, *International Economic Review*, 19, 585-609.

Brock, W.A. (1986), A Revised Version of Samuelson's Correspondence Principle: Applications of Recent Results on the Asymptotic Stability of Optimal Control to the Problem of Comparing Long Run Equilibria, in: H. Sonnenschein (ed.), *Models of Economic Dynamics*, Springer Verlag, Berlin.

Brock, W.A., and J. Scheinkman (1976), Global Asymptotic Stability of Optimal Control Systems with Applications to the Theory of Economic Growth, *Journal of Economic Theory*, 12, 164-190.

Brown, L.R., and J.L. Jacobson (1986), Our Demographically Divided World, Worldwatch Paper 74, Washington D.C.

Buckholtz, P., and J. Hartwick (1989), Zero Time Preference with Discounting, *Economics Letters*, 29, 1-6

Buiter, W.H. (1981), Time Preference and International Lending and Borrowing in an Overlapping-Generations Model, *Journal of Political Economy*, 89, 769-797.

Buiter, W.H. (1985), A Guide to Public Sector Debts and Deficits, *Economic Policy*, 1, 14-79.

Buiter, W.H. (1986), Death, Population Growth, Productivity Growth and Debt Neutrality, Working Paper No. 2027, NBER, Cambridge, Mass.

Buiter, W.H. (1988), Death, Birth, Productivity Growth and Debt Neutrality, *Economic Journal*, 98, 279-293.

Buiter, W.H. (1989), Debt Neutrality, Professor Vickrey and Henry George's 'Single Tax', *Economics Letters*, 29, 43-47.

Buiter, W.H., and K.M. Kletzer (1991), The Welfare Economics of Cooperative and Noncooperative Fiscal Policy, *Journal of Economic Dynamics and Control*, 15, forthcoming.

Cadsby, C.B., and M. Frank (1989), Experimental Tests of Ricardian Equivalence, Discussion Paper #738, University of Guelph.

Calvo, G.A., and M. Obstfeld (1988), Optimal Time-Consistent Fiscal Policy with Finite Lifetimes, *Econometrica*, 56, 411-432.

Cantor, R., and N.C. Mark (1987), International Debt and World Business Fluctuations, *Journal of International Money and Finance*, 6, 153-165.

Canzoneri, M.B., and D.W. Henderson (1988), Is Sovereign Policymaking Bad?, *Carnegie-Rochester Conference Series on Public Policy*, 28, 93-140.

Cass, D. (1965), Optimum Growth in an Aggregative Model of Capital Accumulation, *Review of Economic Studies*, 32, 233-240.

Cass, D., and K. Shell (1976), The Structure and Stability of Competitive Dynamical Systems, *Journal of Economic Theory*, 12, 31-70.

Chakravarty, S. (1969), *Capital and Development Planning*, MIT Press, Cambridge, Mass.

Chakravarty, S., and A.S. Manne (1968), Optimal Growth When the Instantaneous Utility Function Depends Upon the Rate of Change in Consumption, *American Economic Review*, 58, 1351-1354.

Chamley, C. (1985a), Efficient Taxation in a Stylized Model of Intertemporal General Equilibrium, *International Economic Review*, 26, 451-468.

Chamley, C. (1985b), Efficient Tax Reform in a Dynamic Model of General Equilibrium, *Quarterly Journal of Economics*, 100,

335-356.

Chamley, C. (1986), Optimal Taxation of Capital Income in General Equilibrium with Infinite Lives, *Econometrica*, 54, 607-622.

Chan, L.K.C. (1983), Uncertainty and the Neutrality of Government Financing Policy, *Journal of Monetary Economics*, 11, 351-372.

Chari, V.V. (1988), Time Consistency and Optimal Policy Design, *Quarterly Review*, Federal Reserve Bank of Minneapolis, 17-31.

Chari, V.V., and P.J. Kehoe (1989), Sustainable Plans and Mutual Default, Research Department Staff Report 124, Federal Reserve Bank of Minneapolis.

Chari, V.V., and P.J. Kehoe (1990a), International Coordination of Fiscal Policy in Limiting Economies, *Journal of Political Economy*, 98, 617-636.

Chari, V.V., and P.J. Kehoe (1990b), Sustainable Plans, *Journal of Political Economy*, 98, 783-802.

Chari, V.V., P.J. Kehoe, and E.C. Prescott (1989), Time Consistency and Policy, in: R.J. Barro (ed.), *Modern Business Cycle Theory*, Basil Blackwell, Oxford.

Chiswick, B.R. (1978), The Effect of Americanization on the Earnings of Foreign-born Men, *Journal of Political Economy*, 86, 897-921.

Christiano, L.J. (1989), Understanding Japan's Saving Rate: The Reconstruction Hypothesis, *Quarterly Review*, Federal Reserve Bank of Minneapolis, Spring 1989, 10-19.

Clarida, R.H. (1990), International Lending and Borrowing in a Stochastic Stationary Equilibrium, *International Economic Review*, 31, 543-558.

Corlett, W.J., and D.C. Hague (1953-54), Complementarity and the Excess Burden of Taxation, *Review of Economic Studies*, 21,

21-30.

Coughlin, P.J., D.C. Mueller, and P. Murrell (1990a), A Model of Electoral Competition with Interest Groups, *Economics Letters*, 32, 307-311.

Coughlin, P.J., D.C. Mueller, and P. Murrell (1990b), Electoral Politics, Interest Groups, and the Size of Government, *Economic Inquiry*, 28, 682-705.

Cutler, D.M., J.M. Poterba, L.M. Sheiner, and L.H. Summers (1990), An Aging Society: Opportunity or Challenge?, *Brookings Papers on Economic Activity*, no. 1, 1-73.

Dasgupta, P.S. (1988), Lives and Well-Being, *Social Choice and Welfare*, 5, 103-126.

Davis, K. (1945), The World Demographic Transition, *Annals of the American Academy of Political and Social Science*, 237, 1-11.

Deardorff, A.V. (1985), Growth and International Investment with Diverging Populations, mimeographed, University of Michigan.

Deardorff, A.V. (1987), Trade and Capital Mobility in a World of Diverging Populations, in: G. Johnson and R.D. Lee (eds.), *Population Growth and Economic Development: Issues and Evidence*, University of Wisconsin Press, Madison, Wisconsin.

Deaton, A.S. (1981), Optimal Taxes and the Structure of Preferences, *Econometrica*, 49, 1245-1260.

Deaton, A.S. (1989), Saving and Liquidity Constraints, NBER Working Paper, No. 3196, Cambridge, Mass.

Debreu, G. (1954), Valuation Equilibrium and Pareto Optimum, *Proceedings of the National Academy of Sciences*, 40, 588-592.

Debreu, G. (1959), *Theory of Value: An Axiomatic Analysis of Economic Equilibrium*, Cowles Foundation Monograph, Yale University Press.

Dechert, W.D., and K. Nishimura (1983), A Complete Characterization of Optimal Growth Paths in an Aggregated Model with a Non-Concave Production Function, *Journal of Economic Theory*, 31, 332-354.

Diamond, D.W., and P.H. Dybvig (1983), Bank Runs, Deposit Insurance and Liquidity, *Journal of Political Economy*, 35, 401-419.

Diamond, P.A. (1965), National Debt in a Neoclassical Growth Model, *American Economic Review*, 55, 1126-1150.

Diamond, P.A., and J.A. Mirrlees (1971), Optimal Taxaton and Public Production I: Production Efficiency and II: Tax Rules, *American Economic Review*, 61, 8-27 and 261-278.

Dixit, A.K. (1981), The Export of Capital Theory, *Journal of International Economics*, 11, 279-294.

Djajić, S. (1987), Government Spending and the Optimal Rates of Consumption and Capital Accumulation, *Canadian Journal of Economics*, 20, 544-554.

Djajić, S. (1989), Current-Account Effects of a Temporary Change in Government Expenditure, *Scandinavian Journal of Economics*, 91, 83-96.

Dorfman, R., P.A. Samuelson, and R.M. Solow (1958), *Linear Programming and Economic Analysis*, McGraw-Hill, New York.

Drazen, A. (1978), Government Debt, Human Capital and Bequests in a Lifecycle Model, *Journal of Political Economy*, 86, 505-516.

Drazen, A. (1985), State Dependence in Optimal Factor Accumulation, *Quarterly Journal of Economics*, 100, 357-372.

Drissen, E., and F.A.A.M. van Winden (1991), Social Security in a General Equilibrium Model with Endogenous Government Behavior, *Journal of Population Economics*, 4, 89-110.

Eckstein, Z., S. Stern, and K.I. Wolpin (1988), Fertility Choice, Land, and the Malthusian Hypothesis, *International Economic Review*, 29, 353-361.

Eckstein, Z., S. Stern, and K.I. Wolpin (1989), On the Malthusian Hypothesis and the Dynamics of Population and Income in an Equilibrium Growth Model With Endogenous Fertility, in: K.F. Zimmermann (ed.), *Economic Theory of Optimal Population*, Springer Verlag, Berlin.

Ehrlich, I., and H. Chuma (1990), A Model of the Demand for Longevity and the Value of Life Extension, *Journal of Political Economy*, 98, 761-782.

Epstein, L.G. (1987), A Simple Dynamic General Equilibrium Model, *Journal of Economic Theory*, 41, 68-95.

Epstein, L.G., and J.A. Hynes (1983), The Rate of Time Preference and Dynamic Economic Analysis, *Journal of Political Economy*, 91, 611-635.

Ethier, W.J. (1985), International Trade and Labor Migration, *American Economic Review*, 75, 691-707.

Feldstein, M. (1988), The Effects of Fiscal Policies when Incomes are Uncertain: A Contradiction to Ricardian Equivalences, *American Economic Review*, 78, 14-23.

Feldstein, M., and C. Horioka (1980), Domestic Saving and International Capital Flows, *Economic Journal*, 90, 314-329.

Fischer, S. (1980), Dynamic Inconsistency, Co-operation and the Benevolent Dissembling Government, *Journal of Economic Dynamics and Control*, 2, 93-107.

Flemming, J.S. (1987), Debt and Taxes in War and Peace: The Case of a Small Open Economy, in: M.J. Boskin, J.S. Flemming and S. Gorini (eds.), *Private Saving and Public Debt*, Basil Blackwell, Oxford.

Flemming, J.S. (1988), Debt and Taxes in War and Peace: The Closed Economy Case, in: K.J. Arrow and M.J. Boskin (eds.), *The Economics of Public Debt*, MacMillan, London.

Foley, D.K., and M. Sidrauski (1971), *Monetary and Fiscal Policy in a Growing Economy*, MacMillan, London.

Frenkel, J.A., and A. Razin (1985), Government Spending, Debt, and International Economic Interdependence, *Economic Journal*, 95, 619-636.

Frenkel, J.A., and A. Razin (1987), *Fiscal Policies and the World Economy*, MIT Press, Cambridge, Mass.

Friedman, M. (1949), The Marshallian Demand Curve, *Journal of Political Economy*, 37, 463-495.

Friedman, M. (1953), The Methodology of Positive Economics, in: *Essays in Positive Economics*, University of Chicago Press, Chicago.

Friedman, M. (1955), Leon Walras and his Economic System; A Review Article, *American Economic Review*, 45, 900-909.

Friedman, M. (1957), *A Theory of the Consumption Function*, Princeton University Press, Princeton.

Fullerton, D. (1982), On the Possibility of an Inverse Relationship between Tax Rates and Government Expenditures, *Journal of Public Economics*, 19, 3-22.

Gale, D., and H. Nikaidô (1965), The Jacobian Matrix and Global Univalence of Mappings, *Mathematische Annalen*, 159, 81-93.

Galor, O. (1986), Time Preference and International Labor Migration, *Journal of Economic Theory*, 38, 1-20.

Galor, O., and O. Stark (1991), The Impact of Differences in the Level of Technology on International Labor Migration, *Journal of Population Economics*, 4, 1-12.

van Ginneken, J.K.S., A.F.I. Bannenberg, and A.G. Disseveld (1989), Gezondheidsverlies ten gevolge van een aantal belangrijke ziekte-categorieën in 1981-1985, Methodologische aspecten en resultaten, ("Loss of health as a consequence of a number of important categories of diseases in 1981-85"), Nederlands Instituut Preventieve Geneeskunde, Leiden.

Gorman, W.M. (1961), On a Class of Preference Fields, *Metroeconomica*, 12, 53-56.

Greenwood, M.J., and J.M. McDowell (1986) The Factor Market Consequences of U.S. Immigration, *Journal of Economic Literature*, 24, 1738-1772.

de Haan, J. (1989), *Public Debt; Pestiferous or Propitious? On the Economic Consequences of the Creation and Existence of Government Debt*, PhD. Thesis, University of Groningen.

Hagemann, R.P., and G. Nicoletti (1989), Ageing Populations: Economic Effects and Implications for Public Finance, *OECD Economic Studies*, 12, 59-110.

Hahn, F.H. (1973), On Optimum Taxation, *Journal of Economic Theory*, 6, 96-106.

Hall, R.E. (1988), Intertemporal Substitution in Consumption, *Journal of Political Economy*, 96, 339-357.

Halter, W.A., and R. Hemming (1987), The Impact of Demographic Change on Social Security Financing, *IMF Staff Papers*, 34, 471-502.

Hansen, L.P., and K.J. Singleton (1982), Generalized Instrumental Variables Estimation of Nonlinear Rational Expectations Models, *Econometrica*, 50, 1269-1286.

Hansson, I., and Ch. Stuart (1990), Malthusian Selection of Preferences, *American Economic Review*, 80, 529-544.

Harberger, A.C. (1954), Monopoly and Resource Allocation, *American Economic Review, Papers and Proceedings*, 44, 77-87.

Harberger, A.C. (1990), The Uniform-Tax Controversy, in: V. Tanzi (ed.), *Public Finance, Trade and Development*, Wayne State University Press, Detroit.

Harsanyi, J. (1955), Cardinal Welfare, Individualistic Ethics, and Interpersonal Comparisons of Utility, *Journal of Political Economy*, 63, 309-321.

Hartwick, J. (1977), Intergenerational Equity and the Investing of Rents from Exhaustible Resources, *American Economic Review*, 66, 972-974.

Hartwick, J. (1978), Substitution among Exhaustible Resources and Intergenerational Equity, *Review of Economic Studies*, 45, 347-354.

Hayashi, F. (1987), Tests for Liquidity Constraints: A Critical Survey and Some New Observations, in: T.F. Bewley (ed.), *Advances in Econometrics*, Vol. II, Cambridge University Press, Cambridge.

Helmstädter, E. (1973), The Long-Run Movement of the Capital-Output Ratio and of Labour's Share, in: J.A. Mirrlees and N.H. Stern (eds.), *Models of Economic Growth*, MacMillan, London.

Hendershott, P.H., and S.-C. Hu (1980), Government-Induced Biases in the Fixed Capital Capital Stock of the United States, in: G.M. Furstenberg (ed.), *Capital, Efficiency and Growth*, Ballinger, Cambridge, Mass.

Hochman, H.M., and J.D. Rodgers (1969), Pareto Optimal Redistribution, *American Economic Review*, 59, 542-557.

Hoover, K.D. (1988), *The New Classical Macroeconomics: A Sceptical Inquiry*, Basil Blackwell, Oxford.

Horne, J., J.J.M. Kremers, and P.R. Masson (1989), Net Foreign Assets and International Adjustment in the United States, Japan and the Federal Republic of Germany, IMF Working Paper, March 14, 1989, Washington D.C.

Horne, J., and P.R. Masson (1988), Scope and Limits of International Economic Cooperation and Policy Coordination, *IMF Staff Papers*, 35, 259-296.

van Imhoff, E. (1989a), *Optimal Economic Growth and Non-Stable Population*, Springer Verlag, Berlin.

van Imhoff, E. (1989b), Optimal Investment in Human Capital under Conditions of Non-Stable Population, *Journal of Human Resources*, 24, 414-432.

van Imhoff, E., and J.M.M. Ritzen (1988), Optimal Economic

Growth and Non-Stable Population, *De Economist*, 136, 339-357.

Inada, K. (1968), Free Trade, Capital Accumulation and Factor Price Equalization, *Economic Record*, 44, 322-341.

International Labour Office (1986), *Economically Active Population, 1950-2025*, Vol. I-V, Geneva.

Intriligator, M.D. (1971), *Mathematical Optimization and Economic Theory*, Prentice-Hall, N.J.

Kaldor, N. (1961), Capital Accumulation and Economic Growth, in: F.A. Lutz and D.C. Hague (eds.), *The Theory of Capital*, St. Martin's Press, New York.

Kehoe, P.J. (1989), Policy Cooperation among Benevolent Governments May Be Undesirable, *Review of Economic Studies*, 56, 289-296.

Kendrick, J.W. (1961), *Productivity Trends in the United States*, Princeton University Press, Princeton, New Jersey.

Kendrick, J.W. (1973), *Postwar Productivity Trends in the United States, 1948-1969*, Columbia University Press, New York.

Kessler, D., and A. Masson (1988), *Modelling the Accumulation and Distribution of Wealth*, Clarendon Press, Oxford.

Keynes, J.M. (1933), *Essays in Biography*, MacMillan, London.

Keynes, J.M. (1940), *How to Pay for the War*, reprinted in: *The Collected Writings of John Maynard Keynes, Vol. IX, Essays in Persuasion*, MacMillan, London.

Keynes, J.M. (1973), *The Collected Writings of John Maynard Keynes, Vol. XIV, The General Theory and After*, edited by D. Moggridge, MacMillan, London.

Keyfitz, N. (1977), *Applied Mathematical Demography*, John Wiley, New York.

King, R.G., C.I. Plosser, and S.T. Rebelo (1988a), Production, Growth and Business Cycles, I. The Basic Neoclassical Model, *Journal of Monetary Economics*, 21, 195-232.

King, R.G., C.I. Plosser, and S.T. Rebelo (1988b), Production, Growth and Business Cycles, II. New Directions, *Journal of Monetary Economics*, 21, 309-341.

Kingston, G. (1989), Should Marginal Tax Rates be Equalized Through Time?, Discussion Paper 89/8, University of New South Wales.

Klamer, A., and D. Colander (1990), *The Making of An Economist*, Westview Press, Boulder.

Kletzer, K.M. (1988), External Borrowing by LDCs: A Survey of Some Theoretical Issues, in: G. Ranis and T.P. Schultz (eds.), *The State of Development Economics, Progress and Perspectives*, Basil Blackwell, Oxford.

Kondo, H. (1989a), Population, International Trade and Indebtedness: A More General Analysis, in: K.F. Zimmermann (ed.), *Economic Theory of Optimal Population*, Springer Verlag, Berlin.

Kondo, H. (1989b), International Factor Mobility and Production Technology, *Journal of Population Economics*, 2, 281-299

Koopmans, T.C. (1960), Stationary Ordinal Utility and Impatience, *Econometrica*, 28, 287-309.

Koopmans, T.C. (1964), On Flexibility of Future Preferences, in: M.W. Shelly, II, and G.L. Bryan (eds.), *Human Judgements and Optimality*, Wiley, New York.

Koopmans, T.C. (1965), On the Concept of Optimal Economic Growth, in: *The Econometric Approach to Development Planning*, North-Holland, Amsterdam.

Koopmans, T.C. (1967a), Objectives, Constraints, and Outcomes in Optimal Growth Models, *Econometrica*, 35, 1-15.

Koopmans, T.C. (1967b), Intertemporal Distribution and 'Optimal' Aggregate Economic Growth, in: W. Fellner (ed.), *Ten Economic Studies in the Tradition of Irving Fisher*, Wiley, New York.

Koopmans, T.C. (1974), Proof for a Case where Discounting Advances the Doomsday, *Review of Economic Studies*, 41, 117-120.

Koopmans, T.C. (1976), Concepts of Optimality and Their Uses, *Les Prix Nobel en 1975*, Nobel Foundation, Stockholm.

Koopmans, T.C. (1980), The Transition from Exhaustible to Renewable or Inexhaustible Resources, in: C. Bliss and M. Boserup (eds.), *Economic Growth and Resources, Volume 3: Natural Resources*, MacMillan, London.

Koopmans, T.C., P.A. Diamond, and R.E. Williamson (1964), Stationary Utility and Time Perspective, *Econometrica*, 32, 82-100.

Kotlikoff, L.J. (1988), Intergenerational Transfers and Savings, *Journal of Economic Perspectives*, 2, 41-58.

Kotlikoff, L.J., T. Persson, and L.E.O. Svensson (1988), Social Contracts as Assets: A Possible Solution to the Time-Consistency Problem, *American Economic Review*, 78, 662-677.

Kotlikoff, L.J., and L.H. Summers (1981), The Role of Intergenerational Transfers in Aggregate Capital Accumulation, *Journal of Political Economy*, 89, 706-732.

Kremers, J.J.M. (1986a), The Dutch Disease in the Netherlands, in: J.P. Neary and S. van Wijnbergen (eds.), *Natural Resources and the Macroeconomy*, Basil Blackwell, Oxford.

Kremers, J.J.M. (1986b), The Optimality of Dynamic Tax Smoothing and the Cost of Sub-Optimal Budgetary Policy, Working Paper, IMF, Washington.

Kremers, J.J.M. (1989), U.S. Federal Indebtedness and the Conduct of Fiscal Policy, *Journal of Monetary Economics*, 23, 219-238.

Kremers, J.J.M. (1990), External Imbalances and Fiscal Policy in the United States, Japan and Germany: The Role of Stock-Flow Dynamics, in: G. Krause-Junk (ed.), *Public Finance and*

Steady Economic Growth, Foundation Journal Public Finance, The Hague.

Kula, E. (1984), Derivation of Social Time Preference Rates for the United States and Canada, *Quarterly Journal of Economics*, 99, 873-882.

Kydland, F.E., and E.C. Prescott (1977), Rules Rather than Discretion: The Inconsistency of Optimal Plans, *Journal of Political Economy*, 85, 473-492.

Kydland, F.E., and E.C. Prescott (1980), Dynamic Optimal Taxation, Rational Expectations and Optimal Control, *Journal of Economic Dynamics and Control*, 2, 79-91.

Kydland, F.E., and E.C. Prescott (1982), Time to Build and Aggregate Fluctuations, *Econometrica*, 50, 1345-1370.

Kydland, F.E., and E.C. Prescott (1990), Business Cycles: Real Facts and a Monetary Myth, *Quarterly Review*, Federal Reserve Bank of Minneapolis, Spring 1990, 3-18.

Laitner, J.P. (1979), Bequests, Golden-Age Capital Accumulation and Government Debt, *Economica*, 46, 403-414.

Lawson, T. (1987), The Relative/Absolute Nature of Knowledge and Economic Analysis, *Economic Journal*, 97, 951-970.

Lee, R.D., and S. Lapkoff (1988), Intergenerational Flows of Time and Goods: Consequences of Slowing Population Growth, *Journal of Political Economy*, 96, 618-651.

Leeds, M.A. (1989), Government Debt, Immigration and Durable Public Goods, *Public Finance Quarterly*, 17, 227-235.

Leiderman, L., and M.I. Blejer (1988), Modeling and Testing Ricardian Equivalence, A Survey, *IMF Staff Papers*, 1-35.

Lipsey, R.E., and I.B. Kravis (1987), Is the U.S. a Spendthrift Nation?, Working Paper No. 2274, National Bureau of Economic Research.

Lucas, R.E. Jr (1976), Econometric Policy Evaluation: A Critique, *Carnegie-Rochester Conference Series on Public*

Policy, 1, 19-46.

Lucas, R.E. Jr. (1977), Understanding Business Cycles, *Carnegie-Rochester Conference Series on Public Policy*, 5, 7-29.

Lucas, R.E. Jr. (1980), Methods and Problems in Business Cycle Theory, *Journal of Money, Credit and Banking*, 12, 696-715.

Lucas, R.E. Jr. (1982), Interest Rates and Currency Prices in a Two-Country World, *Journal of Monetary Economics*, 10, 335-359.

Lucas, R.E. Jr. (1987), *Models of Business Cycles*, Yrjö Jahnsson Lectures, Basil Blackwell, Oxford.

Lucas, R.E. Jr. (1988), On the Mechanics of Economic Development, *Journal of Monetary Economics*, 22, 3-42.

Lucas, R.E. Jr. (1990a), Why Doesn't Capital Flow from Rich to Poor Countries, *American Economic Review, Papers and Proceedings*, 80, 92-96.

Lucas, R.E. Jr. (1990b), Book review of *Trade Policy and Market Structure*, by Elhanan Helpman and Paul R. Krugman, *Journal of Political Economy*, 98, 664-667.

Lucas, R.E. Jr., and N.L. Stokey (1983), Optimal Fiscal and Monetary Policy in an Economy without Capital, *Journal of Monetary Economics*, 12, 55-93.

Lucas, R.E. Jr., and N.L. Stokey (1984), Optimal Growth with Many Consumers, *Journal of Economic Theory*, 32, 139-171.

Mackenbach, J.P. (1988), *Mortality and Medical Care*, PhD Thesis, Erasmus University Rotterdam.

Maddison, A. (1987), Growth and Slowdown in Advanced Capitalist Economies, *Journal of Economic Literature*, 25, 649-698.

Malthus, T.R. (1798/1971), *An Essay on the Principle of Population*, Penguin Books, Harmondsworth.

Mankiw, G.N. (1981), The Permanent Income Hypothesis and the Real Interest Rate, *Economics Letters*, 7, 307-311.

Mankiw, G.N., J.J. Rotemberg, and L.H. Summers (1985), Intertemporal Substitution in Macroeconomics, *Quarterly Journal of Economics*, 100, 225-251.

Mao, Ching-Sheng (1989), Estimating Intertemporal Elasticities of Substitution: The Case of Log-Linear Restrictions, *Economic Review*, Federal Reserve Bank of Richmond, 75, 3-14.

van Marrewijk, Ch., and J. Verbeek (1991), Endogenous Population Growth: A Problem for Development, Discussion Paper Series, No. 9109/G, Erasmus University Rotterdam.

Masson, P.R. (1989), Equilibrium Net Foreign Assets in a Two-Country Version of the Yaari-Blanchard-Weil Model of Optimizing Consumers, mimeographed, International Monetary Fund.

Masson, P.R., and R.W. Tryon (1990), Macroeconomic Effects of Projected Population Aging in Industrial Countries, *IMF Staff Papers*, 37, 453-485.

Matthews, R.C.O., C.H. Feinstein, and J.C. Odling-Smee (1982), *British Economic Growth 1856-1973*, Clarendon Press, Oxford.

McKee, M.J., J.J.C. Visser, and P.G. Saunders (1986), Marginal Tax Rates on the Use of Capital and Labour in OECD Countries, *OECD Economic Studies*, No. 7, Paris.

McCloskey, D.N. (1985), *The Rhetoric of Economics*, University of Wisconsin Press, Madison, Wisconsin.

McCloskey, D.N. (1990), *If You're So Smart, The Narrative of Economic Expertise*, Chicago University Press, Chicago.

Meade, J.E. (1955), *Trade and Welfare, The Theory of International Economic Policy*, Oxford University Press, Oxford.

Michel, Ph. (1990), Criticism of the Social Time-Preference Hypothesis in Optimal Growth, CORE Discussion Paper, No. 9039, Université Catholique de Louvain.

Modigliani, F., and R. Brumberg (1954), Utility Analysis and the Consumption Function: An Interpretation of Cross-Section

Data, in: K.H. Kurihara (ed.), *Post-Keynesian Economics*, Rutgers University Press, New Brunswick, N.J.

Morison, S.E. (1965), *The Oxford History of the American People*, Oxford University Press, New York.

Munk, K.J. (1978), Optimal Taxation and Pure Profits, *Scandinavian Journal of Economics*, 80, 1-19.

Nerlove, M. (1988), Population Policy and Individual Choice, *Journal of Population Economics*, 1, 17-32.

Nerlove, M., A. Razin, and E. Sadka (1987), *Household and Economy, Welfare Economics of Endogenous Fertility*, Academic Press, New York.

Newman, P. (1987), Frank Plumpton Ramsey, in: J. Eatwell, M. Milgate and P. Newman (eds.), *The New Palgrave*, MacMillan, London.

Ng, Y.-K. (1989), What Should We Do About Future Generations?, *Economics and Philosophy*, 5, 235-253.

Notestein, F.W. (1945), Population: the Long View, in: T.W. Schultz (ed.), *Food for the World*, Chicago University Press, Chicago.

Obstfeld, M. (1983), Intertemporal Price Speculation and the Optimal Current Account Deficit, *Journal of International Money and Finance*, 2, 135-145.

Obstfeld, M. (1986), Capital Mobility in the World Economy: Theory and Measurement, *Carnegie-Rochester Conference on Public Policy*, 24, 55-104.

Obstfeld, M. (1990), Intertemporal Dependence, Impatience, and Dynamics, *Journal of Monetary Economics*, 26, 45-75.

O'Connell, S.A., and S.P. Zeldes (1988), Rational Ponzi Games, *International Economic Review*, 29, 431-450.

OECD (1985), *Social Expenditure, 1960-1990: Problems of Growth and Control*, Social Policy Studies Series, No. 1, Paris.

OECD (1988), *Ageing Populations, The Social Policy Implications*,

Demographic Change and Public Policy Series, No. 1, Paris.

Ohkawa, K., and H. Rosovsky (1973), *Japanese Economic Growth*, Stanford University Press, Stanford.

Ommen, T.K. (1989), India: 'Brain Drain' or the Migration of Talent?, *International Migration*, 27, 411-426.

Oniki, H., and H. Uzawa (1965), Patterns of Trade and Investment in a Dynamic Model of International Trade, *Review of Economic Studies*, 32, 15-38.

Parfit, D. (1984), *Reasons and Persons*, Oxford University Press, Oxford.

Persson, M., T. Persson, and L.E.O. Svensson (1987), Time Consistency of Fiscal and Monetary Policy, *Econometrica*, 55, 1419-1431.

Persson, T., and L.E.O. Svensson (1984), Time-Consistent Fiscal Policy and Government Cash-Flow, *Journal of Monetary Economics*, 14, 365-374.

Persson, T., and L.E.O. Svensson (1986), International Borrowing and Time-Consistent Fiscal Policy, *Scandinavian Journal of Economics*, 88, 273-295.

Persson, T., and L.E.O. Svensson (1989), Why a Stubborn Conservative Would Run a Deficit: Policy with Time-Inconsistent Preferences, *Quarterly Journal of Economics*, 104, 323-345.

Persson, T., and G. Tabellini (1990), *Macroeconomic Policy, Credibility and Politics*, Harwood Academic Publishers, London.

Pestieau, P. (1984), The Effects of Varying Family Size on the Transmission and Distribution of Wealth, *Oxford Economic Papers*, 36, 400-417.

Pezzey, J. (1989), Economic Analysis of Sustainable Growth and Sustainable Development, Environment Department Working Paper No. 15, Worldbank, Washington D.C.

Phelps, E.S. (1961), The Golden Rule of Accumulation: a Fable for Growthmen, *American Economic Review*, 51, 638-643.

Pigou, A.C. (1952), *The Economics of Welfare*, 4th edition, MacMillan, London.

Pitchford, J.D. (1974), *Population in Economic Growth*, North-Holland, Amsterdam.

Pitchford, J.D. (1977), Two State Variable Problems, in: J.D. Pitchford and S.J. Turnovsky (eds.), *Applications of Control Theory to Economic Analysis*, North-Holland, Amsterdam.

Pitchford, J.D. (1989), Optimum Borrowing and the Current Account when there are Fluctuations in Income, *Journal of International Economics*, 26, 345-358.

van der Ploeg, F. (1988), International Policy Coordination in Interdependent Monetary Economies, *Journal of International Economics*, 25, 1-23.

Poeth, G.G.J.M. (1975), *Economic Aspects of Retirement*, Unpublished PhD Thesis, University of Leyden.

Pontryagin, L.S., V.G. Boltyanskii, R.V. Gamkrelidze, and E.F. Mischenko (1964), *The Mathematical Theory of Optimal Processes* (translation of Russian 1961 edition), Pergamon Press, Oxford.

Poterba, J.M., and L.H. Summers (1987), Finite Lifetimes and the Effects of Budget Deficits on National Saving, *Journal of Monetary Economics*, 20, 369-391.

Pozdena, R.J. (1987), Inflation, Age and Wealth, *Economic Review*, Federal Reserve Bank of San Francisco, Winter 1987, 17-30.

van Praag, B.M.S., and G.G.J.M. Poeth (1977), Human Capital Theory and the Theory of Population, in: *Public Economics and Human Resources*, Proceedings 31st Congress IIPF, 1975, Nice.

Prescott, E.C., and J.H. Boyd (1987), Dynamic Coalitions, Growth and the Firm, in: E.C. Prescott and N. Wallace (eds.), *Contractual Arrangements for Intertemporal Trade*, Minnesota Studies in Macroeconomics, Vol. I, Minneapolis.

Quibria, M.G. (1990), On International Migration and the Social Welfare Function, *Bulletin of Economic Research*, 42, 141-153.

Ramsey, F.P. (1927), A Contribution to the Theory of Taxation, *Economic Journal*, 37, 47-61.

Ramsey, F.P. (1928), A Mathematical Theory of Savings, *Economic Journal*, 38, 543-559.

Rawls, J. (1972), *A Theory of Justice*, Oxford University Press, Oxford.

Renaud, P.S.A., and F.A.A.M. van Winden (1987), Tax Rate and Government Expenditure, *Kyklos*, 40, 349-367.

Ricardo, D. (1817), *The Principles of Political Economy and Taxation*, in: P. Sraffa (ed.), 1962, *The Works and Correspondence of David Ricardo*, Vol. I, Cambridge University Press, Cambridge.

Ritzen, J.M.M. (1977), *Education, Economic Growth and Income Distribution*, North-Holland, Amsterdam.

Ritzen, J.M.M. (1987), Human Capital and Economic Cycles, *Economics of Education Review*, 6, 151-161.

Ritzen, J.M.M. (1989), Revenue and Demographic Change, in: A. Chiancone and K. Messere (eds.), *Changes in Revenue Structures*, Wayne State University Press, Michigan.

Ritzen, J.M.M., and H.P. van Dalen (1990), The Economic Consequences of Selective Immigration Policies, in: K.F. Zimmermann (ed.), *Migration and Developing Countries*, Springer Verlag, Berlin, forthcoming.

Ritzen, J.M.M., and B.M.S. van Praag (1985), Golden Rules and Non-Stationary Population, Working Paper, Erasmus University Rotterdam.

Robbins, L. (1935), *An Essay on the Nature and Significance of Economic Science*, MacMillan, London.

Roberts, J. (1987), An Equilibrium Model with Involuntary Unemployment at Flexible, Competitive Prices and Wages, *American Economic Review*, 77, 856-874.

Rodriguez, C.A. (1975), On the Welfare Aspects of International Migration, *Journal of Political Economy*, 83, 1065-1072.

Rodriguez, C.A. (1976), Brain Drain and Economic Growth: A Dynamic Model, in: J.N. Bhagwati (ed.), *The Brain Drain and Taxation, Theory and Empirical Analysis*, Vol. II, North-Holland, Amsterdam.

Rogoff, K. (1985a), Can International Monetary Policy Cooperation be Counterproductive?, *Journal of International Economics*, 18, 199-217.

Rogoff, K. (1985b), The Optimal Degree of Commitment to an Intermediate Monetary Target, *Quarterly Journal of Economics*, 100, 1169-1190.

Romer, P.M. (1986), Increasing Returns and Long-Run Growth, *Journal of Political Economy*, 94, 1002-1037.

Romer, P.M. (1989), Capital Accumulation in the Theory of Long-Run Growth, in: R.J. Barro (ed.), *Modern Business Cycle Theory*, Basil Blackwell, Oxford.

Roubini, N., and J.D. Sachs (1989a), Government Spending and Budget Deficits in the Industrial Countries, *Economic Policy*, 4, 99-127.

Roubini, N., and J.D. Sachs (1989b), Political and Economic Determinants of Budget Deficits in the Industrial Democracies, *European Economic Review*, 33, 903-938.

Ruffin, R.J. (1979), Growth and the Long-Run Theory of International Capital Movements, *American Economic Review*, 69, 832-842.

Sachs, J.D. (1981), The Current Account and Macroeconomic

Adjustment in the 1970s, *Brookings Papers on Economic Activity*, no. 1, 201-268.

Sachs, J.D. (1982), The Current Account in the Macroeconomic Adjustment Process, *Scandinavian Journal of Economics*, 84, 147-159.

Sahasakul, C. (1986), The U.S. Evidence on Optimal Taxation over Time, *Journal of Monetary Economics*, 18, 251-275.

Sala-i-Martin, X. (1990), Lecture Notes on Economic Growth (I): Introduction to the Literature and Neoclassical Models, (II): Five Prototype Models of Endogenous Growth, NBER Working Paper, #3563 and #3564, Yale University, New Haven.

Samuelson, P.A. (1937), A Note on Measurement of Utility, *Review of Economic Studies*, 4, 155-161.

Samuelson, P.A. (1947), *Foundations of Economic Analysis*, Harvard University Press, Cambridge, Mass.

Samuelson, P.A. (1951), Theory of Optimal Taxation, 'unpublished' memorandum for the U.S. Treasury, reprinted in: *Journal of Public Economics*, 1986, 30, 137-143.

Samuelson, P.A. (1954), The Pure Theory of Public Expenditure, *Review of Economics and Statistics*, 36, 387-389.

Samuelson, P.A. (1958), An Exact Consumption-Loan Model of Interest with or without the Social Contrivance of Money, *Journal of Political Economy*, 66, 467-482.

Samuelson, P.A. (1963), Problems of Methodology - Discussion, *American Economic Review, Papers and Proceedings*, 53, 231-236.

Samuelson, P.A. (1965), A Catenary Turnpike Theorem Involving Consumption and the Golden Rule, *American Economic Review*, 55, 486-496.

Sandmo, A. (1985), The Effects of Taxation on Savings and Risk Taking, in: A.J. Auerbach and M. Feldstein (eds.), *Handbook of Public Economics*, Vol. I, North-Holland, Amsterdam.

Sargent, T.J. (1982), Beyond Demand and Supply Curves in Macroeconomics, *American Economic Review, Papers and Proceedings*, 72, 382-389.

Sargent, T.J. (1987), *Dynamic Macroeconomic Theory*, Harvard University Press, Cambridge, Mass.

Scheinkman, J.A. (1976), On Optimal Steady States of n-Sector Growth Models when Utility is Discounted, *Journal of Economic Theory*, 12, 11-30.

Schmitz, J.A., Jr. (1989), Imitation, Entrepreneurship, and Long-Run Growth, *Journal of Political Economy*, 97, 721-739.

Schultz, T.P. (1990), Economic and Demographic Consequences of Educating Women, Social Returns to Women's Schooling, mimeographed, Yale University.

Seierstad, A., and K. Sydsæter (1987), *Optimal Control Theory with Economic Applications*, North-Holland, Amsterdam.

Sen, A. (1977), Social Choice Theory: A Re-Examination, *Econometrica*, 45, 53-89.

Simon, H.A. (1982), Understanding the Natural and the Artificial Worlds, in: H.A. Simon, *The Sciences of the Artificial*, MIT Press, 2nd ed., Cambridge, Mass.

Simon, J.L. (1986), *Theory of Population and Economic Growth*, Basil Blackwell, Oxford.

Simon, J.L. (1990), Bring on the Wretched Refuse, *Wallstreet Journal*, February 1, 1990.

Simon, J.L., and A.J. Heins (1985), The Effect of Immigrants on Natives' Incomes Through the Use of Capital, *Journal of Development Economics*, 17, 75-93.

Skiba, A.K. (1978), Optimal Growth with a Convex-Concave Production Function, *Econometrica*, 46, 527-539.

Solow, R.M. (1956), A Contribution to the Theory of Economic Growth, *Quarterly Journal of Economics*, 70, 65-94.

Solow, R.M. (1960), Investment and Technical Progress, in: K.J.

Arrow, S. Karlin and P. Suppes (eds.), *Mathematical Methods in the Social Sciences*, Stanford University Press, Stanford.

Solow, R.M. (1970), *Growth Theory, An Exposition*, Oxford University Press, Oxford.

Solow, R.M. (1974), The Economics of Resources or the Resources of Economics, *American Economic Review, Papers and Proceedings*, 64, 1-14.

Srinivasan, T.N. (1989), The Theory of International Trade, Steady State Analysis, and Economics of Development, in: G. Feiwel (ed.), *Joan Robinson and Modern Economic Theory*, MacMillan, London.

Stiglitz, J.E. (1983), The Theory of Local Public Goods Twenty-Five Years after Tiebout: A Perspective, in: G.R. Zodrow (ed.), *Local Provision of Public Services: The Tiebout Model after Twenty-Five Years*, Academic Press, New York.

Stiglitz, J.E. (1987), Pareto Efficient and Optimal Taxation and the New New Welfare Economics, in: A.J. Auerbach and M. Feldstein (eds.), *Handbook of Public Economics*, Vol. II, North-Holland, Amsterdam.

Stokey, N.L. (1988), Learning by Doing and the Introduction of New Goods, *Journal of Political Economy*, 96, 701-717.

Strotz, R.H. (1955-56), Myopia and Inconsistency in Dynamic Utility Maximization, *Review of Economic Studies*, 23-24, 165-180.

Sumner, L.W. (1978), Classical Utilitarianism and Population Optimum, in: R.I. Sikora and B. Barry (eds.), *Obligations to Future Generations*, Temple University Press, Philadelphia.

Swank, O.H. (1990), *Policy Makers, Voters and Optimal Control*, PhD. Thesis, Tinbergen Institute, Amsterdam/Rotterdam.

Tabellini, G. (1991), The Politics of Intergenerational Redistribution, *Journal of Political Economy*, 99, 335-357.

Thompson, W.S. (1929), Population, *American Journal of*

Sociology, 34, 959-975.

Tinbergen, J. (1987), Het getal twee is van Keynes (trans. "The number two originates from Keynes"), *Economisch Statistische Berichten*, 72, 1092.

Tobin, J. (1980), *Asset Accumulation and Economic Activity*, Yrjö Jahnsson Lectures, Basil Blackwell, Oxford.

Tu, P.N.V. (1984), *Introductory Optimization Dynamics*, Springer Verlag, Berlin.

Tu, P.N.V. (1988), Migration: Gains or Losses?, mimeographed, University of Calgary.

Turchi, B.A. (1975), *The Demand for Children: The Economics of Fertility in the United States*, Ballinger, Cambridge, Mass.

UNESCO (1989), *Statistical Yearbook 1989*, UNESCO, Paris.

Uzawa, H. (1968), Time Preference, the Consumption Function and Optimum Asset Holdings, in: J.N. Wolfe (ed.), *Value, Capital and Growth: Essays in Honor of Sir John Hicks*, Aldine, Chicago.

van Velthoven, B.C.J., and F.A.A.M. van Winden (1990), A Behavioural Model of Government Budget and Deficits, *Public Finance*, 45, 128-161.

Viscusi, W.K., and M.J. Moore (1989), Rates of Time Preference and Valuations of the Duration of Life, *Journal of Public Economics*, 38, 297-317.

Weil, Ph. (1987), Love Thy Children, Reflections on the Barro Debt Neutrality Theorem, *Journal of Monetary Economics*, 19, 377-391.

Weil, Ph. (1989), Overlapping Families of Infinitely-Lived Agents, *Journal of Public Economics*, 38, 183-198.

Weil, Ph. (1990), Nonexpected Utility in Macroeconomics, *Quarterly Journal of Economics*, 105, 29-42.

Weitzman, M.L. (1976), On the Welfare Significance of National Product in a Dynamic Economy, *Quarterly Journal of*

Economics, 90, 156-162.

Whittington, L.A., J. Alm, and H.E. Peters (1990), Fertility and the Personal Exemption: Implicit Pronatalist Policy in the United States, *American Economic Review*, 80, 545-556.

Wildasin, D.E. (1988), Nash Equilibria in Models of Fiscal Competition, *Journal of Public Economics*, 35, 229-240.

Wildasin, D.E. (1991), The Marginal Cost of Public Funds with an Aging Population, *Journal of Population Economics*, 4, 111-135.

van Winden, F.A.A.M. (1983), *On the Interaction Between State and Private Sector*, North-Holland, Amsterdam.

van Winden, F.A.A.M. (1987), Man in the Public Sector, *De Economist*, 135, 1-28.

Worldbank (1984), *Population Change and Economic Development*, Oxford University Press, Oxford.

Worldbank (1985), *Desertification in the Sahelian and Sudanian Zones of West Africa*, Washington D.C.

Worldbank (1987), *World Development Report 1987*, Oxford University Press, Oxford.

World Resources Institute/International Institute for Environment and Development (1988), *World Resources 1988-89*, Basic Books, New York.

Yaari, M.E. (1965), Uncertain Lifetime, Life Insurance and the Theory of the Consumer, *Review of Economic Studies*, 32, 137-150.

Yotsuzuka, T. (1987), Ricardian Equivalence in the Presence of Capital Market Imperfections, *Journal of Monetary Economics*, 20, 411-436.

SUBJECT INDEX

Adverse selection, 231, 234

Ageing, 7-9, 21, 30, 77

Age-structure, 4-6

Aggregator function, 208

Altruism, 22, 94, 218, 221-225
   impure, 223

Average utility criterion (see social welfare)

Benthamite utility function (see social welfare, total utility)

Bequest motive, 220, 225, 234, 235

Birth, rate, 4, 210, 234

Boundedness assumptions, 135

Brain drain, 45, 46, 193-199, 299

Capital
   dilution, 88, 194
   human, 16, 171-181
   income shares, 92
   physical, 16, 43

Capital market, 20-24
   imperfections, 218, 231-235
   international, 137-139, 294

Carrying capacity, 29, 295

Communication, endogenous, 232-235

Comparative statics, of
   endogenous time preference model, 157-161, 164-167
   human capital model, 181-185, 202, 203
   one-sector growth model, 88-92, 96-98
   two-region world model, 110-114

Complex utility criterion (see social welfare)

Cooperation, 276, 282-286, 288, 302

Credibility, 277-281, 304

Credit rationing, 231

Current Account, 129, 130, 138

Deadweight loss (see excess burden)

Death rate, 4, 227-229, 234

Debt
   foreign, 45, 125-127, 298
   government (see public debt)
   neutrality, 46, 205, 216, 235-241, 299

Default, 232, 310

Printing: Druckhaus Beltz, Hemsbach
Binding: Buchbinderei Kränkl, Heppenheim

E. van Imhoff

Optimal Economic Growth and Non-Stable Population

1989. IX, 218 pp. 27 figs. (Studies in Contemporary Economics) Softcover ISBN 3-540-51556-9

This book studies the consequences of demographic change for optimal economic growth in a closed economy. It connects the analytical tools of traditional growth theory with the actual demographic experience of most industrialized countries. A natural way of incorporating the demographic structure into growth models is by making the model one of overlapping generations, thus allowing for explicit analysis of demographic forces as potential sources of non-stationarities in economic development.
The book offers a number of economic growth models with which the effects on social welfare of demography, investment in physical and human capital, and technical progress can be analyzed. Using these models, rules for optimal economic policy can be derived. The study formulates general guidelines for long-run economic and educational policy, given the available demographic projections.
Two main conclusions are reached. First, a fall in fertility has a beneficial effect on consumption per capita, provided that the population growth rate does not pass below a certain (probably negative) critical level. Second, investment in education is a good substitute for population growth: when the population growth rate falls, investment in education becomes more attractive.

W. Schmähl (Ed.)

Redefining the Process of Retirement

An International Perspective

1989. XI, 179 pp. 16 figs. Hardcover
ISBN 3-540-50826-0

Past and future development as well as possibilities for influencing the process of retirement are discussed, in particular effects on the labour market (supply and demand, behaviour of workers and firms, concerning human resource management and occupational pensions), financing of social security and income of workers. Decisions concerning earlier or postponed, full or partial retirement are the main topic stressing the central role of firms' decisions depending e. g. on their view of the productivity of the elderly. Reports on Scandinavian countries (Sweden, Denmark, Finland) in particular on their approach for partial retirement are included as well as papers discussing possibilities to stop the trend of early exit from the labour force and how to give incentives for a longer working life (e. g. by changes in social security). These topics are discussed in the view of structural changes in demography, economy and society, using – among others – the US and West Germany as examples.

A. Wenig, K. F. Zimmermann (Eds.)

Demographic Change and Economic Development

1989. XII, 325 pp. 45 figs. (Studies in Contemporary Economics) Softcover ISBN 3-540-51140-7

In recent years, population economics has become increasingly popular in both economic and policy analysis. For the inquiry into the long term development of an economy, the interaction between demographic change and economic activity cannot be neglected without omitting major aspects of the problems. This volume helps

to further developments in theoretical and applied demographical economics covering the issues of demographic change and economic development.

Springer-Verlag
Berlin
Heidelberg
New York
London
Paris
Tokyo
Hong Kong
Barcelona
Budapest